THE FAT BOY
WITH THE BOMB

AND 299 MORE OF THE
WORLD'S CRAZIEST POLITICIANS

THE FAT BOY WITH THE BOMB

AND 299 MORE OF THE WORLD'S CRAZIEST POLITICIANS

Compiled by Brian O'Connell

Illustrated by Norm Chung

MYRMIDON

Rotterdam House
116 Quayside
Newcastle upon Tyne
NE1 3DY

www.myrmidonbooks.com

Published by Myrmidon 2014

Typeset by Ellipsis Digital Limited, Glasgow
Printed by Martins the Printers, Berwick-upon-Tweed

A catalogue record for this book is available from the British Library
ISBN 978-1-910183-09-0

1 3 5 7 9 10 8 6 4 2

For Angela, Rachel, Evan and Ellie

CONTENTS

SHELDON ADELSON

POLITICAL PUNTER

DARK MONEY

Adelson shelled out $100 million in the
2014 mid-term elections for a range of
US conservative candidates and causes.
The mysterious casino mogul, who has made much of this money in the murky world
of gambling in Macao, is an ATM for the American right and the Tea Party movement in
particular.

In 2012 Adelson gave $30 million to the *Restore Our Future*, Political Action Committee
(PAC) that supported Mitt Romney's bid for the White House. He gave $20 million to
Winning Our Future, the PAC that supported Newt Gingrich's unsuccessful primary run for
the presidential nomination. In short, Adelson bet a lot of money backing the losing horses.

Besides being in the gambling business, Adelson owns an Israeli newspaper, *Israel
HaYom* (*Israel Today*), which has the highest circulation in the country and is essentially a
mouthpiece for the right-wing *Likud* Party. Adelson used to be a Democrat but switched
to the Republicans because he felt they were more supportive of Israel (70% of Jews in
America voted for Democrat, Barack Obama in 2012).

Not surprisingly, a lot of the politicians Adelson backs are also with him in his effort
to block online gambling, which is cutting into his casino earnings. When asked by *Forbes*
magazine about his efforts to block online gambling, Adelson told the publication 'I'm willing
to spend whatever it takes'. One of the candidates he donated to, Senator Lindsey (he's
straight!) Graham, introduced legislation to outlaw internet betting. Adelson is also a big
backer of the Republican Jewish Coalition – a dwindling organisation, particularly after the
defeat of Eric Cantor, one of the few Jewish Republicans in office. There are some thirty
Jewish members of the US Congress and virtually every one of them are Democrats.

ISAIAS AFWERKI

PRESIDENT OF ERITREA

THE KIM JONG UN OF AFRICA

Eritrea fought a thirty-year war of independence from Ethiopia and what did they get out of it? Not much, after all. It's a place you'd sooner say goodbye to. Thousands have done just that and drowned in the process of trying to migrate to Europe. But it's not all *totally* bad, particularly for Isaias Afwerki, the dickhead president who has ruled the country since 1993.

Afwerki's decided he's mature enough to judge that his people are too immature to vote. Journalists can't enter the country unless they pledge to write positive stories and there's no independent press allowed internally, which assures that all news is happy news.

The events of September 11, 2001 played right into his hands. While the world was concentrated on New York, he put eleven of his closed confidantes and eighteen independent journalists in the clink and charged them with treason, which is subject to a death penalty. All they wanted was a bit of democracy.

Instead of the guerrilla uniform he once wore, now Afwerki prances around in the finest tailored Italian suits while young people are required to do 'national service' in remote rural areas where they can't ferment unrest. Rather than spend money on much needed domestic programs, Afwerki is credited with funding the Al-Shabab group of terrorists in the horn of Africa. He doesn't allow the United Nations in the country to monitor frequent reports of famine or to deliver aid. In August of 2014 President Barack Obama excluded Afwerki from being invited to a global summit on investment in Africa. In 2009 the African Union asked the UN Security Council to slap sanctions on the Eritrean government for threatening the security of northeast Africa. That doesn't matter much to the Eritrean dictator. As Afwerki himself said to the *Los Angeles Times*, 'people may talk about democracy, but even those who pretend to be democratic are not democratic.' Leastwise himself.

ESPERANZA AGUIRRE

**PRESIDENT OF THE
MADRID REGION**

RUN AND HIT

She is the 'Iron Lady' of Spain. According to *IberoSphere,* she is
the scourge of Basque and Catalan nationalists, and an ardent
advocate of free enterprise, the head of the Madrid regional
government has carved out a place for herself in Spain's Popular Party as a
'kingmaker'. They go on to state that, 'Aguirre is an economic liberal, and has steadily
pushed ahead with privatising health and education during her tenure as boss of Madrid;
unlike Thatcher, Aguirre is also a social liberal, believing in the legalization of drugs and
prostitution, for example.'

What Esperanza has that Maggie never did is a touch of glamour and she uses it to her
full advantage. And, unlike the grocer's daughter, she was born into privilege and is married
to a nobleman. Perhaps that gave her enough arrogance to pull off a stunt that captured
the attention of all Spain.

In April, 2014, she parked her car in a bus lane in Madrid and ran out to get cash from
an ATM. Parking in a bus lane can result in a fine of €200. She was nabbed by the cops, but
instead of taking her medicine then and there, she jumped into her car and drove off. That's
when things took a turn for the worse. When she pulled out into the street she ran over
a traffic cop who was sitting on a moped. (He wasn't injured.)

Of course she blamed the cop for the incident, saying he had parked the moped poorly.
'I didn't run over anybody. I started my car and on leaving I brushed against a moped agent
who then fell on the ground,' she told Onda Cero Radio the next day, adding: 'He fell, and
I apologised.' Things could get worse, though. She may be charged with 'disobedience',
which carries a prison sentence of up to ten years.

ATIQ AHMED

PARTY LEADER

DACOITY DAN

It would embarrass some people to file election papers when there are 73 criminal cases pending against you, including six for murder, six for attempted murder and four for kidnapping and abduction.

The most famous murder is that of Raju Pal, who ran on the Bahujan Samaj Party ticket in 2004, and was foolish enough to best Ashraf Ahmed, Atiq's brother.

The *Indian Express* newspaper refers to him as 'mafia-turned-politician' and wrote that the 'candidate from Sultanpur (Ahmed) had, on Sunday, taken out a procession in which his supporters, in a show of strength, were reportedly seen flaunting firearms.' The newspaper also describes Ahmed as a 'history-sheeter', a uniquely Indian term to describe a certain type of criminal who has a spectacularly long criminal record.

In 2012, indicted under what is referred to as the 'Stringent Gangsters Act', Ahmed was given bail to contest an election, even though he had been behind bars since 2008. The leader of the Samajwadi Party's campaigning has not been going spectacularly well as of late. Speaking of the Muzaffarnagar Riots, (named for a city in a city in Uttar Pradesh with a population of 500,000, where 65 people were killed and 50,000 made homeless in clashes between Hindus and Muslims) he described the people who were consequently displaced and living in the relief camps as 'professional beggars'. He was roundly criticised for the remarks. Ahmed has also been charged with 'dacoity', which, according to the *Oxford English Dictionary*, is 'violent robbery committed by an armed gang'.

MIKE ALLEN

ASSEMBLY OF ALBERTA

MR 3-WAY

He's a Member of Alberta's Legislative Assembly, representing the Progressive Conservatives and he's the kind of guy that can get lonely and bored sitting in a hotel room in a strange city.

His 26 year marriage had broken up four years before and, as he told the *Edmonton Sun* newspaper, 'personal circumstances led to my decision to do this and I am just devastated as a result.'

On government business in St Paul, Minnesota in July 2013, he decided that if he couldn't drum up some on his own he would use his wallet to generate some amusement. He let his fingers do the walking and made a phone call to what he thought was an escort and made arrangements for some three-way action with two babes. Unfortunately for Allen, the hooker he called wasn't really a hooker: she was an undercover police officer working for the vice squad on sting operations. She agreed to his request and at 8:00 pm that evening two women showed up to his hotel room door and Allen shelled out $200 in anticipation of a night of fun, and then out popped the cops who cuffed Allen and threw him in the slammer for the night.

At least he didn't feel lonely anymore, although he might have lost out on some sleep that night. He faced a gross misdemeanour charge of solicitation of prostitution which carries a fine of $1,500 but he was given a plea deal and the charge was reduced resulting in a fine of only $500.

Naturally the Progressive Conservatives righteously washed their hands of Allen in the expectation he would lose the next election and he became an independent MLA. But, once it became apparent Allen was still popular in his district, the party became all forgiving and invited him back into their ranks in 2014.

ROB ANDERS

CANADIAN HOUSE
OF COMMONS

AS SHARP AS A MARBLE

The Conservative from Calgary has been dubbed 'Canada's worst MP' and that was by a conservative magazine.

In 2001, Anders was the only MP to vote against giving Nelson Mandela honorary Canadian citizenship because he was a 'communist and a terrorist'. *Press Progress* reported at the time, that Anders had said Mandela was a 'politically correct kind of lib left poster-boy ... I would say that 30 years from now Nelson Mandela will not be lionized as much as he is today.' He elaborated on those remarks a year later, saying, 'Nelson Mandela advocated violence and used violence to achieve his aims ... it is very politically correct to go ahead and lionize him, but there are problems in South Africa today and we are glossing over these things.'

Anders is against gay marriage because he thinks it will undermine society. He's also notorious for dozing off during parliamentary sessions. He was thrown off the Veterans Affairs committee for arriving late, texting during hearings and falling asleep. Before he entered the Canadian Parliament he worked in America as a professional political heckler for the campaign to elect the Republican, Jim Inhofe, in Oklahoma.

He's not afraid to give America advice either. Anders issued a statement after the Russian annexation of Crimea saying: 'I also agree with the idea that military action should not be ruled out because I think for somebody who is a thug like Putin, it's what he understands and I think that message is not just words. I would very much like to see the US Fifth Fleet move into the Black Sea and the George W Bush aircraft carrier move into the eastern Mediterranean.' (He must have meant the USS George H.W. Bush, named after the elder Bush president.)

His voters responded by voting him down in the 2014 primary for the Calgary Signal Hill constituency. Since then he has decided to run in the rural area of Bow River, east of Calgary, for the 2015 elections.

JOSÉ DOMINGO ARIAS

**FORMER MINISTER AND
PRESIDENTIAL CANDIDATE**

MIMITO

He was front man for the former Panamanian president, Ricardo Martinelli, who couldn't run in the 2014 presidential elections because the constitution forbids a president to serve a consecutive term. In fact, Martinelli made Arias take his wife, Marta Linares de Martinelli, as his running mate, just to make sure he pulled the strings even while out of office.

Arias only joined the *Cambio Democrático* (Democratic Change) party in 2006 and three years later he was appointed Minister of Foreign Trade and then Minister of Housing and Land Management, which is where he made his biggest impact, leading an urban development program to provide flooring to the rural poor who still lived in houses with dirt floors.

The Martinelli presidency was a boom time for the country and Panama City is now seen as the Miami of Central America. But there was trouble in the corridors of power. The president and the vice president became *peores enemigos* (bitter enemies), which is why Arias was picked for the party nomination. The Vice President, Juan Carlos Varela, ran on the *Partido Panameñista* ticket against Arias and Martinelli's wife. Despite the fact the Varela is under investigation for money laundering, he alluded to the corruption that Martinelli failed to combat during his presidency, when he promised to make government 'pass from being a business to being a service'.

Something happened along the way to Arias's presidential coronation: he ran a miserable campaign based on the flawed advice of his mentor and his political consultants. When the dust finally settled, Varela pulled out a stunning upset that saw him capture 39% of the vote against 32% for Arias. The former president only had this to say about Varela's win, 'I know the candidate, and really, may God help us.' Meanwhile, Arias, who is known as Mimito in Panama, has turned on his old boss, declaring he, not Martinelli, will be the next nominee for the *Cambio Democrático*.

BÜLENT ARINÇ

DEPUTY PRIME MINISTER OF TURKEY

DR NO

There are a lot of things Bülent Arınç doesn't want Turkish women to do. In fact, the list seems endless. The dour Vice Prime Minister of Turkey wants to abolish fun.

The co-founder of the Justice and Development Party, along with Recep Tayyip Erdoğan, he is particularly worried about 'moral corruption'. In 2014 he admonished Turkey's women for what he considers to be their lax morals. During the Eid-al-Fitr holiday he said that of the ideal woman: 'She will not laugh in public. She will not be inviting in her attitudes and will protect her chasteness.'

Referring to the kind of Turkish woman he abhors, he said they 'leave their husbands at home, and go to vacation with their lovers. They can't wait to climb poles when they see someone,' he said, referring to every Turkish woman's secret desire to become a pole dancer. Bülent is also an opponent of mixed sex housing at Turkey's universities. He has called for chastity in both men and women and blamed television and the media for turning teenagers into 'sex addicts'. As far as his advice goes to Turkey's young men, he thinks 'he should not be a womaniser. He should be bound to his wife. He should love his children. Men and women should know what is haram and not haram.'

Of course all of Bülent's suggestions have backfired with Turkey's youth, who are also not big fans of his boss, Recep Tayyip Erdoğan. According to the *Guardian* newspaper, Erdoğan's chief political rival tweeted: 'more than anything else, our country needs women to smile and to hear everybody's laughter.' The *Guardian* further reported that one of the opposition MPs, Melda Onur, wrote this on Twitter: 'we would have left Arınç to his fantasies and wouldn't even have laughed about it, but while so many murders are being committed he makes (women) a target by stressing the need for chastity.'

BASHAR AL-ASSAD

PRESIDENT OF SYRIA

A LESSER EVIL

He *almost* had a tolerable reputation until the Arab Spring came along and he proved to be the same murderous monster his father was. But his reputation went through another re-evaluation in 2013-2014 thanks to the unwelcome arrival of the Islamic State of Iraq and Syria (ISIS) who have proved to be even worse than Assad, and that takes some doing.

A coalition of Western and Arab states found themselves the unwitting allies of the Syrian president who, despite all the atrocities he's committed, is perhaps the only leader in Syria who can save the country's minority populations.

It should have come as a warning to the world that the Christian population of Syria allied themselves with the Assad regime at the outset of the Syrian Civil War, as did the Alawites who form his base of support. They have found themselves the victims of the worst of the atrocities committed by the fanatic Sunni ISIS followers.

The sanctions imposed on Assad by the European Union and the United States have done little to stop the flow of aid the regime receives from Russia, Iran and *Hezbollah*. Rational assessments of the situation in Syria in 2012 all predicted that Assad would be out of power by 2014 and probably either dead or under trial at the International Criminal Court. Now, the situation looks entirely different and the world looks like it is beginning to resign itself to at least a negotiated settlement of the civil war and possibly a continuation of the Assad regime.

Perhaps the Syrians themselves look wistfully backwards to the relative peace and tranquillity their country lived under before the arrival of the Arab Spring in Damascus.

DAUREN BABAMURATOV

KAZAKH MAJILIS

PAINT IT PINK

It may have escaped your gaydar but Almaty, Kazakhstan, is supposedly the hot new gay weekend getaway place, or at least that is what Dauren Babamuratov fears. The country that has now banned lace underwear for women is now 'the gay capital of Central Asia' according to Babamuratov, who claims there are 14 gay clubs in the capital. (Almaty has a population of 1.4 million –that's 100,000 people for every gay hangout).

The MP is the leader of *Bolashak*, a Kazakhstan nationalist movement that also is keen to have former police chief, Rakhat Aliyev extradited from Austria (Aliyev is not only married to the current president's daughter but he is also wanted on two murder charges).

According to the AKI press agency, *Bolashak* 'organized a press-conference in Almaty on September 11, 2014, urging the Parliament of Kazakhstan to work out amendments to certain laws of Kazakhstan in order for the gay propaganda [to] be banned and they seek to prohibit gay people to work at public offices or serve in the Kazakh army'.

According to the *Independent*, Babamuratov said, 'homosexuality is a threat to the nation' and 'I think it is very easy to identify a gay person by his or her DNA. A blood test can show the presence of degeneratism in a person.'

Think Progress quotes *Bolashak* as saying, 'we have stooped so low that LGBTs no longer hide their orientation and young people in coloured pants hang out in the city's malls and other public places.' Despite Babamuratov's concerns there have been no 'gay pride' events or LGBT marches in Kazakhstan to date, although the nation's women are pretty upset that they are barred from wearing sexy knickers. The ban took effect in July of 2014. According to the BBC, 'the authorities in Kazakhstan have detained several women protesting against a ban on lace underwear.'

PAUL BABEU

SHERIFF OF PINAL COUNTY, ARIZONA

NO WAY JOSE

He was the Republican party's great hope in 2012. He not only was the co-chairman of Mitt Romney's campaign in Arizona, but he was up for a congressional seat. The ultraconservative Arizona Sheriff was first elected to the post in 2008 and seems to court publicity.

His law and order message is firm: illegal aliens should be deported. He portrays his Democrat opponents as weak on immigration. In response to the wave of unaccompanied minors who flooded across the US-Mexican border in the summer of 2014, he thinks 'the most humanitarian response would be to place these children on planes and return them back to their country of origin.'

Back in 2012 the outspoken sheriff was just vociferous about the issue, which is why it was a bit unfortunate that a certain 'Jose' started spilling the beans about his love affair with Babeu. Up until that point, his electors just assumed that the sheriff was as straight as a board and not the kind of guy to meet up with another guy on gay.com.

To make matters worse, 'Jose' was a Mexican with a dubious legal right to live in the United States and he also worked on Babeu's congressional campaign. According to 'Jose', he was pressured to keep quiet about the relationship or be kicked out of the country. Babeu was forced to admit he had been dating 'Jose' for three years and that he was gay, but he angrily denied that his lover was an illegal alien or that he had threatened to have him deported. Babeu resigned from Romney's campaign and decided to end his bid for congress.

The conservative voters of Pinal County re-elected him as their sheriff and he's still holding anti-immigration rallies.

MICHELE BACHMANN

US HOUSE OF
REPRESENTATIVES

MARCUS'S BEARD

She's one of a kind: a combination of suburban beauty teamed up with a bat shit crazy view of the world. For one brief, shining moment she was the Republican darling of the presidential primaries in 2012. Barack Obama must have been hoping beyond hope that she would make it through and lead the ticket against him, but that didn't happen. There was a revelation somewhere along the way. The voters realised that being hot was just not enough: they wanted a candidate who actually had a sufficiently generous amount of cerebrum in their skull.

The US Representative from Minnesota isn't a big fan of the LGBT movement, which might seem something as a conflict of interest inasmuch as her husband, Marcus, is in the controversial business of counselling gays to turn them into heterosexuals. Marcus Bachmann's mannerisms and a tape of him dancing caused the gay journalist, Dan Savage, to say in 2011 that Marcus might have 'tiptoed down the road to homosexuality just a couple of inches . . . maybe six or seven.'

'What a bizarre time we're in', said Michele Bachmann recently. 'When a judge will say to little children that you can't say the pledge of allegiance, but you must learn that homosexuality is normal and you should try it.'

Bachmann is also hyped up about people crossing the Mexican border illegally and she thinks the best way to stop it is to take all their money. She compares the wave of recent migration to a war. 'What we have to recognize is that this truly is a war against the American people', Bachman said to *Right Wing Watch*. 'And if we don't act like it and take this border seriously, we're going to have even more gangs.'

Global warming is another issue to get Michele hot under the collar. She's convinced it's 'all voodoo, nonsense, hokum, a hoax' and to show her dedication to the cause, she introduced a much needed law: HR 849, the Light Bulb Freedom of Choice Act (it didn't pass). She's an Obama-hater too and thinks he is both un-American and a socialist. But the best idea Michele has come up with yet is to introduce an amendment to the constitution to bar America ever giving up the dollar and adopting a 'global currency' – whatever that is.

LEADER OF ISIS

CALIPH IBRAHIM

It's not easy to crack wise about Baghdadi and it's seems pretty unlikely that he has a self-deprecating side. That said, he is a nonetheless absurd figure leading an equally absurd group of losers in some sort of effort to establish a caliphate and murdering as many people as they can before the US drops a big one on top of their heads.

In reality, though, America and the rest of the world should just leave him and his followers alone, walk away and wash their hands of the whole business. They are the product of their parents, the static society in which they live and the idiots in the Gulf States that provide their funding.

It's no secret that the educated Arabs in the Levant hold the Gulf Arabs in utter contempt. Sure, they're richer but that's about all they have going for them. Even the natural resources they produce have to be brought out of the ground by more resilient and innovative people: either Westerners, educated Arabs, the Chinese or the Japanese. There's nothing else produced in the Gulf States that is exportable except loony nutcases like Baghdadi.

There are two Sunni universities in the Middle East where an Imam is supposed to be educated: the Islamic University of Medina or the al-Azhar University of Cairo. He went to neither but claims he is a direct descendent of Mohammed (there's no evidence of that) and got a PhD from the Islamic University of Baghdad (he might have, but Harvard, Cambridge, or the Sorbonne it ain't).

After the incredibly inept US invasion of Iraq, Baghdadi got together with some of his mates and created the Army of the Sunni People, which has now morphed into the Islamic State of Iraq and Syria (ISIS). Baghdadi's delusional declaration of a caliphate has done one thing: it has awakened the normal Arab world to the dangers of extreme Wahhabism and jihadism once and for all. That's a good thing, and means it's likely that Baghdadi and his ilk will be virtually forgotten in a couple of years.

FRANK BAINIMARAMA

PRIME MINISTER OF FIJI

BAINIMARAMA REPUBLIC

He is the Prime Minister of a middle-income country with a per capita GDP of about $4,500. His salary, according to Radio New Zealand, comes in at about $700,000 and his second-in-command pulls in a cool half million. Bainimarama must think he's stepped in shit because with a population of just 881,065 it's as if every Fijian is giving him almost a buck a year to sit in the presidential palace.

Like most military strongmen, he has a gripe or two. As he told the Australian Broadcasting Company, 'we are shown on the TV and in the papers every day as dictators, dictators in the sense that we go round abusing the powers that we have. That doesn't happen here.' Pressed about the fact that he had put the islands under a state of emergency, he replied, 'is that what dictatorship is about? Then if that is a definition of dictator, then I guess most of the countries in the region have dictators.'

Having overthrown the government in 2006, Bainimarama has been both the head of the military and interim Prime Minister up until 2014 when 'elections' will be held. He had to resign his military post in March 2014 in order to comply with Fijian election law. He's got a big thing for royalty and keeps pictures of the Queen and Prince Philip, although his country was suspended from the Commonwealth of Nations in 2009. His recent trips to Australia and New Zealand were met by protests from expat Fijians. The *New Zealand Herald* thinks Bainimarama faces a possible backlash by native Fijians because the Prime Minister abolished the traditional Great Council of Chiefs and gave full citizenship to the ethnic Indian population. It reports that, 'one of the questions concerning Fijians is the likelihood of another coup – particularly if Bainimarama loses the election and calls in the armed forces, now run by his hand-picked successor, Brigadier-General Mosese Tikoitoga.'

UZAIR BALOCH

PARTY BOSS

TONY SOPRANO

Lyari Town is one of the oldest neighbourhoods in Karachi and one of the poorest in Pakistan's administrative region of Sindh, stronghold of the ruling Pakistan People's Party (PPP).
It's also home to the notorious warring Baloch and Baba Ladla criminal gangs that have murdered hundreds in their struggle to dominate the crime scene in the neighbourhood.

Crime in Pakistan usually revolves around heroin brought across the border from Afghanistan. Close to 11% of the residents of Lyari are heroin addicts and the illicit trade in Pakistan is estimated to generate $2 billion per year.

Uzair Baloch not only runs his criminal enterprise, he's also put his hat into the political arena. He runs the People's Peace Committee, which has aligned itself with the ruling PPP. According to a National Public Radio (NPR) report filed in 2013, 'to the PPP, he provides votes. To the people of Lyari, he provides schools, hospital services and food stamps. In return, he gets unquestioned loyalty. Baloch and his men control Lyari Town so completely, the police no longer go into it. The last time they tried, in April (2013), they were met with a hail of bullets. The Lyari operation went on for days before the police returned to their posts.'

That was before the crime war with the Baba Ladla gang broke out. The Karachi police have filed charges against Baloch for murder and tax evasion. After the NPR journalist interviewed Baloch, she noted that 'just when she was leaving, he was joined by another visitor: the city government's top man in Lyari Town, the local administrator. He [said he was] there to discuss development projects with Baloch.'

According to the Pakistani newspaper, *The Nation*, 'the absconder and notorious chief of Lyari gang, Uzair Jan Baloch, reached United Kingdom leaving the gang war between the Baloch and Baba Ladla groups to continue in the area, which claimed three more lives here on Wednesday (9 September 2014)'. They further reported that, 'the escape of Uzair abroad proved the leniency of the Sindh government towards the Lyari gangsters'. It probably says something about the British government, too.

MAMATA BANERJEE

CHIEF MINISTER OF
WEST BENGAL

JIHAD PARADISE

She is affectionately referred to as Didi (big sister) in West
Bengal, where she has been Chief Minister since 2011 when she
ousted the longest standing democratically elected communist
government in the world. Before that she was Minister of the Railways,
Minister of Coal and Minister of State for Human Development.

Time magazine named her as one of the '100 most influential people in the world' in
2012 and is generally rated as one of the most honest politicians in India. She founded her
own political party in 1997: the All India Trinamool Congress. None other than Bill Gates
has praised her efforts to eradicate polio in her state. She is known as a street fighter with a
mercurial temper, but virtually nobody has anything bad to say about Banerjee – at least up until
September 2014. That's when the 'what the fuck' moment happened.

Banerjee was accused of collusion in the funding of the Bangladesh *Jamaat-e-Islami*,
which is a banned political party that was once linked to forced conversions of Hindus
to Islam, rape and war crimes. They also aren't big fans of India. The purported reason for
funding the banned group was to destabilize the Awami League led government which won
a majority of the parliamentary seats in Bangladesh's 2014 elections. Reports of Banerjee's
involvement in this were allegedly leaked to the press by the security services. She has
now been accused of running a 'Jihad Paradise' and allowing the *Jamaat-e-Islami* and other
radical groups to freely operate in West Bengal and work to undermine the government of
neighbouring Bangladesh, but that may be the last thing that will happen.

On 2 October 2014 a blast tore through a house in Burdwan in West Bengal. When
the dust settled 50 improvised explosive devices were found and the National Intelligence
Agency concluded that the homemade bombs were meant to be placed in Kolkata during
the *Durga Puja*, an important annual Hindu festival.

MARION BARRY

WASHINGTON DC
CITY COUNCIL

THE BITCH SET HIM UP

India's Prime Minister Manmohan Singh earns just $4,000 a year but Marion Barry, one of 13 councilmen who govern Washington DC, makes $125,583 per year. That's more money than the governors of Colorado, Maine, Kansas and about a dozen more American states make.

But Barry is unrepentant about the salary he takes home, telling the *Washington Post* that: 'we deserve more, quite frankly. We put in 40 or 50 hours a week in addition to constituent service. I think we are really underpaid.'

Barry is probably the best-known city councilman in America, for all the wrong reasons. He released a book, *Mayor for Life*, in 2014 that suggests substantial memory loss. In 1990, when he was mayor of Washington, the FBI filmed him secretly in a room in the Vista Hotel and recorded him smoking a crack pipe with his girlfriend Hazel Diane 'Rasheeda' Moore. He was arrested *in situ* and Barry was videotaped muttering under his breath, 'bitch set me up ... I shouldn't have come up here ... goddamn bitch.' He was put on trial for that and sentenced to prison but in his new book he claims he never smoked crack. Ever. He now claims 'the federal government never proved there was a crack pipe' and 'the jurors didn't believe it.' Whatever they believed, they nevertheless found him guilty as charged.

Even though a convicted criminal, he was re-elected to a fourth term as mayor when released from federal prison, although Congress, which has oversight over the federal district, took away all his authority because of his financial mismanagement.

During his heady booze and cocaine-fuelled days, Barry would seldom show up to work before noon and he wasn't in great shape then. In 2014 he also produced a documentary about Ward 8, the area he represents in Washington. It has a 25% unemployment rate and the average household income is $44,076, just over a third of Barry's salary.

VIT BARTA

**FORMER MINISTER,
CZECH REPUBLIC**

PAPER TRAIL

This should have been a warning sign: according to the *New York Times*, 'the (transport) minister, Vit Barta, has been banned from driving for six months and fined 5,000 koruna, about $280, for using a phoney license plate on his car' in November, 2010. He was one of the founders of the *Věci veřejné* (Public Affairs) party in the Czech Republic that managed to become part of the ruling coalition. Public Affairs was all about tranparency, direct democracy, wiping out political corruption and, most importantly, about Barta himself.

The problem with Barta was that he was really just a businessman who used politics to feather his nest and the mistake he made was working with colleagues that really believed in the party's message and who turned on him in the end.

He founded a company called ABL a.s. in 1992. The company's web site, boasts among other things that it provides security to the Czech Nightingale Mattoni competition or the Czech Miss Beauty Contest. But, if you type in the founder's name into the search engine on the site, you are directed to a different page that informs you of this: 'under its new trading name, M2.C, the holding (ABL a.s.) remains compliant with all existing processes, standards, codes of ethics as well as the generally recognised UK Bribery Act, Sarbanes-Oxley Act and Foreign Corrupt Practices Act'. There's a reason for this ...

According to the *Economist*, Barta's party, Public Affairs, was eventually killed off by internal feuds that 'came to a head after the conviction for bribery of its leading light, Vit Barta.' (The conviction was overturned because of Barta's parliamentary immunity.) The *Wall Street Journal* reported that, 'the scandal involving Mr Barta and his Public Affairs party, also known as VV, escalated late last week after a leaked internal memo from Mr. Barta's former security company, called ABL a.s., showed that as early as 2008 he was instructing his employees to seek public offices to influence the award of public contracts to ABL.' Despite this, Barta remains active in politics and is leading a crusade against gambling and for more affordable food.

NAFTALI BENNETT

ISRAELI KNESSET

KILL THEM DEAD

If you want to take a spin down the far-right highway watch
out when you get to the Israeli part of the road: that's when it gets quite perilous. In his own
words, he's 'killed lots of Arabs in [his] life and there's no problem with that.' Those are just
the platitudes of peace and forgiveness that the Middle East needs nowadays.

Bennett would reportedly rather kill Palestinian prisoners than return them in prisoner
swaps. According to the *Huffington Post*, Bennett allegedly told the Tel Aviv daily, *Yedioth
Ahronoth* that 'if you catch terrorists, you have to simply kill them.'

He's head of the Jewish Home Party and Israel's Minister of Industry, Trade and Labour.
The software tycoon was formerly head of the Judea and Samaria Settlement Council, so you
know where his head is at when it comes to West Bank settlements. His spokesperson later
retracted the statement Bennett made about killing the terrorists, saying that he only meant
that they should be killed in the course of military operations instead of being taken prisoner.

When commenting on the August 2014 confiscation of West Bank land by the Israeli
government the *Jerusalem Post* quoted Bennett as saying, 'what we did yesterday was a
display of Zionism', further adding that, 'building is our answer to murder'.

Perhaps Shaul Magid sums Bennett up best in his profile of him for the *Daily Beast*.
According to Magid, he likes Bennett, 'because if he and his party are as successful as polls
predict, it will put a clear choice before the American Jewish community and the United
States government. No more evasive language. The Jewish/Israel lobby will have to throw
away its handbook. Its slogans will become obsolete. Bennett's Israel does not want peace.
It is not waiting for the other side to denounce violence. Two states? That was something
from the last century. One state? Yes, but not one many American Jews will feel proud of.
And not one the US government will easily support.'

JOHN BERCOW

SPEAKER OF THE
HOUSE OF COMMONS

MR SQUEAKER AND LONG TALL SALLY

The office of Speaker in Britain's parliament has a long and noble history, and it's usually been filled by those who can command the respect and affection of the whole House. More recently, though, things have rather gone off the rails.

To some John Bercow is a fair-minded, good-natured moderniser, a Jewish taxi driver's son made good. To others, he's 'Mr Squeaker', a pompous upstart that they'd love to drag from his chair at the first opportunity. Prime Minister, David Cameron, is particularly thought to loathe the diminutive Bercow with a passion.

Then there's his statuesque wife. Sally Bercow is a big story just waiting to happen and editors salivate at the prospect that, one day, she'll drop right into their nets. The first thing about Sally is that she's an increasingly public and committed Labour supporter, which reinforces to many Conservative MPs that her husband is biased against them in the Speaker's chair. The second thing is that she likes to party.

In 2011, after Bercow became Speaker, she did a photo spread for the *Evening Standard* just wearing a bed sheet and was quoted as saying, 'becoming Speaker has turned my husband into a sex symbol'. Shortly after that she appeared on *Celebrity Big Brother 2011* (she was the first to be evicted). In 2012 she libellously tweeted that Lord McAlpine was implicated in a report on paedophiles. She was sued and found guilty. In October 2013, she was photographed getting into a taxi after a magazine launch with her skirt hiked up to her knickers while she was giving the finger to the press. In February 2014, she was snapped snogging a muscle bound fitness trainer in a West End nightclub and, later that month, sipping champagne while sitting on another geezer's lap. When rumours started that her marriage was in trouble, Sally tweeted that all was 'innocent, totally out of context' and said that her marriage was stronger than ever.

GURBANGULY BERDIMUHAMMEDOV

PRESIDENT OF
TURKMENISTAN

RIDER OF THE STORM

Surely he couldn't be any worse than Turkmenistan's last dictator –
er … president, Saparmurat Niyazov. Niyazov had a rotating golden
statue of himself erected in the central square of the capital and changed all the names of the
months, naming January after himself (he also renamed the days of the week).

When Niyazov died in 2008 and Berdimuhammedov took over after an election that
he won with an astounding percentage of the vote, he did away with all the new names for
the days and months and went back to the traditional ones. But, as the *Guardian* reported,
US diplomatic cables revealed by Wikileaks, described the Turkmenistan leader as 'vain,
suspicious, guarded, strict, very conservative, a practiced liar, a good actor and vindictive'. The
cables further stated that Berdimuhammedov is 'not a very bright guy' and he 'reportedly
has a Turkmen wife and a Russian mistress'. He was re-elected in 2012 to the office with
(you guessed it) 97% of the vote.

Forbes magazine ranks Turkmenistan as the sixth most corrupt country on earth and reports
that 'oil and gas surpluses are supposedly stored in a "Stabilization Fund" although *Global
Witness* reports there is no evidence, other than the president's word, that such a fund exists.'
The 2013 parliamentary elections yielded less than surprising results: Berdimuhammedov's
Democratic Party of Turkmenistan won all of the 125 seats in the assembly.

The president also likes racehorses and fancies himself as a jockey. He gave it a go
in 2013 but things didn't work out so well. In a fixed race the *Telegraph* described how
'three strides after the winning post his mount crossed its legs, turned a somersault and
planted the president turban first into the all-weather surface.' The paper then reported
that, 'state television showed the big man's great victory on the news, cutting to beautifully
choreographed cheering crowds (even the fir trees are beautifully choreographed in the
background) as he crossed the line. Though all journalists were taken to a windowless room
and body-searched at the races for footage.'

LUCIANA BERGER

UK HOUSE OF COMMONS

HOT, HOT, HOT

According to the *Mirror*, the Labour MP for Liverpool Wavertree is 'Britain's sexiest MP'. The paper reported that, 'she is one of a dozen Labour lookers in the poll, proving the party's MPs are red hot compared to the Tories, who are feeling blue with just nine entries in the coveted table.'

Being 'hot' is no sin, but that's not the problem. Berger was raised in Wembley; a neighbourhood in London where a two-bedroom flat will set you back only about £425,000 ($685,000). That's *an apartment*, not a house with a nice garden to frolic in. In the constituency Berger now represents, you can pick up a modest two bedroom for around £89,000 ($143,000). That's because the people who live there don't have the £14,502 ($23,330) every year that it takes to send their child to Haberdashers' Aske's School for Girls where Berger went before she went to the University of Birmingham. She also spent a year at ICADE in Madrid and then took her leisurely time to get a post graduate degree from the University of London while nurturing her contacts among Labour's political elite.

Berger is just another example of how the mainstream political parties in Britain couldn't give a hot damn about the constituencies they represent. The former friend of ex-Prime minister Tony Blair's son, Euan, was foisted on to a 'safe Labour' seat and breezed her way into the House of Commons in 2010 and now she is the Shadow Minister for Public Health, even though she has no qualifications in the medical field at all. To be fair to her, she's by no means unique: this is Britain, where they have no primaries, where local party involvement is weak and where, perhaps more than any other western democracy, the mainstream parties' headquarters pretty much inflict whomever they please on local electors. Usually though, the carpetbaggers do some homework and make a show of it. Not Berger: she'd never heard of Bill Shankly, Liverpool's legendary football manager and didn't know who sang *Ferry Cross the Mersey* – imagine standing for a congressional seat on the Texas Panhandle if you're clueless about Buddy Holly or the Dallas Cowboys.

SYLVIO BERLUSCONI

**FORMER ITALIAN
PRIME MINISTER**

MR LIBIDO

'I say it's better to like girls, than to be gay,' said Sylvio, probably during one of his hectic 'bunga bunga parties' where a lot of girls (of course they're not hookers) vied to be around the former Italian Prime Minister.

It really must irk Sylvio that the new Prime Minister, Matteo Renzi, is actually the darling of Europe now for actually trying to do something to kick start the Italian economy (his magic isn't quite working yet).

Italian politics are now a running gag with sex scandal after sex scandal (and an occasional tax evasion issue) filling the newspapers. He has not given up politics; he's the current leader of the *Forza Italia* (Forward Italy party), which won 16% of the vote in the 2014 European elections.

Let's just review some of the headlines while Sylvio was in power: Berlusconi convicted of having sex with underage prostitute; Berlusconi accused of paying showgirls to lie at 'bunga bunga' prostitution trial; former premier's sexual instincts stimulated in exchange for payment; Berlusconi convicted of tax-fraud. Let's compare the headlines now the Matteo Renzi is the man in charge: Renzi promises 'open door revolution'; Renzi defends pace of Italian reform and Bono praises Renzi's leadership (that's not a joke).

Sylvio is still in the news but for all the wrong reasons. The latest from the *Telegraph* is a story about the ageing politician paying Karima El Mahroug, a Moroccan exotic dancer known in Italy as Ruby the Heartstealer, 'between five and seven million euros' during his most recent trial although he says it was less and it was to provide her 'a head start in life and ensure she did not fall into prostitution' (a little late there). He can afford it. Berlusconi's media network is said to be worth something approaching $9 billion.

KIZZA BESIGYE

UGANDAN PARTY LEADER

GLUTTON FOR PUNISHMENT

Someone should tell Kizza Besigye that it might be time to call it a day. Every time the opposition leader of the Forum for Democratic Change steps out of his house or returns to Uganda he gets thrown in the clink.

His opponent, Yoweri Museveni, has been president of the country since 1986 and he has the magical ability, common to many tyrants, to win elections by truly massive margins. That's not going to change any time soon, no matter how many protests Besigye mounts or how many more days he spends in jail.

Besigye, three-time contender for president, was once a member of the ruling party, the National Resistance Movement, but split with them and mounted a challenge for the presidency in 2001. He lost, but challenged the election results in the Supreme Court. They ruled that there was massive vote rigging but would not invalidate the result. Shortly after that, the cops took Besigye, beat him up, and threatened him with arrest for treason. Besigye fled to the US and then South Africa.

He returned to a tumultuous welcome in Kampala in 2005 – and was soon arrested for treason, rape and concealment of treason. He spent six months in prison before he was acquitted of all the charges. Besigye ran again for president in 2006, lost and challenged the election again in the Supreme Court. The court ruled that there were indeed considerable irregularities but upheld the results. He ran again for president in 2011, but lost by such a wide margin he didn't challenging the outcome. Nevertheless, the cops pepper-sprayed and arrested him.

He was jailed again in 2013 for leading protests against high prices. Now, the perennial candidate is losing popularity rapidly because of his support for gay rights and his opposition to Uganda's anti-homosexuality legislation. After three presidential runs, months spent in exile or jail and frequent beatings at the hands of the police, Besigye seems further from the presidential palace than he ever was.

VINAY BIHARI

BIHAR LEGISLATIVE ASSEMBLY

THE CROONER

In May of 2014 Bihari was granted bail by an Indian court for a case relating to recording 'obscene' lyrics for an album he had made in the Bhojpuri language ten years previously. He is one of 13 people being charged in the case. The album has been described as being chock full of 'obscene, raunchy songs'. He has recorded over 300 songs and written over a thousand.

He's also a strict vegetarian. The independent MLA has been appointed Minister of Art, Culture and Youth Affairs in the Jitan Ram Manjhi government. He's also a filmmaker who claims his movies wipe out sleaze. He produced and directed a Bhojpuri film in 2014 with 12 Bihar MLAs acting in it. He's won the Bhojpuri Film Award as 'Best Lyricist' twice and he's worked with the famous Indian singer, Damodar Raao. So, he's a fairly sophisticated guy, tuned into culture and has had a rich diverse life.

He should understand what motivates the young. Obviously with 'youth affairs' in his portfolio, the minister is surely concerned about the rise in sexual violence towards women in India. Bihari thinks he's pinpointed the cause of the problem: mobile phones and non-vegetarian food.

He told the *Telegraph* newspaper that, 'I believe that youths use the mobile to watch blue films. Youths don't use the Internet service on their mobile phones to educate themselves but to watch pornography which encourages them to commit rape'. He further added that, 'people who eat more non-vegetarian food like chicken and fish are inclined towards carrying out molestation and rape'. Bihari has a reasonable side, though. He's led the effort to turn George Orwell's birthplace in Motihari, in the eastern Indian state of Bihar, into a museum.

JEJOMAR BINAY

VICE PRESIDENT OF THE PHILIPPINES

SOMETIMES IT PAYS TO PLAY

There are two things that are almost certain to happen to a Filipino politician: they'll end up in bed with someone that isn't their wife at least once during their political career and they'll almost certainly end up in court when that career nears its end.

Binay is the current Vice President of the Philippines but getting elected to that office wasn't a sure thing. He's also President of the Boy Scouts of the Philippines as well as being the former mayor of the city of Makati. In 2006, when he was still a mayor, he was charged with graft and was officially suspended from office, but he barricaded himself inside his office until the case was dropped because of insufficient evidence.

He ran for the office of Vice President under the PDP-LABAN banner. Initially, things didn't look good for him. In public opinion polls he trailed way behind Senators Loren Legarda and Mar Roxas but then the pictures came out.

In April of 2010 pictures of Binay with his mistress began to fill social media. They weren't particularly tawdry but they forced him to admit adultery and that he had adopted a child. Though Binay called the pictures 'black propaganda', his opponents claimed that they were deliberately leaked in order to boost his popularity. Whatever the truth is, it worked. He went from the most unlikely choice for the job to bookies favourite inside a week.

In 2014 Binay had to face a Senate Blue Ribbon sub-committee that was called to investigate irregularities regarding the construction of the Makati City Hall building. His former vice-mayor claims Binay took a 13% kickback on the construction costs, which would have made him a millionaire many times over. Binay claims the charges are hearsay.

ROBERT BLEAKLEY

WIGAN TOWN COUNCIL

TRUE GRIT

There are 40 people on Wigan Town council as opposed to 50 New York City aldermen which says something about the UK: there are so many MPs, Lords, ministers, councillors and too much bureaucracy altogether. When you have 40 people representing a city of 97,000 you're taking representative government a bit too far. Plus, you'll inevitably get a weirdo in there somewhere and quite likely there'll be something strange going on in the sex department.

Bleakley is the kind of guy that makes any tabloid editor's day. First of all, there was an incident where he altered an email in order to get someone sacked. Then there was the online porn he accessed on the computer the council provided him. But the real story was the sex chat lines: the same chat lines that advertise in the back of most British tabloids (the same tabloids that like to do salacious exposés about politicos and celebs), promising one-on-one hot talks with ultra horny babes. Bleakley racked up a bill of £2,400 ($3,800) on premium sex chats, all charged to Wigan council. One such chat line, *Get Naughty*, which promises to deliver 'hundreds of girls who want to get laid', only costs about £1 per every three minutes. That means that Bleakley was on the premium sex chat lines for the equivalent of 8 hours a day for 20 working days.

When Bleakley was caught he got all remorseful and said he'd pay back the money, but in September 2014 he actually got some backbone. The council circulated a letter asking him to resign and he refused, then they passed a motion asking him to resign which he still refused to do. They told every female member of the council staff not to speak to him but he still stayed on the job and they finally passed a motion disallowing him from speaking during council sessions but he still clung on to his job. If that's not true grit, what is?

CHRISTOPH BLOCHER

VICE-PRESIDENT OF THE SWISS PEOPLE'S PARTY

THE BILLIONAIRE BLOWHARD

According to the Germany's *Der Spiegel*, he's against the 'European Union, immigration and Islam' and just blew €2.45 million to prevent 'mass migration' to Switzerland. (He can afford it, he built up the international chemical company, EMS-CHEMIE, and is reckoned to be worth billions.) He's so incensed about the EU, he resigned from politics in 2014 to dedicate himself to a campaign against Switzerland's eventual membership. The *Daily Mail*, noted this message on his web site: 'The main threat to Switzerland consists of the planned institutional linking of Switzerland and the EU.'

He was recently kicked out of the Swiss Cabinet, which may have something to do with getting out of politics altogether, although he will still maintain his as Vice President of the *Schweizerische Volkspartei* (Swiss People's Party.) In an interview with *Der Spiegel*, Blocher said that claims that the *Schweizerische Volkspartei* was a far right party amounted to 'vilification from opponents and journalists'. But in 2009 his political party led the effort to ban minarets in Switzerland and produced a political campaign that, according to the *Financial Times*, included a 'poster of a woman in a burqa, standing on a Swiss flag, flanked by minarets looking like missiles.' It worked a charm and the vote to ban minarets on mosques won 57% of the vote.

According to the *New York Times*, Blocher lost a case to a Swiss newspaper, *SonntagsBlick*, 'which published an article under a headline taken from a phrase he used in a 1997 speech about the Holocaust accounts: *Blocher: The Jews Are Only Interested In Money*'. According to *Business Week* magazine, Blocher 'believes the Swiss central bank should not contribute to a separate $185 million fund for Holocaust survivors and their heirs', even though they probably still hold untold amounts of gold that was taken from Jews during the Holocaust.

**PRESIDENTIAL CANDIDATE:
CZECH REPUBLIC**

THE TV READER

She leads the *Suverenita* (Sovereignty) party in the Czech Republic, is a former television newsreader, an ex-MEP and she's kind of hot. It must be disappointing for liberals out there that, invariably, the hottest female politicians are conservatives.

Bobosikova's Sovereignty party is a Eurosceptic, populist party but it has not really broken through into the ranks of national politics, garnering under 6% of the vote in the last election. The tagline on the party's website says 'Law, Labour, Order', as if that isn't some sort of message that every other political party out there is putting out. It's also pro-Christian and anti-Muslim — as if the Czech Republic is at risk of being turned into a caliphate. It's anti-immigration too, which is a bit much for a country that sends so many of its professionals to other European countries to get work.

The former member of the Czechoslovak Socialist Union of Youth has denounced EU declarations on human rights, among other things. Bobosikova has also been quick to criticise members of the government she thinks are living high on the hog whilst ignoring their struggling constituents and, in a bid to capture the senior vote, opposes any sort of pension reform. She had a brief flirtation with the Communist Party in 2008, first entering the race as an independent presidential candidate with the party's backing but later pulling out when it was obvious how badly she would perform.

Although she is a minor figure in Czech politics, the fact that she has media savvy makes her a potential future contender, and as a political outsider she has the ability to unite both left and right in the cause of Czech nationalism, which always has an appeal to the disenfranchised.

JOHN BOEHNER

**SPEAKER OF THE
US HOUSE OF
REPRESENTATIVES**

TEARS OF A CLOWN

First of all, the name is supposed to be pronounced as 'Baner', not 'boner' as anybody unfamiliar with Mr Speaker might assume. He's a cigarette-smoking, perma-tanned, country club Republican who likes his booze – and there's nothing wrong there. He's been in politics for almost thirty years and was elected to the House in 1991.

He cries.

A lot. He cried at a Taco Bell event when he was praising the Boys' & Girls' Clubs of America. He cried at an event in 2012 honouring the painter, Constantino Brumidi and at another event while he was listening to Irish music. He got teary eyed when Neil Armstrong was given the Congressional Gold Medal in 2011. When he became Speaker of the House in the same year he was all tears again.

The list of tearful moments is endless; Boehner is one guy who's clearly not afraid to show his emotions. Even inanimate objects, like the bust of Winston Churchill, make the Speaker break down and the statue of Rosa Parks almost sent him into convulsions in 2013.

It may seem irrelevant to some readers that Boehner has a propensity to cry like a little girl but it becomes a bit more important when, under the current order of succession in the United States, he is third in line if the president resigns or something worse happens to him. That means that, if the Vice President resigns after the president resigns, then Boehner becomes head of state. That means that every time he would address the country there would be tears. He would also never get elected again, because he would lose the female vote. As the saying goes: every woman wants a man who can ruin her lipstick and not her mascara.

SULTAN OF BRUNEI

SPOILSPORT

In April of 2014, Sultan Hassanal Bolkiah imposed Sharia Law on his tiny state of Brunei. That means, according to the *Telegraph*, he has instituted a 'penal code, which punishes adultery with death by stoning, theft with amputation by sword and drunkenness with 40 lashes from a rattan cane.'

There's something very wrong with that.

First of all, the Sultan is the absolute leader of the country but he has had himself appointed Prime Minister, Minister of Defence and Minister of Finance by the thirty-six member legislative council that is handpicked by the Sultan, meets for only two weeks a year and doesn't really have any power.

Second of all, it does seem somewhat hypocritical for someone who has lived a graced life of excess to impose such a Spartan code on his people. According to the *New York Post*, 'the Sultan and his equally decadent brother, Prince Jefri, were dubbed *constant companions in hedonism* in 2011 by Vanity Fair. The Sultan lives in a palace with 1,788 rooms, 257 bathrooms, five swimming pools, a mosque, a banquet hall that holds 5,000 people and a 110-car garage. When he turned fifty, the Sultan built a stadium, invited Michael Jackson to perform in it and paid him $17 million for three concerts.'

The newspaper further reports that, '(Prince) Jefri, 59, maintains a separate pleasure palace and once owned a 152-foot yacht called *Tits*; he named its tenders *Nipple 1* and *Nipple 2*, and could never understand why others often found that juvenile and crass. Here and abroad, the brothers are infamous for their sex parties and their harems composed mainly of underage girls.' Of course it is illegal in Brunei to criticise the Sultan or to report about his lifestyle abroad.

For the country's 400,000 inhabitants life is pretty dull: no nightclubs, no alcohol and no fun.

UMBERTO BOSSI

**ITALIAN CHAMBER
OF DEPUTIES**

PADANIA

The Bossi-Fini law is one of the harshest anti-immigration acts in Europe. It criminalises illegal entry into Italy with prison sentences of up to four years for repeat offenders and stops Italian boats and ships from helping immigrants who are stranded at sea.

It's the work of Umberto Bossi, an Italian politician and the former head of the *Lega Nord* (Northern League) party that ultimately wants the northern Italy to break off from the rest of the country and form the magical kingdom of Padania. It's Italy's version of the Scottish National Party and according to Reuters, Bossi was 'saddened' by the outcome of the 2014 referendum in which Scots voted to preserve their union with the rest of the UK.

Only in Italy can a politician who has been convicted for taking a bribe present himself as a reformer. He also had a one-year prison sentence (suspended) for inciting violence at a political meeting. Like the American libertarian politician, Ron Paul (who named his son Rand, after the novelist Ayn Rand), Bossi chose uniquely absurd names for his children, like Libertà (freedom – a feminine noun) for one of his sons.

The anti-immigration stance of the *Lega Nord* often morphs into outright racism, although Bossi is quoted as saying, 'to me the blacks are nice'. *Reuters* news agency reports that *Lega Nord* 'party members have been accused of racism over grossly insulting attacks on Integration Minister Cecile Kyenge, Italy's first black minister, who was born in the Democratic Republic of the Congo.'

Bossi had a spectacular run as head of his political party up until 2012 when a judicial inquiry began looking into the finances of the *Lega Nord* and Bossi himself. As the BBC reported, 'according to court documents, Mr Bossi's wife bought no fewer than eleven houses and apartments with Northern League party funds.' They further reported that the 'Bossi family is revealed as being every bit as corrupt as the thieving Rome politicians it boasted that it wanted to unseat.'

ILLINOIS HOUSE OF
REPRESENTATIVES

FAST AND FURIOUS

His explosive rages are legendary to YouTube viewers prompting some commentators to suggest that he switch to decaf. In 2014 Bost ran for the US Congress on a Republican ticket in the southern part of the state that's sometimes called 'Little Egypt' because of the intense summer heat.

Besides saying 'the federal government has basically blown everything they are doing right now' he didn't present much more of a platform than promising to create jobs. His colourful past includes an incident where he shot a dog to death that had bitten his daughter. In 1986 a beagle named Rusty became aggressive after Bost's four-year-old had chased it and it turned on her and bit her face that later needed 19 stitches. Bost got his gun, found the dog and fired on it until it was dead. He was brought to trial for that incident but acquitted of any crime. He also had a .357 Rossi revolver stolen from his gun safe, which he didn't report to the police. It was used later in a criminal incident. In fact, he didn't know the gun was missing until the cops showed up at his door. He has a couple of car crashes to his credit and a mysterious incident where someone kicked in the door of his home when he was gone.

His incidents on the floor of the Illinois legislature are widely watched. In one debate he smashed his microphone and in another rage about pension legislation he screamed, 'I feel like somebody trying to be released from Egypt! Let my people go!' He came in second for that particular rage in a CNN compilation of 'Best Celebrity Flip-Outs of All-Time'. He went into an angry tirade about a concealed weapon bill that would require the local sheriff to decide if a person was stable enough to be armed which prompted one opposition member to say about Bost, 'so here's my point, members, we don't want someone like that carrying a concealed weapon.'

DESI BOUTERSE

PRESIDENT OF SURINAM

SOMETIMES YOU GET WHAT YOU WISH FOR

He was elected President in 2010, although he had been the *de facto* military head of state from 1980 to 1987. The fact that he was chosen the leader of the country makes you wonder about the sanity of some of the electors. According to the *New York Times*, 'Desi Bouterse has been a soldier, a coup plotter, the military ruler of the former Dutch colony, a convicted drug trafficker and, for more than a decade, a fugitive from Interpol.'

In 2000, the Dutch courts found him guilty of smuggling 474 kilos of cocaine into their country and sentenced him to eleven years in prison. Though Europol have a warrant for his arrest, his status as Surinam's Head of State gives him immunity. He was the prime suspect in the torture and killing of fifteen political opponents in December 1982, although he never attended the trial and claimed he was not present when the murders took place. In 2012 the Surinam Parliament granted amnesty to all those accused of the murders, rendering any further legal action redundant.

According to the *Times*, shortly after taking power again in 2010, Bouterse also began remodelling Surinam's governing institutions, frequently with his own family. He put his wife, Ingrid Bouterse-Waldring, on the government payroll at about $4,000 a month for her duties as first lady. He also named his thirty-eight-year-old son, Dino Bouterse, convicted by the Dutch in 2005 of leading a cocaine and illegal weapons ring, as part of the command of a new Counter-Terrorism Unit.

Choosing Dino to head that unit was not the smartest thing Desi Bouterse ever did. Dino wandered Panama with a diplomatic passport, found himself arrested and was extradited to the US. According to the *Associated Press*, in September 2014, Dino, 'pleaded guilty to US charges that he sought to offer a home base in his South American country to the Lebanese militant group Hezbollah'. Dino told a Manhattan federal court that 'as part of the scheme he provided a false Surinamese passport to a person he believed was a Hezbollah operative. He also pleaded guilty to drug trafficking and firearms charges.'

CHRISTINE BOUTIN

**LEADER OF THE FRENCH
CHRISTIAN DEMOCRATIC PARTY**

CATHOLIC CRUSADER

Who said only America had Jesus freaks? Ultra-catholic Rick Santorum, runner-up in the 2012 Republican presidential primaries, would certainly feel at home talking to Christine Marcelle Valérie Cécile Marie Martin – or Christine Boutin, as she's been known since 1967, when she married her first cousin, Louis, with whom she has three children.

A law graduate who switched to journalism before running for – and winning – a city council seat in a Parisian suburb in 1977, the short and chubby-cheeked Boutin is known for her extremely strongly conservative views. The defining moment of her political career is perhaps her brandishing of the Bible in the French National Assembly in her five-hour diatribe against the passage of civil unions in the late 1990s. Strongly against abortion and gay marriage, she has publicly stated that the 'homosexual problem' and the 'gay invasion' was at the heart of the 'collapse of society' and also tweeted that Angelina Jolie's voluntary mastectomy for fear of breast cancer was so that 'she would look like a man'.

A 9/11 'truther', she stated in 2006 that it was possible George W. Bush was responsible for the attacks on the World Trade Center. Boutin is a staunch royalist in a country that last had royals in 1848, and has stated that she has 'never fully accepted the death of Louis XVI and Marie Antoinette'. A member of the French parliament for many years, she was chosen as Housing Minister in 2007, serving under Nicolas Sarkozy. She only lasted two years in the job, and since founded the Christian Democratic Party – as party chair, she has advocated in the last five years for an end to birthright citizenship and the return of military service.

PATRICK BRAZEAU

CANADIAN SENATE

THE BRAZMAN

He's got the best of both worlds. The suspended Canadian Senator doesn't have to attend any of the Senate's sittings anymore, which leaves him free to collect a second pay check for his work as a day manager at the BareFax strip club in Ottawa's ByWard Market.

Brazeau faces charges of fraud and breach of trust for tax evasion and allegedly claiming false expenses in his role as Senator. Furthermore, in April of 2014 he was done for two counts of assault, uttering threats, cocaine possession and breach of bail conditions. He pleaded not guilty to all counts.

He is the youngest Senator ever appointed and controversially took his seat while he was also getting paid for being the Chief of the Congress of Aboriginal Peoples. Before he was kicked out of the Conservative caucus he had one of the lowest attendance ratings in the Senate, which was pointed out by a journalist, Jennifer Ditchburn. Brazeau didn't take that well and called her a 'bitch'. He did the obligatory rehab facility in Saint-Andre-d'Argenteuil but the Senate wants him to pay back $50,000 he has claimed in expenses and they're taking payments out of his salary.

Since his suspension, he challenged the WWF's 'Honky Tonk Man' to a public wrestling match that took place in May 2014 in Smith Falls, Ontario. To further burnish his image he claimed to be attending university in the latter part of 2014, although he never revealed either the university or his course of study. He has to be in court on June 1, 2015, to address the fraud charges he faces.

In April of 2014, Stephen Maher from *Postmedia News* photographed a slew of personal items that had been thrown in the snow outside of the Brazman's house near Ottawa. The Senator apparently had been kicked out of his own house and his possessions were hurled out after he left, including 'a bag of what looked to be marijuana'.

PAUL BROUN JR

US HOUSE OF
REPRESENTATIVES

THE PIT OF HELL

Broun isn't just impassioned. He's livid. Speaking at the
Sportsman's Banquet at the Liberty Baptist Church, the
Georgia congressman said, 'All that stuff I was taught about
evolution and embryology and the Big Bang Theory, all that is lies straight from the pit of Hell.'

Broun earns top marks for craziness. He thinks Planned Parenthood and National Public
Radio are 'unconstitutional'. He has said that the Civil War was just a 'Yankee War of
Aggression'. What should worry Americans is that Broun serves on the House Science,
Space, and Technology Committee, a position that would suggest some basic aptitude for
rational thought. But Broun doesn't need 'so-called-scientists' to tell him why the world
turns, he's got a book at home that tells him everything. 'And what I've come to learn is
that it's the manufacturer's handbook, is what I call it,' says Broun. 'It teaches us how to run
our lives individually, how to run our families, how to run our churches. But it teaches us
how to run all of public policy and everything in society. And that's the reason as your
congressman I hold the Holy Bible as being the major directions to me of how I vote in
Washington, D.C., and I'll continue to do that.'

There's nothing in the Bible about 'global warming', so you can forget about that. He
proposed to make 2010 the 'Year of the Bible', but that piece of legislation is still languish-
ing. Broun's biggest concern is that President Obama is secretly trying to turn the United
States into a Marxist Dictatorship. When asked on Sirius XM satellite radio if he thought
Obama was really American, he replied, 'I don't know'. During Obama's 2011 State of the
Union address, Broun tweeted, 'Mr President, you don't believe in the Constitution. You
believe in socialism.' The congressman is also big on 'family values' and is currently married
to his fourth wife.

It's estimated that in the last election for congress in 2012, almost 5,000 of his constituents wrote in the name 'Charles Darwin' on their ballot papers.

LEN BROWN

MAYOR OF AUCKLAND

THE DRAGON LADY

You have to admire a politician who gets caught with his pants down, runs up some questionable expenses and just shrugs it off as another day in the life.

That's particularly true if you come from a country as staid as New Zealand. The Mayor of Auckland, Len Brown, was first elected to the post of the amalgamated Auckland 'Super City' in 2010 and re-elected in 2013. Cameron Slater, who writes the widely read political blog, *Whaleoil*, had Brown in his sights for years, and in 2013 he hit pay dirt and published lurid details of Brown's affair with a younger council advisor, Bevan Chuang. That affair involved sex in the Mayor's chambers and lots of other places.

Chuang is an unusual woman. In 2012 she made a public appeal on radio and television for sperm donors so she could get pregnant in the Year of the Dragon. A lot of people volunteered for the job and she interviewed twenty of the most promising, although nothing came out of it in the end.

She also has a criminal conviction for illegally accessing emails. She was having an affair with the mayor at the same time she asked for sperm donors, but she was also seeing Luigi Wewege, who was the close advisor to Brown's political opponent, John Palino. It was Wewege who clued in Cameron Slater about the Mayor's affair. He also released nude photos he had taken of Chuang to the media. After the details of the affair broke, Stephen Cook, the journalist who had written the story on *Whaleoil* and was also organising a $25,000 contest for *New Zealand's Next Top XXX Model*, offered Chuang a job as a porn star, which she politely declined.

Meanwhile, Len Brown made all the necessary apologies and carried on in his job and continues to rack up some rather big expenses on the mayoral credit card.

MARIE BURKE

BELLEVILLE TOWN
COUNCIL, NEW JERSEY

'N' OR NOT 'N'

Belleville, New Jersey, is a peaceful little place within the New York City commuter belt. It was settled in 1796 and has about 35,000 people within its tree-lined streets who have a standard of living well above the national average. It's mainly a white town but 10 % of the population are African American and there is a significant Asian population.

Marie Burke is a local Democratic politician in the town, representing the first ward on the town council. She's lived in Belleville for 45 years and has a regular column in the *Belleville Times* about life in her local neighbourhood, Silver Lakes. Burke launched a campaign for mayor in 2014 but ran into some problems right away.

In 2013 Burke allegedly left a voicemail on Councilman Kevin Kennedy's phone in a conversation about upcoming tax changes. In the recording, she supposedly said, 'this is terrible. This is terrible. This is gonna be a fucking nigger town.' Burke denied that the voice was hers but, according to the *New York Daily News*, 'a forensics lab based in Michigan confirmed the voice on the tape was Burke's'.

Her opponent in the mayoral race, Raymond Kimble, called for her resignation from the town council but Burke was adamant it was all a set-up. According to the *Star Ledger*, when Burke found out the tape had been sent to a forensic lab for analysis, she said, 'I am 100% certain that Kimble's fingerprints are all over this report.' Kimble was convinced it was Burke's voice on the phone asserting that, it was, 'her speaking style, her pacing. The delivery of all the words spoken in both samples are identical.' A petition to recall Burke was launched in 2014 but did not garner enough signatures to warrant action. The councilwoman is adamant that the tape was forged by her political opponents, saying, 'this is just political retaliation because I wanted to run for mayor.'

ITALIAN CHAMBER
OF DEPUTIES

PAINT IT BLACK

The Italian MP, Gianluca Buonanno, once produced a makeup kit in Parliament and started to dab his face in order to make it darker, in protest at immigrants to Italy receiving state benefits. He famously told the chamber of deputies that: 'to get money, perhaps we all need to make ourselves darker'.

Buonanno's political party, *Lega Nord* (the Northern League) are notoriously xenophobic, but Gianluca always seems to take things a step beyond the limit of sanity. To make matters worse, he's also the mayor of Borgosesia and one of his ambitions is to make gay kisses illegal and subject to a €500 fine. He's got a picture of Russian President Vladimir Putin in his office because he admires his anti-gay stance. 'I don't like that two people of the same sex exchange public displays of affection,' said Buonanno. 'It's a matter of respect and I am convinced that it is morally harmful to children.' One of his fellow MEPs said 'it would be an interesting psychological exercise to ask why Mr. Buonanno is so obsessed with homosexuality.'

Buonanno also has a thing about Viagra, once proposing that the city subsidise the cost of the drug by 50% to promote the fertility of the Italian people. One of the many insane proposals Buonanno has made was to change the name of one of the city's squares to honour Benito Mussolini. He also proposed to fine anyone from €100 to €200 if they insulted the Catholic religion.

He is something of a dancer and performed on the Italian television show, *Let's Dance*, but his real passion is homosexuality. 'At the Gay Pride we see scenes that are disgusting, horrifying scenes,' said Buonanno. 'The Pride sucks. It is a carnival with gays and lesbians and the children see everything, they see the ass, kissing in the street. If a gay guy comes up and tries to piss me off I give him a kick in the balls.'

TROY BUSWELL

WESTERN AUSTRALIA ASSEMBLY

THE DRY HUMPER

Australians like their politicians to be on the crazy side
and they certainly got their money's worth with Troy Buswell.
Because of their inflated egos, many 'responsible married' politicians who 'treasure family
values' still have to have a little something on the side. The trouble is that when you dump
them they get angry and want some payback.

Adele Carles was the first Green Party member to get elected to the Western Australian Legislative Assembly. That's where she met Troy Buswell and sparks begin to fly. The two
lovebirds didn't try to make a big secret about their affair but Buswell vigorously denied it
until 2010 when Carles admitted to a 'mutual, albeit stupid' romance with the Treasurer of
Western Australia. That was the end of both of their marriages.

According to the *Australian* newspaper, Carles then went on the radio and social media
and talked how her ex-lover sniffed 'the seat of a female staffer while moaning in mock pleasure' and 'of dry humping a businessman and being an alcoholic with psychological issues'.
The paper went on to explain that 'it is less known that he thought it was terrifically funny
when he grabbed the testicles of a fellow MP during a sitting of the Legislative Assembly and
that he unfastened the bra of a Labour staffer through her shirt at parliament as a party trick.'

Buswell sued Carles for defamation but that was settled amicably a couple of years later.
Then came the incidents with the ministerial car. According to the *Guardian*, 'Buswell quit
cabinet following revelations he had a mental breakdown after crashing into parked cars, a
pole and the front gate of his Subiaco home while returning from a wedding in the early
hours of February.' A legislative committee looked into the incident and, as Opposition
Leader, Mark McGowan, said in conclusion to a report being issued about the matter, which
laid the blame solely on Buswell, 'it's not the committee that got drunk at a wedding and
then crashed a government vehicle.'

At this time, Buswell was Western Australia's Transport Minister.

FRANK BWALYA

ZAMBIAN PARTY LEADER

THAT'S FREE SPEECH

The former Australian opposition leader, Mark Latham, who once called another former opposition leader, Bob Carr, a 'grade A arsehole' and referred to former prime minister, John Howard, as 'an arse-licker', wouldn't fare too well in Zambian politics. Zambian politicians are a sensitive lot as Frank Bwalya found out in 2014.

Bwalya is the leader of the opposition party, the Alliance for a Better Zambia, and also an ordained Roman Catholic priest. He made a seemingly innocuous remark about the president of the country, Michael Sata, during a radio interview in January. He called Sata a *chumbu musholdolwa*, which translates into 'a sweet potato that breaks when it is bent'. That Zambian idiom actually means not heeding or listening to advice, it doesn't mean 'arse licker' or 'grade A arsehole', but it was enough to get Bwalya arrested and charged with defamation of the president.

Bwalya is no stranger to bizarre arrests. In 2010 he was participating in an anti-government rally in Kitwe, which is north of Zambia's capital, Lusaka, when he flashed a red card to the crowd. The police interpreted that as an indication that Bwalya wanted to remove the government from power and threw him in the clink.

Bwalya actually supported Sata when he was in the opposition, but since Sata took power he has been Bwalya's political opponent. Bwalya was eventually acquitted of the charge of defamation but that didn't stop him from criticising President Sata. In April 2014 he called on the president to resign because he was destroying the democracy of the country and said the government was feeding the people 'a diet of lies' and that Sata was 'out of touch with reality'.

SPANISH CONGRESS OF DEPUTIES

BUMMER

Voters, particularly Spanish Catholic ones, generally like to see their elected MPs maintain a certain level of decorum.

Not so with Toni Canto. The openly gay Spanish MP is proud of his acting ability and would like nothing better than to once again appear naked in a hard core gay porno film.

A member of the Union, Progress and Democracy Party, Canto's film career was launched in 2011 when he played a Spanish sex tourist in *The Last Match,* which was shot in Havana, Cuba.

According to *Gay Star News*, the film was made, 'just a few months before [his] being elected to office, but [Canto] says if offered a similar role now he'd have no hesitation about taking it'. He told the Spanish news agency EFE, 'if you're asking me if I would have played a gay character in sex scenes while being an MP, the answer is yes.' He clarified that remark by adding, 'I'm aware of the fact that I live in a society where people are more shocked by seeing an MP's backside than by one who robs or is paid under the table.'

The Last Match was released in Spain in March of 2014 and tells the story of two soccer-crazed male prostitutes who live in Havana.

Canto says, 'I need to express my artistic side, otherwise I go a bit mad.' Anyway, it's not all gay; in one scene, Canto has his clothes taken off by a naked woman and another guy comes in to watch the action.

JOHN CARNEVALE

RHODE ISLAND CONGRESS

PUTTING PUBLIC FIRST

There are 7,382 state legislators in the US, so there's a good chance that some of them will turn out to be bad eggs.

John Carnevale is a Democrat representing the 13th District in the smallest of America's states: Rhode Island. His motto is 'putting public first' and he has a strange way of demonstrating that.

In November of 2011, Carnevale was indicted by a grand jury on three counts of sexual assault. According to the *Johnston Sun Rise*, 'the victim claimed she received a phone call from Carnevale, who she says is the Godfather to her son, just before midnight, asking her where she was.'

The woman said Carnevale arrived at her apartment building shortly thereafter and smelled of alcohol. She said he told her she was beautiful and proceeded to pull her down on an air mattress in the living room. The report describes a struggle, 'during which the victim claims that Carnevale fondled her and attempted to rape her. When she resisted, the victim said Carnevale masturbated in front of her and forced her face up to his genitalia. When Carnevale was finished, the victim said he threw a $20 bill down and told her to take her kid out to eat.' (What a gent!)

The victim died shortly after the court proceedings of a pulmonary embolism. According to NBC News, 'the attorney general said the state cannot proceed with the case without the woman's testimony.'

That's not all the former cop has been accused of, but never convicted. According to the *Boston Globe*, 'In 1999, Reed (former wife, Jennifer Reed) told police that Carnevale grabbed her by the wrist, dragged her out of the house and hung up the phone when she called the police. Reed told police the fight started after Carnevale woke her up and asked for money. When she refused, Reed said Carnevale told her to call his girlfriend. When she picked up the phone to call, Reed said Carnevale pulled the phone off the wall, according to a transcript of a police interview.'

PRESIDENTIAL ASPIRANT

THE GREAT BLACK HOPE

He's the darling of the American right and first came
to fame when he gave a speech at the 2013 National
Prayer Breakfast, with President Barack Obama in the
audience that described the Affordable Care Act as being at
the heart of the 'moral decay and fiscal irresponsibility' that was destroying the country.

He's announced that it's very likely he will run for president in 2016. He was placed
second in the Republican Leadership Conference's straw poll in 2014 behind Texas Senator
Tom Cruz, despite the fact that he has never held public office. The son of a Baptist preacher,
Carson became one of America's most talented and respected neurosurgeons. He was
the first to successfully separate conjoined twins that were joined at the head and was
awarded the Presidential Medal of Freedom in 2008.

He hung up his surgical gloves and retired in 2013 to concentrate on his political career
and he's crisscrossing the country telling audiences that Obamacare, which has helped
insure 9 million Americans who were previously uninsured, is morally equivalent to slavery
and thinks its implementation has done more damage to the country than 9/11. He's called
for the dismantling of Social Security, Medicare, Medicaid, public assistance and he wants to
institute a flat tax. He describes abortion as a 'human sacrifice' and goes off on vicious riffs
about the LGBT community and likens homosexuality with 'bestiality'. He's even got a Euro-
style crush on Vladimir Putin because of the Russian leader's stance on gays.

The fact that he has a book that is number one on the *New York Times* bestseller list,
One Nation: What We Can All Do To Save America's Future and has appointed a professional
manager (talk show host Armstrong Williams) may reveal a different agenda. Maybe it's not
so much the conservative fervour that is motivating the doctor, but the money he could
make from the rubes who believe him.

DOUGLAS CARSWELL

UK HOUSE OF COMMONS

THE FLIGHT OF THE LOONS (PT 1)

In October 2014, Douglas Carswell became the first Member of Parliament for the United Kingdom Independence Party (UKIP) after winning the seat of Clacton, from the Conservatives with a historic 44% swing. One Clacton resident said he voted UKIP because 'the Conservative never done much for people around here.' The Conservative was none other than … Douglas Carswell. He jumped ship from his old party and resigned as an MP to cause the by election, which he then fought under new colours.

Why he did so is anybody's guess. The jutting jawline suggests too much grit to run scared of being unhorsed by UKIP in 2015. He's also a very intelligent and perceptive man; he'd been a veritable think tank while in the Conservative party, credited with pioneering localism and direct democracy long before they became fashionable. He also favours open primaries for political candidates – something the Brits don't have. Up to now, the UK political parties tend to pretty much dump candidates on localities – frequently party favourites from hundreds of miles out of town – and this has been a cause of growing public discontentment with Britain's political elite. He's big on civil liberties too, opposing ID cards, uncontrolled fingerprinting and the holding of biometric data and the unrestricted expansion of CCTV (it's said that the Brits live under more surveillance cameras than the rest of Europe put together). He also wants to roll back the incursions made over the years against the principles of trial by jury and habeas corpus. So why in the name of all things cerebral did Carswell decide to sign up with the political nuthouse?

It could be that he's following the maxim that in the country of the mad, the half sane man is king – or maybe he simply lost patience with the Etonian clique that now runs his old party.

Either way, the UKIP leader, Nigel Farage, ought to be wetting himself with joy. He's not only acquired his first MP but a degree of respectability – and a one-man policy machine too, something the one-plank party badly needs.

HORACIO CARTES

PRESIDENT OF PARAGUAY

EL PRESIDENTE

According to the *Independent*, 'in 2011, WikiLeaks cables originat-
ing from the US embassy in Buenos Aires placed him at the centre of a drugs and money-
laundering network operating out of the lawless frontier with Argentina and Brazil.' They
further reported how, 'in 2000, drugs enforcement officers intercepted a small plane on
one of Mr Cartes's farms carrying a cargo of cocaine and marijuana. Mr Cartes said that an
unknown plane landing on his property had nothing to do with him.' (Of course it didn't.)

Paraguay's new president didn't have any political experience before he took the job.
In fact, he had never voted before he put his hat in the ring for the Colorado Party, which
shows his historic civic commitment.

He's the kind of guy that respects traditional family life rather than the 'monkeys' who
belong to the LGBT community. He even said he'd shoot the balls off of his children
entering into a same sex marriage. He did time in 1989 for currency fraud but was later
acquitted and bounced back to create a tobacco empire. The *New York Times* reported that
allegations of 'money laundering and the smuggling of cigarettes into neighbouring Brazil'
were made against Cartes during the 2013 campaign.

CTV of Canada reported that, 'Before taking office as president, his family became an
issue . . . when uncle Juan Viveros Cartes was arrested in Uruguay for allegedly violating its
airspace. Uruguayan officials allege the uncle was using a small plane to look for clandestine
landing strips for drug smuggling.' According to Adrienne Pine on Al Jazeera, 'this is somebody who the DEA has investigated for drug trafficking, who set up a bank with no actual
building, and no employees on the Cook islands, which was basically for laundering money
in the 90s and follows a pattern of wealthy land owners and businessmen in Latin America,
who have come to power, and who have received the support of the United States.'

CHANG AN-LO

PARTY LEADER, TAIWAN

THE WHITE WOLF

The leader of the China Unification Promotion Party has an interesting past. Described as erudite, educated and polite, he's the former head of the biggest triad in Taiwan and, as the *Sydney Morning Herald*, pointed out, 'is a convicted kidnapper, extortionist and heroin trafficker who has been mobilising muscular protests and intimidating pro-democracy activists on the island.'

He's also an ally of the Chinese Communist Party, who see him as a tool to reunify the two countries by popular vote instead of by force. As the *Economist* reports, Chang was, 'incarcerated in a maximum-security American penitentiary for ten years on drug-trafficking charges.' He spent the last 17 years in mainland China as a fugitive and was arrested on his return to Taiwan in 2013. In April of 2014 he addressed a group of anti-unification students in Taipei and told them, 'You are all fucking offspring of China, but do not deserve to be Chinese.' The *Economist* also observed that video footage from Taiwan's *Apple Daily* newspaper 'shows members of Mr Chang's entourage beating a lone student caught up in their throng.'

Besides heading his new political party, Chang is also said to be the 'spiritual' leader of a Taiwanese triad that smuggles drugs into the country. According to the *Washington Post*, Chang 'was one of nine men convicted on drug and racketeering charges for their part in a Taiwan-based international crime ring, the Bamboo Union gang, which, according to US and Taiwanese court records, also carried out a politically motivated killing in Daly City, California in 1984. The victim, Henry Liu, was a crusading Taiwanese American journalist.' The *Taipei Times* tells of how police raided one of Mr Chang's political campaign offices in 2013. According to the paper, it was a front for the Bamboo Union to 'engage in extortion, possess guns illegally and hold drug parties'.

AUSTRALIAN HOUSE OF
REPRESENTATIVES

TWO CHINS

The further down America's eastern seaboard you go, the crazier the politicians get. That's true — in reverse — of Australia's east coast. George 'two chins' Christensen is a Liberal MP representing the area around Dawson, Queensland. He's been described as an outstanding player on 'team idiot' by his colleagues.

Just as Australia was preparing to join America, Britain and France to battle ISIS in 2014, Christensen made a stirring speech in parliament when he said, 'The greatest terrorism threat in north Queensland, it is sad to say, comes from the extreme green movement.' He was speaking about opposition to the expansion of the seaport at Abbot Point that is meant to enable huge shipments of Australia's coal to China and the rest of Asia. Opposition mainly concerns the vast amount of dredging underway that may affect the nearby Great Barrier Reef.

As the port is located in Queensland and Christensen is not what one would call an environmentalist, he strongly supports the construction of the massive facility no matter what the environmental costs. He stated that the 'well-organised eco-terrorists who use fear and blackmail to coerce government and the public into adopting their extreme political and ideological viewpoints' were set to destroy the economy. Furthermore, the Liberal MP wants Queenslanders to 'call out the gutless green grubs for the terrorists that they really are.'

Other issues bother him too, like the Muslims who he recommends should 'jump on the first plane and head back to where you come from.' He's also dead keen on bringing back the death penalty and was the only MP to see the Dutch ultra-nationalist, Geert Wilders, when he visited Australia. One of his favourite issues is opposing the Health Department's recommendations on reducing sugar in the diet. His defence of the Queensland sugar producers has earned him the nickname of the 'sugar plum fairy'.

AHMED CHALABI

IRAQ PARLIAMENT

APOCALYPSE THEN AND NOW

The bullshitter from Bagdad is a bad memory for those who led America into war in Iraq in 2003. In fact, they conveniently forgot about him until he was mentioned in 2014 as a bizarre possible replacement for the screw-up, Nouri al-Maliki, who is personally credited with single-handedly enabling the Islamic State of Iraq and Syria. He used to be the head of the Iraqi National Congress (INC), which was based in Washington DC and provided much of the 'intelligence' about Saddam Hussein's stockpile of weapons of mass destruction and his ties to al-Qaeda, all of which proved a load of horse shit.

He was reverently referred to as the 'George Washington of Iraq' in the right-wing isolation ward that governed the US at the time. He had been convicted *in absentia* for bank fraud in Jordan, but that didn't stop him in his drive to have America invade his country of birth. In fact, the US government paid the INC millions, which Chalabi cleverly used to employ the lobbying firm of BKSH & Associates to push his agenda in the capital. Although he was seen as a natural leader for post-invasion Iraq, the Iraqis themselves saw him as a 'convicted fraudster' who had helped bring hell to their doorstep.

After the invasion, the US put him in charge of the ill-conceived Higher National De-Ba'athification Commission, but he used his role as a means to shake down wealthy businessmen. In the Iraqi elections of 2005 he failed miserably, but the Americans virtually forced the new government to appoint him Deputy Prime Minister and acting Oil Minister. The year before, Chalabi had been invited by the First Lady, Laura Bush, to hear her husband give the State of the Union address to congress. Now Chalabi is just one member of the Iraqi Parliament, and not a very significant figure in the minds of Iraqis but it is said that he made a fortune on the back of the American invasion.

BUDDY CIANCI

FORMER MAYOR OF
PROVIDENCE, RHODE ISLAND

RASCAL KING

He's running again for mayor and some people in
Providence, Rhode Island aren't too happy about that.
The reason is that, somehow, the rug-wearing Cianci
always ends up in prison at the end of his term.

Originally winning the post as a Republican in this heavily Democratic city, he ran the
second time as an independent. According to National Public Radio (NPR), 'the 73-year-old
Cianci served over two decades as mayor of Providence, though his time in office was split
up by a felony conviction for assault, another for corruption, and time in federal prison.'

Darrell West, a political science professor at Brown University told NPR, 'this is a guy
who has been convicted twice and spent four and a half years in federal prison, but despite
that kind of background, it's not inconceivable that this guy could end up becoming the next
mayor of Providence.'

After becoming mayor in 1974 he had a fairly uneventful ten years before he assaulted
someone who he thought was getting it on with his estranged wife. He had to resign then
because he was convicted of a felony assault. He ran again in 1990 and won by a slim
margin. Cianci was indicted by a federal grand jury in 2001 on 27 felony counts, which
ranged from mail fraud, extortion, and witness tampering. He was acquitted on 26 counts
but convicted in 2002 for the 27th and got four and a half years in the slammer.

When he was released from federal prison in 2007 he began co-hosting a talk show
on WPRO, a local Providence radio station. He announced on air in June, 2014, that he
was, once again, running for mayor. According to the *Associated Press*, Cianci calls his
prison term 'a bump in the road' and says what's more important is the good he did in
'overseeing visionary changes, including moving rivers, building a huge shopping mall and
investing in arts and preservation.' That 27th count was for racketeering.

BARBARA COMSTOCK

US CONGRESSIONAL CANDIDATE

ATTACK DOG

Barbara Comstock has a surprisingly short memory. The Republican nominee for a US Congressional seat representing northern Virginia in 2012 was all for the 'mandatory ultra-sound' legislation that would have required every woman in the state seeking an abortion to submit themselves to a humiliating transvaginal ultrasound. It didn't pass but a version requiring a normal ultrasound did, and that required Virginia's 23 abortion clinics to make expensive changes.

It's what the Democrats have dubbed the Republicans' 'War on Women'. Two years after that, Comstock is now for over-the-counter contraceptives instead of prescription based pills as a means to win back the support of women. However, she is against expanding Medicare to the 400,000 uninsured Virginians of which 200,000 are women and she's dead keen on repealing the Affordable Care Act (Obamacare) if she wins the election in 2014.

The former lobbyist for the Koch brothers, 'forgot' to report that a PR company she owns took $85,000 from the 'Romney for President' campaign, which was a potential violation of ethics. She's got a lot of smart ideas, though, like keeping track of illegal immigrants the same way Federal Express or DHL tracks its packages. She told a campaign gathering that, 'Fed-Ex can track packages coming in here all of the time, we can track people who are coming into the country and we can do that right' (as long as we tattoo a bar code on them?).

Comstock is a former GOP researcher and was one of the behind-the-scenes players in the drive to impeach Bill Clinton. She was also a key figure in the 2000 campaign of George W. Bush and prepared all the attack information about his opponent, Al Gore. She once admitted she stayed up late at night trying to find dirt on the Clintons, particularly Hillary, because she reminded her so much of herself.

ANTONIO GARCIA CONEJO

CONGRESS OF MEXICO

STRIPSHOW

It says a lot about someone if his favourite book is *Jonathan Livingston Seagull*. Garcia is a Deputy in the Mexican Congress representing the Free and Sovereign State of Michoacán de Ocampo for the Party of the Democratic Revolution (PRD). Nominally a part of the Socialist Alliance, it's famous for videos of its members gambling large sums of money in Las Vegas.

Garcia wasn't involved in that little scandal but he didn't like the idea of opening up the energy sector and possibly allowing Petroleos Mexicanos, (PEMEX) to be bought by a foreign oil giant. The bill also would remove five members of the PEMEX board who were from the notoriously corrupt oil workers union.

The PRD came out strongly against the legislation. Garcia's comrade, Carlos de Jesus Alejandro, also of the PRD, stated that he was 'against those who would sell their mother, their motherland'. The bill also included a provision that would end the monopoly of the national electricity utility, known as CFE. Cries of 'traitor' interrupted the voting and scuffles broke out, but Garcia took the day when he gave an opposing speech while he was stripping off his clothes. Thankfully, the chunky lawmaker stopped the show when he got down to his underwear. Asked by *Vocativ* why he put on the strip show, Garcia said, 'some of it was personal frustration, I had the feeling no one was listening to me, so I had to catch the attention of the floor in some way.' He further added that 'the government is trying to strip the country of its resources, so I thought I might as well strip myself.' Asked if he would ever strip again, Garcia said, 'I'm not sure if I'll do something like this again, but the most important thing is to continue creating awareness amongst Mexicans about this nefarious reform.'

RAFAEL CORREA

PRESIDENT OF ECUADOR

CRITICISM WILL COST YOU

Countries should start to worry when their presidents contemplate keeping their job forever. Rafael Correa, is thinking of doing just that because he 'believes' in democracy.

He first came into office in 2007 and is credited with taking Ecuador into the 21st century. One of his first acts of power was an audacious bluff. He declared the $3 billion the country owed to overseas creditors an 'illegitimate debt'. He said he wasn't going to pay it and would fight in the international courts to have it cancelled. Bondholders all over the world panicked and sold their bonds at huge discounts, allowing Correa to effectively cancel the debt for peanuts.

Irritated by satirical cartoons and virulent media criticism, Correa established the press authority, Supercom, ostensibly to guarantee freedom of the press, but in reality to regulate it through a sense of self-censorship among the media. Supercom fined the magazine *Vistazo* $80,000 in 2012 for printing an article advocating a 'no' vote against the president. *El Universo* was nailed for $40 million and three of its directors and journalists were sentenced to three years in the clink for an article that accused Correa of abusing human rights (he later pardoned them). This wouldn't all be so bad if Correa hadn't offered asylum to the self-righteous tosser, Julian Assange, in his embassy in London. Assange is cowering away in the tiny consulate because he is convinced that the rape charges against him in Sweden are part of a devious plot to extradite him to the United States. Correa now blames Britain for violating Assange's human rights.

He tried to support a $9 billion class action suit against the American oil giant, Chevron, for pollution but that was thrown out by an arbitration panel in The Hague. Correa has a television show where he sings songs and criticises the press. If he gets his way, the Supreme Court of Ecuador will shortly send a law to its parliament allowing Correa to carry on as president for as long as he wants.

MIKE CRAPO

US SENATE

BOOZE HOUND

Let's not call it a cult because that would be insulting to the 7 million Mormons in the world. After all, wearing magical underwear, believing that the dead can be baptised in your faith, that every star in the universe has its own god, that coffee, tea and especially booze shouldn't ever be consumed and dinosaur bones came from other planets are all just part of a normal rational belief system.

Furthermore, having a name that looks like it should be pronounced as 'crappo' and claiming it really should be said as 'cray-po' is no worse than the speaker of the US House of Representatives saying his surname shouldn't be pronounced as 'boner'. Where's the reality? Only 2% of the US population is Mormon but 7% of the US Senate are members of the Church of the Latter Day Saints. They also make up a good portion of the Secret Service and the CIA, although they probably make the most unlikely spies.

Mike Crapo is a Mormon and US Senator for the state of Idaho. He's not a particularly outstanding member of the upper chamber of the legislature but he presents himself as a rock solid kind of guy. He's been Idaho's senior senator since the retirement of Larry Craig, who was arrested for soliciting an undercover police officer for sex in a men's restroom at Minneapolis-St Paul Airport in 2007.

Crapo, who told the voters he was a strict teetotaller, got stuck into a bottle of white lightning in December of 2013 in his house outside of Washington, DC, and decided to go out on the town. He didn't make it very far. He was pulled over by the Virginia cops, tested for alcohol and came up with a blood reading of .11%; Virginia's legal limit is .08%. He was nicked for drunk driving and had his licence revoked for a year and was fined $250. Thankfully for him, it was right after Christmas and it didn't make many headlines.

TED CRUZ

UNITED STATES SENATE

MR UNPOPULARITY

He's only been a senator for a few years but you could already write a book about him. Unfortunately, it would be a tragedy of epic proportions. Everybody hates him on both sides of the aisle.

He's obviously got big political ambitions – or at least the Democrats hope so, because if Ted Cruz led the Republican ticket in the 2016 presidential elections, he'd be hard pressed to pick up one state.

GQ magazine calls him the 'Distinguished Wacko Bird from Texas' and *Mother Jones* magazine says he's 'the thinking man's tea partier'. There's no doubt he's intelligent, graduating from Princeton and Harvard Law School, but he's also incredibly abrasive. Cruz habitually wears a pair of black, ostrich-skinned cowboy boots that he calls his 'argument boots'. But in September 2013 he famously abandoned these in favour of a comfortable pair of tennis shoes when he gave the fourth longest speech in the history of the Senate. In a filibuster attempt to strip 'Obamacare' of funding, he was on his feet for 21 hours and 19 minutes. At one point he read Dr Seuss's *Green Eggs and Ham* because he said his kids might be watching and need a bedtime story.

The *New York Times* says he is 'the least popular person in Washington', but then they would say that. Fellow Republicans say worse things but only off-the-record. When it comes to getting things done, Cruz isn't your 'go-to' guy. But, when it comes to shutting the government down, he's your man. He did just that in 2013 in a ridiculous bid to stop the Affordable Care Act. And that's pretty much his entire legislative record. He's cast 500 votes in the Senate and, as you can guess, most of them were a resounding 'no'. As far as taking responsibility for the hugely unpopular government shut-down, Cruz isn't having any of that. He blames it all on President Obama.

JOSEPH CURTATONE

MAYOR OF SOMERVILLE, MASSACHUSETTS

TROUBLE IN HIPVILLE

He became Mayor of Somerville, Massachusetts in 2004 and has been re-elected six times. So, who's complaining?

Well, one of the first things he did as mayor was up his salary by $45,000 and hire one more assistant. His brother, Cosmo, just got done for assault and rape in 2014. Oh, and larceny too. And he called his ex-girlfriend a 'hunk of shit', according to the *Somerville Times* newspaper. But, what the brother does should not tar the Mayor. In fact, he thinks family matters don't warrant a public comment.

The town of 80,000 has been losing population, probably because the property taxes only go one way . . . up. They have to, since they fund the $300,000 media budget for the city. But what's not to like about the head of the Massachusetts Mayor's Association and a leading member of Mayors Against Illegal Guns. *DigBoston* did an excellent piece on Curtatone and revealed that the head of Hipville isn't so hip at all. He's got that 'progressive' thing going (although he used to be a Republican), but he's also an enabler for big business. That's particularly true for the real estate business.

According to *Dig*, 'contractors contributed tens of thousands of dollars to Curtatone' to help him pay his campaign expenses. *Dig* further reveals that 'attorneys from Palmer & Dodge, for example, gave a total of $4,000 to Curtatone in 2005; that same year, the firm was paid more than $500,000 to re-write zoning for Assembly Square, a real estate development – changes that were later ruled illegal by a Massachusetts land court.' *Dig* also found that the mayor used 'campaign funds to visit Washington DC for a Bruins (Boston ice hockey team) game, and to travel abroad to Tiznit—a ceremonial Somerville sister city on the coast of Morocco—where he stayed at the Hilton in Casablanca.' It was his third visit there in four years.

There's no doubt Curtatone has ambitions to be the governor of his state and many think he has his eyes set on the the White House in a few years.

SIMON DANCZUK

UK HOUSE OF COMMONS

HOOTERS AND SHOOTERS

First of all, there's the wife. She likes to show off her tits. Karen Danczuk, a Rochdale councillor and wife of Rochdale Labour MP Simon Danczuk, has 10,000 followers on Twitter. According to the *Mirror* newspaper, 'the Rochdale councillor . . . hit the headlines and gained thousands of followers on Twitter earlier this year after posting a string of revealing shots showing off her ample cleavage.'

Defending the pictures, she told the newspaper that 'times are changing, things are different now. I've had so many young girls and women saying I'm an inspiration.' Not only does she feel the necessity to fill the airwaves with pictures of her knockers, she likes to vent about her husband's drug-imbibing past. According to the *Daily Mail*, the 'outspoken Labour MP has admitted going on ecstasy-fuelled nights out when he was younger, and smoking cannabis twice a week'. The paper further added that, 'Danczuk's first wife Sonia Milewski, 37, claims they used to have ecstasy-fuelled nights out in Manchester before they were married. Ms Milewski, who has two children by the Rochdale MP, alleges that he took drugs while a councillor for Blackburn and Darwen and a mature sociology student at Lancaster University.' She told the *Sun* newspaper that, 'We'd go out and do pills a couple of times a week. I think because he was a mature student, it was his way of catching up.'

Danczuk divorced his first wife in 2010 and married Karen Burke, who is, frankly, much hotter than he deserves. She claims the cleavage shots are accidental although she can't seem to stop sending them out. Defending herself in the *Daily Mail*, she said, 'they're not supposed to be sexy. I'm not an attention seeker. I don't roll out of clubs drunk. I'm not silly. I'm not a crazy party animal. I'm not a girly girl and I rarely wear make-up. In fact, I'm quite a tomboy.'

GOVERNOR OF GEORGIA

FOETUS FARMS

Just as there isn't an ethics investigation where his name doesn't pop up regularly, there isn't a gun that Nathan Deal doesn't love. He signed House Bill 60, which came into effect in 2014. This sensible piece of legislation allows Georgians to carry heat into churches, airports, bars, cafes, nightclubs and virtually all the other places.

The Governor of Georgia must be getting tired of saying it's all politically motivated every time another grand jury convenes to look into his doings. He resigned from the US Congress and ran for governor of the state just at the time the Ethics Committee was going to come full on for him.

He's getting crazier as the years roll on. His latest concern is 'foetus farming' which he thinks isn't such a good idea, describing the imaginary threat as, 'the creation and development of a human foetus for the purposes of killing it later for research or for harvesting its organs,' adding that, 'just because scientists have the knowledge to do it, does not make it right.'

He also claims to have the ability to spot future criminals, saying, 'my wife tells me she could look at her sixth-grade class and tell ya which ones are going to prison and which ones are going to college.' His latest money saving scheme is to prevent the poor from going to the emergency room. Under US law, emergency treatment cannot be refused because of financial reasons. Deal would like to overturn that.

In 2014 Deal faced Jason Carter in his battle for re-election. Carter is the grandson of US President Jimmy Carter, who also came from Georgia. The first debate centred on unemployment and came just after Georgia employment bucked the national trend and saw unemployment figures rise. Deal blamed the figures on a devious plot masterminded by the US Department of Labor, which had set out to personally embarrass him.

SCOTT DESJARLAIS

**US HOUSE OF
REPRESENTATIVES**

THE LOVE DOCTOR

His own campaign website states that, 'Congress-man DesJarlais believes that all life should be cherished and protected. He has received a 100% score from the National Right to Life Committee.' The Republican congressman from Tennessee is also a medical doctor who obviously interprets the Hippocratic Oath in his own unique way. He's anti-abortion but that doesn't extend to his own sex life.

The number of patients he's bonked keeps on rising but not his offspring. During an acrimonious divorce from his wife it was revealed that he had four affairs during his marriage and when one of his mistresses got knocked up he pressured her into getting an abortion. She was also his medical patient.

Another ex-girlfriend claimed that she and the congressman got stoned together and he gave her pain relievers. When the divorce proceedings were made public in 2012, it was revealed that he had admitted to six extramarital affairs and also had pressured his ex-wife to have two abortions. In 2014 the Tennessee Board of Medical Examiners slapped him with a fine of $500 for getting it on with two patients, which is about how much it costs to spend an hour with a high-class hooker in Washington. DesJarlais faced a primary challenge in 2014 and eked a 38 vote win but he is expected to return to Washington in 2014 by a wide margin in the reliably Republican state. Perhaps they just love his caring nature. In 2013, in a town hall meeting, he told an eleven-year-old girl that her father, an undocumented alien, should be deported. That comment actually generated a round of applause from his Tea Party supporters.

FILIP DEWINTER

MEMBER OF THE
FLEMISH PARLIAMENT

MINDER, MINDER, MINDER

You can buy a Belgian coffee cup in France that is symbolic of what the French think of their neighbour to the north: the handle is on the inside. Belgium divides into three lingual areas: Flemish in the north, Walloon in the south and a small German-speaking minority in the east. And they all hate each other. Add to this mix a sizable North African Muslim immigrant population, an enclave of Hassidic Jews in Antwerp and a moderate Christian African population left over from the days when the country ran the Congo like a slave camp.

It's perfect territory for a small-minded racist like Filip Dewinter to prosper. He is a member of the *Vlaams Belang*, a Flemish nationalist party that is the successor to the *Vlaams Blok* that was banned in Belgium in 2004 because of its racist beliefs. Dewinter was recently questioned by Antwerp prosecutors over the release of a computer game on the party's web site that was said to be racist. The game is called *minder, minder, minder* (fewer, fewer, fewer in English) as a reference to Dewinter's often-stated question as to whether the voters want more or fewer Moroccan immigrants. In the game, players swat flies that are either identified as Dewinter's political opponents, mosques or Islamic terrorists.

In 2009 he published a book entitled *Inch'Allah*. 'With mass immigration and Islamisation we invite in a Trojan horse,' said Dewinter when talking about the tome. 'It is an insidious poison, and nothing less than the third Islamic invasion in the history of Europe.'

Dewinter also tried to honour the few Flemish Nazi collaborators buried with 40,000 Wehrmacht soldiers in the Lommel cemetery in Belgium although his father had been captured by the Nazis and forced into a labour camp during the Second World War. When asked why he wanted to honour the collaborator's graves, he said to *Haaretz* newspaper: 'Flemish nationalists collaborated during the war because they thought—and now it is clear that they were wrong—that this would help them achieve independence for Flanders.'

NADINE DORRIES

UK HOUSE OF COMMONS

LIVER BIRD OR JUNGLE PARROT?

Channel 4 presenter, Cathy Newman, described her as 'a tropical bird in amongst all that dull, grey, plumage on the Commons benches.' Less appreciative journalists refer to her simply as 'Mad Nad'.

The bus driver's daughter from Liverpool is a right-wing Eurosceptic, a committed Christian and a passionate pro-lifer – though she attributes her stance on abortion to her experiences as a nurse. She's also fiercely proud of her roots and has never been at ease in a party that now seems to be dominated by a privileged elite. In April 2012, she grabbed the headlines and shocked the mandarins of her local party by damning Prime Minister, David Cameron, and Chancellor, George Osborne, as 'two arrogant posh boys' with 'no passion to understand the lives of others.'

Six months later, Dorries caused another furore by taking part in the jungle survival reality TV show: *I'm a Celebrity Get Me Out of Here*. She said she hoped it might help promote her ideas to a wider audience. When not buried in cockroaches or chewing kangaroo penis, maybe there could have been an opportunity to share her views around the campfire – with millions tuning in.

As it was, she never got the chance. First to be voted from the jungle by the viewing public, she was exiled to the famously luxurious Queensland Palazzo Versace Hotel. After a hysterical outcry, she was drummed out of the parliamentary Conservative Party and forced to sit as a nominal independent. Five months later she was readmitted, but this may be attributed to a growing panic that she might be on the brink of finding a home with UKIP to give them what would then have been their first parliamentary seat.

Her first novel, *The Four Streets*, was published in 2014. Like her political career, it seems to have gone down better with the masses than with the Tory press. *Daily Telegraph* reviewer, Christopher Howse, described it as 'the worst novel I've read in ten years'. Dorries, whose tale deals in part with child abuse by catholic priests, asserts that the editor deliberately stitched her up in his choice of Howse, alleged to be an ultra-catholic and former member of Opus Dei.

RENEGADE HACKER AND PARTY FOUNDER

A WANTED MAN

He is potentially a political kingmaker. The founder and funder of New Zealand's Internet Party has a very unusual past and he's not even a Kiwi. The German internet mogul has been convicted of computer fraud, data espionage, insider trading and embezzlement. He is wanted in the United States for criminal copyright charges that have cost Hollywood hundreds of millions of dollars in royalties through the now defunct cloud storage site, Megaupload.

Dotcom also goes by the names of Kimble or Kim Tim Jim Vestor; his birth name is Kim Schmitz. He was locked up by the New Zealand authorities in 2012 and is now fighting extradition to the US. The Internet Party has formed an alliance with the Mana Party, a Maori nationalist movement that has a seat in parliament. The party platform calls for copyright reform, low cost internet access, less government surveillance, free university education and programs to tackle poverty.

The 2014 elections in New Zealand should have been a walk in the park for the centre-right Prime Minister, John Key, but Dotcom may have thrown a spanner in the works. It is alleged that he broke into the files of the well-known blogger, Cameron Slater, who publishes the widely read *Whaleoil*. The files have been detailed in a book, *Dirty Politics*, written by investigative journalist, Nicky Hager. It reveals a relationship between a top Prime Ministerial aide, a government minister – and Slater. Judith Collins, the Justice Minister, has admitted to being friends with Slater and has already resigned her post.

Dotcom was filmed at a political event where he said, 'Fuck John Key'. If he is successful in doing that his party could pick up three or four seats in parliament and become part of a governing coalition. Dotcom was granted residency in New Zealand in 2010 and his extradition hearing has been postponed until 2015.

MIKE DUFFY

CANADIAN SENATE

HI DAD!

It's not just 31 counts of fraud, breach of trust and bribery. You can even overlook the supposed expense fiddling, the allegedly rigged contracts and the $90,000 cheque he got from the Chief of Staff to the Canadian Prime Minister, Stephen Harper. That's all the bad news.

The good news is he might have a daughter. It seems Mike had a thing with Yvette Benites Ruiz, a convicted Peruvian drug smuggler, a few years back. Mike Duffy found Karen Duffy on Facebook and they've been talking 'in general terms about family and other matters,' said Duffy to the Canadian Broadcasting Corporation (CBC).

Although he has yet to admit paternity, he's being sued by Karen's mother. The Senator was actually appointed to his seat by Prime Minister, Stephen Harper, so the opposition naturally can't resist the opportunity to question Harper's judgment. Duffy's defence lawyer, Donald Bayne, told the *Huffington Post*, that, 'those, including many in the media, who have been so eager and quick over the past year and a half to malign and even libel Senator Duffy without his ever having had a fair hearing, should slow down their rush to judgment and let fair process determine this matter.'

Though Duffy worked in the media before becoming a senator – while with the CBC, he was one of the last to leave Saigon when it fell to communist forces – he has criticised journalism schools for teaching the beliefs of Noam Chomsky and promoting critical thinking. Whatever happens in the courtroom, Duffy is going to have some difficulty restarting either his political or journalistic career.

RUSSIAN PARTY LEADER

PUTIN'S RASPUTIN

The *National Review* describes Alexander Dugan as 'the mad philosopher who is redesigning the brains of much of the Russian government and public, filling their minds with a new hate-ridden totalitarian ideology whose consequences can only be catastrophic in the extreme, not only for Russia, but for the entire human race.' If that doesn't get your attention, what will?

The Moscow-based founder and leader of the Eurasia Party, the National Bolshevik Party and the National Bolshevik Front believes in the restoration of the Russian Empire, which is surely not good news for the Ukraine, Georgia or the Baltic states. He is fervently anti-American and anti-West in general. 'If you are in favour of global liberal hegemony, you are the enemy,' Dugan said recently at a speech in Moscow.

He also recently told the BBC that war with the Ukraine was 'inevitable'. The *Moscow Times* newspaper quotes Dugan as posting this message on his website: 'there never was . . . a Ukrainian ethnicity, a Ukrainian nation, a Ukrainian civilization. Just western Russian lands.' The *National Review* further states that Dugan believes that 'Russia must unite around itself all the continental powers, including Germany, Central and Eastern Europe, the former Soviet republics, Turkey, Iran, and Korea, into grand Eurasian Union strong enough to defeat the West.'

His political philosophy is actually quite simple: Dugin is an out and out fascist and the kind of person that the West should be very worried about.

Hardly surprising, then, that the 'National Policy Institute', a white supremacist think tank (if that isn't too much of an oxymoron) with headquarters in Montana, has invited Alexander Dugin to speak at a conference they are organising in Hungary and which will also be attended by basket cases from across Europe.

DANE EAGLE

FLORIDA STATE ASSEMBLY

IRRIGATED WITH HORIZONTAL LUBRICANT

Eagle represents the 77ᵗʰ District in Florida's House of Representatives. The Republican says on his re-election website that he'll 'fight' for good paying jobs, spending cuts, student-focused education and the environment. The site further states that his values, from Day 1, are all about hard work and serving the community.

There's no mention of his co-sponsorship of House Bill 1435. That particular piece of legislation is the 'Drug Free Public Officers Act,' which requires every elected public officer of the state, including politicians and mayors, to take periodic drug tests to make sure they aren't snorting crystal meth or something equally evil on the job within 60 days of taking office or being re-elected.

In April 2014 Eagle's car was stopped by the cops after he had popped out for some fine Mexican cuisine at his local Taco Bell at around 2:00 am. He was observed 'driving all over the road' and 'running a red light'. According to the police report, 'when the defendant exited (the car), he stumbled to his left and fell against the rear passenger door of his vehicle'. The report further stated that there was a 'strong odor of alcoholic beverages' emanating from the representative. Eagle refused to take a breathalyser or a sobriety test and assured the cops he was 'good to go' but they took him to the clink and booked him. He issued a statement subsequent to his arrest for driving under the influence of alcohol saying, 'I did not drive under the influence. I did, however, exercise poor judgment that night, and in my carelessness I drove recklessly.'

He refused to resign over the incident. In June of 2014 he appeared in court and accepted a plea bargain and pled guilty to reckless driving and got six month's probation under the condition that he is tested regularly for alcohol and performs 100 hours of community service.

RENEE ELLMERS

US HOUSE OF
REPRESENTATIVES

RENEE, GET YOUR GUN!

The Republican congresswoman from North Carolina is also Chairwoman of the Republican Women's Policy Committee, created in 2012 to counteract claims by the Democrats that Republicans are waging a 'war on women'. According to Ashe Schow, journalist from the *Washington Examiner*, her address to an audience of Republican ladies in July 2014 included some astonishing remarks.

'Men do tend to talk about things on a much higher level,' she said. 'We need our male colleagues to understand that if you can bring it down to a woman's level and what everything that she is balancing in her life – that's the way to go.' Ellmers denied afterwards that she was suggesting that politics and things pertaining to the economy need to be dumbed down for women and claimed she was stitched up by the 'liberal media', although the *Washington Examiner* is anything but liberal. The publication is owned by the billionaire, Philip Anschutz who also owns the neoconservatives' favourite read, the *Weekly Standard*.

Ellmers also supports 'responsible gun ownership' although it wasn't so responsible for an unsecured AR-15 assault rifle to be stolen from an unlocked garage at her home in 2013.

When Texas senator Ted Cruz decided to shut the government down over Obamacare, Ellmers was on board, with a minor caveat: she still wanted to be paid. 'Thing is . . . I need my paycheck,' she said at the time – the government workers obviously didn't need theirs.

She thinks that most Muslims are terrorists and the idea of a 'victory mosque' near Ground Zero in Manhattan is a bad idea. 'The terrorists haven't won and we should tell them in plain English, "no, there will never be a mosque at Ground Zero",' she said, although the proposal was not for a mosque but for a Muslim community centre.

PHILIPPINES SENATE

SHAG-A-THON

The Filipino Senator is getting on in age now and his memory may not be what it used to, which is why it's fortunate his long suffering wife, Cristina Ponce Enrile, has kept a list of all the women her husband has shagged while she's been married to him.

During their fifty-six-year marriage she's counted thirty-eight of them and she's given each one a nickname. She claims that some of the women were her close friends and, as they advanced through the years, some of their daughters also succumbed to the senator's charms.

Christina was, at one time, the Philippine ambassador to the Vatican, but that didn't deter her from packing a gun and firing it at the house of one of her husband's more serious lover's. She actually went to the US after she found that Juan had a thing with his chief of staff, Gigi Reyes, and filed for divorce only to return and find out that there was no way the Lothario was going to let her go. He now lives in a different house in their family compound.

The happy couple have dinner with each other every night, but that may not last long. Enrile had to resign his position as speaker of the Senate in 2013 when rumours of corruption began to surface. In September of 2014 the police took him into custody at Camp Crame and put him on trial, along with his ex-lover, Gigi Reyes, over a $225 million corruption case. The two are facing 62 counts of fraud for skimming money off the Priority Development Assistance Fund. They both assert their innocence. The Senator is using his time inside to write a book of memoirs – which he only wants published after he dies.

RECEP TAYYIP ERDOĞAN

PRESIDENT OF TURKEY

THE PHANTOM MENACE

Turkey jails more journalists than any other country. You'd think President, Recep Tayyip Erdoğan would have little to worry about: of his two main political rivals, one is in exile half a world away and the other has been dead since 1938.

No statesman's memory is more revered by his countrymen than Kemal Attaturk. His stern, but somehow reassuring face looks down from every government office and company reception area. It was Turkey, a Muslim country, that provided the blueprint for the modern secular state and Attaturk is its architect, but Turkey's current president has a different agenda.

Erdoğan wants to show his conservative supporters in rural and eastern Turkey that he's the moral man and good Muslim they voted for but, especially to young and cosmopolitan Turks, Erdoğan's restrictions on liquor sale, his attempts to criminalise adultery and to repeal the ban on women's headscarves in government buildings signals a shift away from Western laws and values and a betrayal of Attaturk's legacy.

Also, Erdoğan's one-time ally, Fethullah Gulen, a moderate Muslim cleric, has been accusing Erdoğan of corruption from his base in Pennsylvania. Gulen still has lots of friends in Turkey's police and judiciary and Erdoğan is tormented by conspiracies, real or imagined. Like Putin, he's not squeamish about changing the constitution to stay in control, shifting from prime minister to president and rewriting the respective job descriptions to enjoy another ten years of power. What title he assumes after that is anybody's guess.

In September 2014 his nephew, Ali, led a group of his bodyguards to assault two journalists in New York as they tried to cover Erdoğan's meeting with the US Vice President. But his suppression of media criticism extends wider. As reported by BBC News he said: 'There is now a menace that is called Twitter… the best examples of lies can be found there. To me, social media is the worst menace to society.' It's hardly surprising Twitter and YouTube are forced off the air from time to time in Turkey – usually at election time or when the Erdoğans are under legal investigation.

JONI ERNST

IOWA STATE SENATE

LIKE AN ONION OF CRAZY

Democratic National Committee Chair, Debbie Wasserman Schultz, called her 'an onion of crazy; the more you peel back the layers, the more disturbing it is.'

Joni Ernst had a TV commercial out in 2014 in which she pointed an assault rifle at the camera and the narrator said, 'once she sets her sights on Obamacare, Joni's gonna unload', and she shot off the gun. She's talked of her life growing up on a farm and castrating pigs and how she's an expert on cutting pork, in a reference to pork barrel spending.

She's been filmed talking about 'Agenda 21', a right-wing fantasy that the United Nations is going to take over the United States that's stridently believed by a sliver of the conspiracy-minded American population. She's warned farmers that 'Agenda 21' will force Iowa's farmers off their land, dictate where people can live and restrict Iowans from travelling freely. When discussing the imaginary threat, she stated that, 'the United Nations has imposed this upon us, and as a US senator, I would say, "No more. No more Agenda 21".'

Ernst has spent over 20 years as a Lieutenant Colonel in the United States Army Reserves and the Iowa Army National Guard and served 14 months in Kuwait during *Operation Iraqi Freedom*, and she's also incredibly attractive. So, when she says judges should be aware that America's laws 'come from God' and when she calls President Barack Obama a dictator who should be impeached, a lot of male voters in Iowa forgive her. She ran for the US Senate in 2014 after beating a field of candidates in the Republican primary.

Despite Ernst's attractiveness and as much as Iowans say they want the government off their back they are addicted to the subsidies the state gets, particularly for the price of its main agricultural crop: corn, which is used to produce federally mandated ethanol as a fuel additive. If the federal government really wanted to cut out pork, the first thing they would do would be to end that multi-billion dollar program that makes Iowa's farmers the richest in the nation.

ENRIQUE SERRANO ESCOBAR

ENRIQUE SERRANO ESCOBAR

**CIUDAD JUÁREZ
MUNICIPAL COUNCIL**

AWOL

Ciudad Juárez – plain Juárez to its local residents, was the murder capital of Mexico and Enrique Serrano Escobar is the president of the city's municipal council. Since 2009, after the drug wars broke out, something like 400,000 people have left the city. It used to be that a murder would take place every hour.

The Sinaloa Cartel has been battling local drug lords for control of the trade that crosses the Bridge of the Americas linking Juárez with its American sister city, El Paso. Serrano was elected in 2013. After he took office the murder rate plummeted. In 2013 there were *only* 497 murders. He won the election the old-fashioned way – with money. His opponent, Maria Antonieta Perez, was accused of promising gifts to supporters and offered a cash reward for proof of vote buying. Serrano offered to double the reward.

In May 2014, Serrano's father, Juan Gayton Adrian Cisneros was arrested for theft, but his biggest challenge has been in knowing where his staff are at any point in time. While the mayor was meeting officials from Major League Baseball, reporters for *El Diario de Juárez* were trying to trace the often-absent environmental officer, Laura Yanely Rodríguez Mireles. When asked by a reporter about her whereabouts, Serrano said she was at 'an event that has to do with her official duties, but I don't remember the name of the event.' He further added that, 'she's going in representation but I don't remember what the event is called. I saw it once but right now I don't remember.' It turned out that she was attending a 'legal summit' in Cuba at the city's expense. The reporters pressed her direct supervisor, Alejandro Gloria Gonzaléz, who said that he did not send her to Cuba and he said that he did not know why she went, but that she had properly filled out the expense form.

JOSEPH ESTRADA

MAYOR OF MANILA

ERAP'S A PLAYER

He's held virtually every office in the Philippines. He's a former Senator, Vice President and President of the country and now he's the capital's mayor. He's also held a lot of women in his arms. Erap, as he is known in his country, is a former actor, having starred in over a hundred films. He is a legend in the love department and has twelve children from six different women.

He was sentenced to life behind bars in 2007 for plundering something in the range of $80 million from government coffers and taking bribes from illegal gambling rackets. He spent some time in prison but was later pardoned by President Gloria Macapagal-Arroyo. Undeterred by that, he ran for president for the second time in 2010 and lost. He captured the job as Mayor of Manila in the mid-term elections of 2013.

He has three children from his marriage to his wife, Luisa, and nine children from extra-marital relationships, including three ex-actresses, Peachy Osorio, Laarni Enriquez and Mary Ann Murphy, a former mayor, Guia Gómez, and two former air hostesses, Joy Melendrez and 'Larena'. It must be difficult for the mayor to keep track of it all. He is the object of ridicule in the Philippines over his lack of command of the English language and there is even a book of jokes written about him titled, *ERAPtion: How to Speak English Without Really Trial*.

In 2014 Estrada faced a disqualification case at the Supreme Court brought by a former mayor of Manila and a political rival, Alfredo Lim. The basis of Lim's case is that Estrada should be barred from holding public office because he is a convicted criminal. There's also an arrest order out for his son, Senator Jinggoy Estrada, for corruption and graft. Jinggoy is in lockup at the Philippine National Police Custodial Center.

BILL ETHERIDGE

EUROPEAN PARLIAMENT

GOLLIWOGS

For those unfamiliar with what a golliwog is, they are rag dolls that were once considered to be suitable to give to children, like teddy bears. That was a few decades ago. Now they are considered a closeted sign of racism and used only to cause offense. Bill Etheridge might not have had that in mind when in 2011 he posed with a golliwog for his Facebook page but the British Conservative Party promptly threw him out and before you could whistle Dixie he wrote a book celebrating golliwogs and joined the UK Independence Party (UKIP). He's currently a UKIP MEP for the West Midlands and living large in Brussels.

In 2014 he doubled down on his dumbness and, during a seminar for the Young Independence Conference in Birmingham, he exhorted his audience to emulate the style of Hitler when speaking in public. The *Mail on Sunday* newspaper quoted him as saying: 'look back to the most magnetic and forceful public speaker possibly in history' and that the Nazi 'achieved a great deal'. The newspaper further quotes him as saying, 'when Hitler gave speeches, and many of the famous ones were at rallies, at the start he walks, back and forth . . . looked at people – there was a silence. He waited minutes just looking out at people, fixing them with his gaze.'

Etheridge himself says he's a simple guy with three stepchildren and a dog named Bruce. Etheridge also organises the Black Country branch of the Campaign Against Political Correctness. In his own words he says, 'I know that being skint doesn't mean only 2 holidays abroad this year! It means watching the pennies and bargain hunting, deciding which red demand to pay first whilst still keeping your family fed and your heads above water.' Now with a monthly salary of €7,957 plus €4,299 in expenses and a daily allowance of €304, the Hitler-admiring Etheridge won't have to hunt for bargains anymore.

MICHAEL FABRICANT

UK HOUSE OF COMMONS

BAD HAIR DAY

Is it a wig or just a weird bouffant? As Marina Hyde put it in the *Guardian*, 'Fabricant looks like he should be *in* an establishment'. He's the perfect example of why Brits are increasingly turning on their politicians and voting for the UK Independence Party (UKIP) even if they couldn't care less about the EU one way or the other.

Marina Hyde was writing specifically about a 'tweet' Fabricant sent out while viewing a debate between two writers, Rod Liddle and Yasmin Alibhai-Brown, on Britain's Channel 4. After explaining why he could never appear in a discussion with Alibhai-Brown, he tweeted that, 'I would either end up having a brain haemorrhage or by punching her in the throat'.

Alibhai-Brown is a Liberal Democrat and a founder of *British Muslims for Secular Democracy* (which sounds laudable enough). Presumably, Fabricant could not lower himself to debate someone who didn't buy into his worldview. As irritating as some people can be, rational men don't threaten violence against a woman, nor do they do their hair in a style reminiscent of a 1950s suburban housewife. He's also got a major thing for the House of Commons Speaker, the diminutive John Bercow. According to the *Birmingham Post*, Fabricant, 'accused the Speaker of being abusive to his clerk, spelling out an obscenity one letter at a time'.

The *Daily Mail* has suggested that he is on a target to defect from the Conservatives to UKIP but, in the *Guardian*, Marina Hyde writes that she would deselect Fabricant anyway for the Alibhai-Brown tweet alone 'despite the increasingly poignant range of non-apology apologies and arse-coverings he offered'. But of course this is Britain, where locals have very little say about mainstream party candidates – which is how a wiggy from Brighton can represent a seat 180 miles away in Staffordshire.

MIKE FAIR

SOUTH CAROLINA STATE SENATE

FAIRLY INSANE

Mike Fair is of the school that believes dinosaurs and
humans once frolicked in the forest together just a few thousand years ago.

He's also not a big fan of the gay, lesbian and transgendered citizens of his state. When
the University of South Carolina Upstate had a two-day LGBT symposium he said, 'it's just
not normal and then you glorify, or it seems to me, that the promotion at USC Upstate is
a glorification of same-sex orientation.' When he heard that there was going to be a light-
hearted one-hour program entitled *How to Become a Lesbian in 10 days or Less* he grew
even more outraged and said 'that's recruiting'.

Though gays may make him angry, it's evolution that's the real anathema to Senator Fair.
When eight-year-old Olivia McConnell wrote to her state representative and pointed out
that South Carolina did not have a state fossil, a bill was introduced to fulfil Olivia's wish
and designate the woolly mammoth for the role, but it met with opposition from Fair and
fellow god-bothering senator, Kevin Bryant, until public ridicule forced them to back down.

The senator once compared Barack Obama to Osama Bin Laden, despite the president's authorisation of the raid that killed the arch-terrorist. He's called climate change a
hoax and blocked funding for a rape crisis centre.

In terms of teaching evolution in South Carolina's schools he has said, 'I don't have a
problem with teaching theories. I don't think it should be taught as fact. After all, what's
science without Jesus?'

Fair also blocked a bill that would have required South Carolina schools to teach sex
education, informing parents what was to be taught, despite the fact that South Carolina
has the 11th highest teen birth rate in the nation. To be Fair, he has proposed certain
changes in the way sex education is taught in the Palmetto State: he wants legislation that
mandates that sex education classes include information that homosexual behaviour is
'unnatural, unhealthy and, most importantly, illegal'.

NIGEL FARAGE

EUROPEAN PARLIAMENT

KING OF THE LOONS

His wife is German and he is a Member of the European Parliament but he wants Britain out of the EU. He also drinks, smokes and is an incredibly likeable guy who just happens to be head of a political party that has been described as a collection of loons and crazies. He famously said on LBC radio that he felt 'uncomfortable' hearing foreign languages spoken on the train and then floundered when the interviewer asked him how he felt about his wife speaking on the train.

The UK Independence Party's manifesto includes compulsory uniforms for taxi drivers, giving MPs more freedom with their expenses, making the Circle Line into a real circle, repainting trains in traditional colours and having a maximum of three foreign players in British football teams. But, when asked by a reporter what was in the manifesto, Farage was stumped. Nevertheless, a segment of the British public adores Farage and is able to shrug off his and his cohorts gaffes, which are endless. The Energy Secretary for the party doesn't believe in climate change, one UKIP candidate was pictured giving a Nazi salute, one called a room full of women 'sluts', another isn't in favour of giving aid to 'Bongo-Bongo Land' and one blamed the floods of 2014 on gay marriage laws (the next day Farage humorously gave a weather report that was broadcast on television).

The ability to laugh at the errors of his fellow party members, and to laugh at himself, earned him an invite to host the popular British news parody show, *Have I Got News For You*. Much to the embarrassment of the Labour, Conservative and Liberal Democrat party, UKIP came ahead in the 2014 UK European elections and Farage himself returned to Brussels to all perks and bonuses. He has one of the lowest voting and attendance rates in the European parliament, which gives him plenty time to enjoy the wonders of Belgian beer.

BLAKE FARENTHOLD

US HOUSE OF
REPRESENTATIVES

ROYAL REGENT

Esquire magazine calls him the 'Royal Regent of the Crazy People'.

'What message do we send to America if we impeach Obama and he gets away with what he's impeached for and he is found innocent?' asks Farenthold rhetorically, without a hint of sanity or intelligence in his voice.

The gargantuan congressman from Texas sports more than a few chins and has that idiotic smile that's sure to get him re-elected in crazy country. Anyone who is a descendent of a man called Sissy might be a little suspect.

Farenthold is also a Benghazi truther, insisting there was a massive cover up to hide the truth that the president was not born in Hawaii, and therefore not eligible for the presidency. No amount of hard evidence would convince Farenthold that Obama was anything but a Kenyan Muslim bent on destroying America – but he thinks it's too late to address the matter. 'I think, unfortunately, the horse is already out of the barn on this, on the whole birth certificate issue,' said Farenthold.

Of course the pictures of him in pyjamas with ducks on them alongside scantily clad women that came out in 2010 were completely innocent in nature. When questioned about the wave of illegal children that have crossed the border from Mexico to Texas, the congressman said, 'these children are being used as pawns by the amnesty-or-nothing folks.' Of course he knows who to blame for the influx: 'It makes me angry that the Obama administration has let it get to this point.'

He's also naturally against gun control although his sister's house was raided in 2012 and, according to *Politico,* the police were 'acting on information that there was gang activity and drugs in the home'. They found two illegal guns, heroin and methamphetamine. Interestingly enough, Farenthold is a law and order kind of guy and supports mandatory sentencing for drug crimes.

AYO FAYOSE

GOVERNOR OF EKITI

IDI AMIN AGAIN

He should have been a happy man. The governor of the Nigerian state of Ekiti was re-elected to the post again in 2014 but not sworn in until October 16th.

Fayose was a busy man between the election and his inauguration. He even fitted in a few moments to join his band of thugs and allegedly beat up a judge, Justice Adeyeye, on the premises of the State High Court on September 25th.

The judge in question was leading a tribunal that was starting proceedings on a petition filed by the opposition All Progressives Congress (APC) Party, challenging the victory of the People's Democratic Party (PDP) candidate, Fayose. Things went from bad to worse after that. The day after, the former leader of the National Union of Road Transport Workers (NURTW) and big supporter of Fayose was shot and killed on his way to meet the governor-elect. He was one of the thugs in the gang that beat the judge on the previous day.

For his part, Fayose said that all the talk about whacking around a judge was opposition propaganda and he called for an investigation by the National Judicial Council. Of course he knows an investigation will take some time. When he assumed office on the 16th of October he was immune to prosecution. He told members of the press that, 'the current crisis is an agenda of the APC and their sole aim is to try and get through the back door what the people of the state did not give them on June 21 when they voted overwhelmingly for me and the PDP'.

As far as what kind of guy Fayose really is we have to look no further than the man he chose to be his deputy governor, Kolapo Eleka. He says all the talk about Fayose controlling a gang of thugs who beat up judges is nonsense and says 'I have moved close to Fayose, he is a real prayerful man.'

MAYOR OF SANTA
CRUZ DE LA SIERRA

THOSE HANDS WERE MADE FOR GROPING

At 75 years old he should know better than to let his hands wander over the body of any woman that comes near him, or at least do it in a place where he won't be caught. But, it's as if those hands have a libido of their own; they just can't stop groping.

The mayor of the Bolivian city of Santa Cruz has a long political career behind him. He has been a national senator, a minister and president of the Development Corporation of Santa Cruz. He has his own political party, Santa Cruz for All, and he was elected mayor with 52% of the vote in 2010.

In May of 2014, CNN reported that 'in a video that's gone viral, Santa Cruz Mayor Percy Fernandez is seen placing his hand on the thigh of journalist Mercedes Guzman.' It goes on to say that, 'it's not the first time Fernandez's advances have been seen on video. In 2012 he was caught on camera – also at a public event – touching city council President Desireé Bravo's bottom twice'. The mayor apologised to Guzman saying, 'I'm worried that I might've disrespected you while you were performing your duties. I apologize again to you and your dignified family.'

The *New York Daily News* reported that 'opposition politician Marcela Revollo Fernandez (no relation) has filed a complaint in La Paz, the Bolivian capital, accusing him of 'sexual harassment, sexual violence and discrimination'. *Global Voices* reported on another incident 'on March 29, 2012, at a public event, where he appeared with suspended city council member Desirée Bravo. When Bravo got up to address the assembled crowd, the tape clearly shows the hand of Fernandez near Bravo's rear end, and it appeared that Bravo attempted to brush his hand away, which led to many to believe that Fernandez was sexually harassing the council member. To add to this bizarre behaviour, Fernandez could be seen kissing and caressing her hand, while laughing with those sitting nearby.'

Despite his antics, Fernandez has been rated Bolivia's top mayor and has an approval rating of over 80%.

LEVY FIDELIX

POLITICAL ASPIRANT

I'LL BE BACK

Fidelix should have stuck to journalism instead of becoming the perpetual losing candidate in any given Brazilian election. He has run for Mayor of São Paulo twice, Governor of São Paulo once, once for parliament and twice for president. In every election bid he's made he's never got through the 1% barrier.

His big dream, if he wins the presidential one day is to build a bullet train between Campinas, São Paulo and Rio de Janeiro. Oh, there's another minor thing he wants to do: lock up the homosexuals as far away from the general population as possible. He lovingly wants to provide them with 'psychological care'.

He established the Socialism and Liberty Party so as to better convey his unique message of delivering fast modern rapid transit and homophobia. His participation in the 2014 presidential debates was contentious at best. Because of the rules of the debates, he got equal footing with President Dilma Rousseff and her closest rival, Marina Silva. While they debated crucial issues such as corruption and the whereabouts of the missing 70 million reals ($28 million) from the oil giant, Petrobras, Fidelix said, 'those people (gays) who have those problems should receive psychological help and very far away from us, because here it is not acceptable.' His statements provoked outrage in the commentariat but drew uproarious laughter in the studio where the debate was held.

In previous statements he's made no distinction between homosexuality and paedophilia and thinks the best cure for both is some good old-fashioned religion. Fidelix knows he was far away from the victory line in 2014 elections but, as he said in the last presidential debate of 2014, 'I know I won't win on this occasion but I will be back.'

BOB FILNER

**FORMER MAYOR OF
SAN DIEGO**

HE'S BACK

He didn't have to go inside but it was a close call.

Filner, the former Democratic Mayor of San Diego, is a touchy feely sort of guy and wasn't afraid to ask his female assistants to come to work sans knickers. He was elected to the US House of Representatives repeatedly and by large margins but it was when he opted to become mayor of San Diego that the wheels started falling off the bus.

According to the *New York Daily News*, it all began to unravel when, 'Filner's former communications director, Irene McCormack Jackson, expedited the mayor's downfall by becoming the first to go public with sexual harassment allegations in July. She has filed a lawsuit against Filner and the city (in 2013), claiming her boss asked her to work without panties, demanded kisses, told her he wanted to see her naked and dragged her in a headlock while whispering in her ear.'

The newspaper further reported that, 'nearly 20 women have publicly identified themselves as targets of Filner's unwanted advances, including kissing, groping and requests for dates. His accusers include a retired Navy rear admiral, a San Diego State University dean and a great-grandmother who volunteers answering senior citizens' questions at City Hall.'

Filner went through what he described as 'intensive therapy' to rid himself of his behaviour and asked the City Council to cover his legal costs for the harassment trial. They refused. He was convicted of felony false imprisonment for putting a woman in a headlock and a couple of misdemeanour counts for kissing a woman who didn't want to be kissed and for grabbing a woman's buttocks. He escaped prison but was given four months house arrest which expired in June 2014, allowing him to re-enter politics. He may decide to run again for his old congressional seat. If so, his opponent novice would be an 88-year-old, married, cross-dressing Republican, Stephen 'Stephanie' Meade.

ROB FORD

MAYOR OF TORONTO

THE DRUNK HUNK

It's hard to imagine a more flawed politician than Rob Ford. MacLean's Magazine says he's 'like a monster delivered in a wooden crate and Toronto is still unpacking him' and says he has the appearance 'of something that's just crawled up from out of the ooze, half-formed and shapeless'.

Toronto used to be unofficially ruled by an old boys' club make up of the patrician descendants of the founders of the city, but Ford broke that monopoly of power with his election as mayor of the city in 2010. Ford is enormously popular with the working class and immigrant population, who choose to ignore his crack-smoking, drunken behaviour. 'The reason I drank or did drugs was not because of stress, it was out of sheer stupidity,' he said in 2014. He has recently apologised for 'lying, conniving and hiding to cover up' his cocaine problems.

Regarding reports that he wanted to have sex with his special assistant, Ford said, 'Oh and the last thing was, um, Olivia Gondek. It says that I wanted to eat her pussy. Olivia Gondek? I've never said that in my life to her. I would never do that. I'm happily married; I've got more than enough to eat at home.' He has a violent side too. When someone caught him on camera Ford is quoted as saying, 'I'm gonna kill that fucking guy. I'm telling you, it's first-degree murder.' When speaking about the dangers of cycling in Toronto, Ford famously said, 'my heart bleeds for them when someone gets killed. But it's their own fault at the end of the day.'

Despite his behaviour, there is a 'Ford Nation' in Toronto which still backs the mayor and thinks he looks out for the 'ordinary guy'. Ford pulled out late from the 2014 mayoral race due to ill health and the Ford Nation failed to turn out in enough numbers to elect the brother who stood in his place.

TRENT FRANKS

US HOUSE OF REPRESENTATIVES

THE SAGE OF SUN VALLEY

The Pain-Capable Unborn Child Protection Act was proposed by Trent Franks, a congressman from Arizona who considers himself something of an expert on things like rape. If passed, it would have banned abortion past 20 weeks, regardless of how the child was conceived.

When pressed on the matter of rape, Franks said, 'the incidence of rape resulting in pregnancy are very low'. It's when he speaks about the special plight of African Americans that you know there's some depth to his soul. 'Half of all black children are aborted,' says Franks. 'Far more of the African American community is being devastated by the policies of today than were being devastated by policies of slavery, and I think, what does it take to get us to wake up?'

When Franks seeks wisdom he needs no further to search than Sarah Palin, a women he particularly respects. 'If every person in the world was like Sarah Palin, there probably wouldn't even be need for government because no one would be in danger of any kind,' Franks said to the American web site, *POLITICO*. 'If every person were like Sarah Palin, this world would be a peaceful, beautiful world to live in.'

But if Palin represents the absolute good in the world, there has to be a counterweight that represents the ultimate evil, and Trent need look no further for that in the person of the President, Barack Obama. Speaking at the *How To Take Back America Conference* in 2009 he called Obama, 'an enemy of humanity'. He further added that, 'President Obama is the greatest threat to the United States Constitution – and one of the nation's worst enemies.' Franks has an impressive insight into things nautical. 'It's always the water on the inside of the ship that sinks it,' he explains, 'And Barack Obama, I have to tell you, is water on the inside of the ship of America.'

DENNIS GABRYSZAK

FORMER MEMBER OF NEW YORK STATE ASSEMBLY

WHAT'S UP, BITCH?

What is it with New York Democrats? Elliot Spitzer, the former Attorney General for New York, was famously caught using hookers while simultaneously trying to prosecute prostitution rings. He had to resign because of that but still had the chutzpah to run for the job of City Comptroller for New York City. (He lost.) Dennis Gabryszak, though, took sexual harassment to a whole new level in the Empire State.

The New York Assemblyman would regularly greet his female staff by asking them, 'what's up, bitch?' The *Village Voice* devoted an article to the accusations of sexual harassment made against him by four female members of his staff (they were later joined by three more former staffers) 'by order of creepiness'. They included, 'joking with interns about having a tattoo on his penis', 'telling female staffers to wear bikinis to political events', 'talking about prostitutes and regaling staff with stories of his regular visits to a strip club', 'sending a video of himself in a bathroom stall receiving fellatio' and 'telling a staffer [he] got a boner when [she] walked into the office'.

The *New York Daily News* reported that, 'the latest claim was filed last week (7 January 2014) by former communications director Kristy Mazurek, 43, who claimed Gabryszak wanted her and another female staffer to dress as sexy elves and sit on his lap in an office Christmas photo.'

In his letter of resignation published in the *Buffalo News*, Gabryszak really didn't get that the world had moved on since the 1950s, adding, 'there was mutual banter and exchanges that took place that should not have taken place because it is inappropriate in the workplace even if it does not constitute sexual harassment.' In the letter he also stated that, 'in fact, there are allegations that have been made that are demonstrably false.'

GEORGE GALLOWAY

UK HOUSE OF COMMONS

GORGEOUS GEORGE

There's no doubt who loves George most: it's the man he sees in the mirror every morning.

The Scots-born MP was always on the far left of the Parliamentary Labour Party in whose ranks he dwelt for 18 years. He wasn't the only MP to oppose the Iraq invasion but his apparent cosying-up to Saddam Hussein and especially his exhortation to British troops that they 'refuse to obey illegal orders' proved too much for Tony Blair's party and they kicked him out in 2003.

In 2005 he volunteered to attend a US Senate Investigations Committee hearing enquiring into rumours that he'd dipped his fingers into the Oil for Food Program (he'd already successfully sued both the *Telegraph* and the *National Enquirer* for making allegations to that effect). From the outset, it seemed as if Galloway was living out an often-indulged fantasy in which he bravely faced down persecution by Joe McCarthy himself. 'I have not, nor have I ever been . . .' was the inevitable beginning. His eloquent if stagey performance brought him many admirers but he then blew much of this collateral by appearing on the reality show, *Celebrity Big Brother*. His performance as a cat, licking milk from the fingers of actress Rula Lenska, was summed up by one YouTube commentator as 'barf inducing'. It certainly shouldn't be watched on an empty stomach – much less a full one.

In 2012, he won the parliamentary seat of Bradford West with a staggering 36% shift in the vote and for the Respect Party that he had founded. But there have been significant defections since then, especially after he upset many supporters by supplying a controversial analysis of the Julian Assange rape allegations from which he opined that Assange could be guilty of little more than 'bad sexual etiquette'.

In August 2014 he announced that Bradford would become an Israeli-free zone, a city in which Israeli goods, Israeli services and Israeli visitors would not be welcome. It's hardly surprising that a few days later Galloway was given a thumping by a Jewish man in London's Notting Hill. Least surprising of all, though, was the fact that he was posing for photographs at the time.

JESUS REYNA GARCIA

FORMER GOVERNOR OF
MICHOACAN

SOMETHING ROTTEN IN THE STATE
OF MICHOACAN

Reyna got a little too close to his buddies in the drug cartel, the *Caballeros Templarios* (Knights Templar) and even went to the funeral of the gang's leader, Servando 'La Tuta' Gomez's father and had several meetings with him.

Federal troops and vigilantes have been systematically decimating the leadership of *Caballeros Templarios* in 2014, killing three of its four leaders in the southwest Mexican state, but the cartel fought back by getting intelligence in return for cash from politicians. In early 2014 the central government created the Commission for Security and Integral Development to both fight the *Caballeros* and control vigilantes. The interim governor, Reyna, was taken into custody in April of that year and held for forty days. Reyna, a member of the Institutional Revolutionary Party had been appointed to the job when the incumbent governor, Fausto Vallejo, fell ill in April 2013. After it emerged that Reyna had numerous meetings with the *Caballeros* and they weren't all about civic duty, he was tossed into the clink at the Altiplano maximum security prison.

In the same month, Arquimedes Oseguera, the mayor of Lazaro Cardenas in the state of Michoacan, was detained on charges of kidnapping, extortion and drug ties. The city treasurer, Omar Alejandro Soto, was also nicked for collusion and both are said to be under the control of the *Caballeros*. In the same month, too, the Mayor of Apatzingan, Uriel Chavez Mendoza, was done for extortion and links to the cartel. In September 2014, the Mayor of Huetamo, Dalia Santana Pineda, a friend and political ally of Reyna, was slapped up for murder, extortion and links to the *Caballeros* and Rodrigo Vallejo, the replacement for Reyna as interim governor of Michoacan, was locked up because he refused to answer questions about his dealings with the cartel.

POLISH PARTY LEADER

KOSHER MEAT

He's the former leader of the League of Polish Families, a far right political party that promotes family values and thinks the European Union is a communist plot. It's the same party that came out with one of the most anti-Semitic television advertisements shown in Europe and they did it when he led the party.

According to the *Washington Post*, the ad, which ran in 2007, 'showed President Lech Kaczynski, first at a meeting with President Bush, and then with Orthodox Jews at Israel's Wailing Wall, where he donned a yarmulke ... the words *Our allies* are flashed across the screen, followed by: *they put us in the line of attack*.'

Before Giertych entered the political arena he founded 'All Polish Youth', which had some crazy Nazi sounding beliefs and rituals. He's also a creationist. When he entered parliament in 2007 and joined a coalition government, taking a post in the cabinet, the Israeli embassy in Warsaw lodged a protest and vowed never to deal with him. The League of Polish Families has largely fallen out of fashion but Giertych remains active on the political scene.

He has also startled the country, Israel and much of Europe by his appointment to a very unlikely task. The *Times of Israel* reported in 2013 that 'The European Jewish Association, a Brussels-based group, has hired the former leader of a political party that has been accused of anti-Semitism to launch a legal challenge to the *shechita* (ritual slaughter for Kosher meat) ban in Poland.' When asked by the newspaper about his anti-Semitic views and those of his father, he admitted that his father was prejudiced but said, 'It is not the history of myself, there is no anti-Semitism in my life.' A spokesman for the Jewish Congress said, 'I wouldn't say he is personally anti-Semitic, but the League of Polish Families is not the kind of political group known for its closeness to the Jewish community.' The head of the European Jewish Association defended the decision, saying, 'Some of our best friends in the European Parliament are former anti-Semites who want to fix the past and help us.'

CARLO GIOVANARDI

ITALIAN SENATE

TESTA DI CAZZO

It's no great secret that the Holocaust doesn't solely belong to the Jews. Although the Jews suffered most in greater numbers, the Nazis also targeted the Roma people, the Poles, homosexuals, Ukrainians, communists and Jehovah's Witnesses.

Carlo Giovanardi, who is an Italian Senator with the New Centre Right party, is hardly the most LGBT friendly politician in Italy. When interviewed on *KlausCondicio*, he stated that there was no 'Homosexual Holocaust', it was only the Jews that were persecuted. (He's wrong, but homosexuals were normally jailed under the Nazis, not usually sent to concentration camps.) He went on to add that: 'we can't forget that there were some gays also among Nazi leaders'. (This is true, but the logical point seems disturbingly elusive.)

But Giovanardi really got hot under the collar when the Swedish furniture maker, IKEA, ran some 'gay friendly' television advertisement in Italy. He told the newspaper, *Repubblica*, that, 'the term "family" is used by a multinational detrimental to the Italian Constitution, because it is meant only for one formed by the marriage between man and woman'.

Nor is the senator one for recreational drugs of any sort. In 2006, Giovanardi helped introduce the Fini-Giovanardi law, which considerably ramped up punishment for any type of drug possession in Italy. According to *Al Jazeera*, 'that law was overturned in 2014 because it equated "soft" drugs, such as cannabis, with hard ones, such as heroin or cocaine.' Speaking about the decision to *Al Jazeera*, Giovanardi said 'In the scientific literature there are no light drugs, there is only one UN chart, and only one European chart, and cannabis has always been the front-door entrance to cocaine or heroin.' The good news is the repeal of the law could mean the release of up to 10,000 prisoners from Italy's overcrowded jails.

BRANIMIR GLAVAS

FORMER MEMBER OF THE CROATIAN PARLIAMENT

THE TERMINATOR

According to the Croatian newspaper, *Dalje*, 'Former Croatian lawmaker Branimir Glavas, who is serving a prison term in neighbouring Bosnia and Herzegovina for war crimes committed in Croatia, has sued Croatia before the European Court of Human Rights in Strasbourg for violating his right to a trial within a reasonable time.'

That's all a bit rich coming from a guy who was found guilty of the torture and murder of innocent Serbian non-combatants in the city of Osijek in 1991 during the Croatian War of Independence when he held the rank of general.

Of course Glavas claims it's all a frame-up and was a politically inspired conviction to kick him out of the Croatian Democratic Union Party, which he helped found. Nevertheless, the Croatian National Police, the International Criminal Tribunal for the former Yugoslavia and Serbian Public Prosecutor amassed 45 witnesses to the events, which seems like an incredible conspiracy just to get someone to leave a political party.

With the writing on the wall but before he was brought to trial, Glavas formed a new political party, the Croatian Democratic Assembly of Slavonia and Baranja and was re-elected to parliament while the trial was going on. Many of his Croatian supporters refer to him as the 'Father and Mother of Slavonia'. Due to his parliamentary immunity, Glavas did not have to be present while the verdict was given at his trial, but when he discovered he was found guilty he fled to Bosnia-Herzegovina where he also holds citizenship. It was later discovered that certain members of his political party, in true Croatian fashion, tried to bribe judges in the Croatian Supreme Court to sway the verdict. It didn't and neither did fleeing to Bosnia-Herzegovina. He was arrested and imprisoned there, although he hopes an appeal will free him. He also wants his back salary paid by the Croatian Parliament.

LOUIE GOHMERT

US HOUSE OF
REPRESENTATIVES

THE MOUTH

There are more than a few nutcases in the United States Congress, but Texas Republican Representative Louie Gohmert sets the bar for lunacy. He also has a serious case of oral diarrhoea, exacerbated by paranoid tendencies that manifest themselves by even accusing members of his own party of colluding with America's enemies. It's not just that he's a full-blown 'birther', he's also convinced that the White House is run by members of the Muslim Brotherhood.

Gohmert lives in Tyler, Texas and represents Texas' First Congressional District, which, thanks to extreme gerrymandering, will never, ever elect someone sane. They went whole hog crazy when they elected Gohmert Representative in 2004 and they have been re-electing him by big margins ever since. As you would expect he thinks talk of global warming is a huge conspiracy to fraudulently cripple economic growth.

On the plus side, he is firmly against limiting the number of bullets that go into the magazine for an assault rifle. In fact, in defence of allowing Americans to have unlimited rounds in their magazines, he said this: 'once you make it ten, then why would you draw the line at ten? What's wrong with nine? Or eleven? And the problem is once you draw that limit – it's kind of like marriage when you say it's not a man and a woman anymore, then why not have three men and one woman, or four women and one man, or why not somebody who has a love for an animal?'

Grassroots America, a tea party group, obviously understands and appreciates Representative Gohmert's political thinking and awarded him the 'Champion of Freedom' award in 2013. He also received the International Foodservice Distributors Association's Thomas Jefferson Award for his support of delaying the employee mandate to provide employee health insurance under the Affordable Care Act.

ZAC GOLDSMITH

UK HOUSE OF COMMONS

DOM OR NON-DOM

What do you do if you are a patriotic Brit and have a fortune estimated to be in the range of £200 million ($321 million), and you want to run for public office? If you are the son of the billionaire, Sir James Goldsmith, and Lady Annabel Vane-Tempest-Stewart, you probably don't expect to get caught out by the *Sunday Times* for having a hunk of your fortune offshore in a 'non-domiciled' (tax free) corner of the world.

If you are the former editor of *The Ecologist* and an ardent campaigner for things like pollution-free public transport, then you don't, as the *Daily Mail* reported in 2014, get 'banned from driving and ordered to pay £570 after getting three speeding tickets in as many months'. That's not what a hybrid Toyota Prius was meant to do.

The Conservative MP from Richmond, a very wealthy borough in West London, certainly has good looks going for him and he is rumoured to have been hand picked to replace Boris Johnson as Mayor of London. Goldsmith is perfect fodder for the *Daily Mail*, combining glamour, wealth and fame. He's the sort of eye candy the paper's readers can't get enough of. That's why one of their columnists, Quentin Letts, could write this: 'David Cameron (the Prime Minister) treated Mr Goldsmith with seriousness.' No serious journalist could pen that sentence and keep a straight face.

The pretty boy who was expelled from Eton for having some weed in his possession didn't quite make it to university but he managed to get a job in publishing thanks to his uncle who was founding editor of *The Ecologist*.

He gave *Daily Mail* readers another thrill in 2010 when, 'four days after becoming a Tory MP, he publicly confessed to adultery'. The paper reported that, 'in court, there was no mention of the identity of the other woman in his marriage. But she is understood to be blonde heiress Alice Rothschild, 25.' Goldsmith later married her. The man-boy recently told the *Telegraph* that politics was 'childish, superficial and rotten'.

BRUNO GOLLNISCH

FRENCH NATIONAL ASSEMBLY AND EUROPEAN PARLIAMENT

THE NUTTY PROFESSOR

He once held the Jean Moulin Chair for Japanese Language and Civilisation at the University of Lyon. For those who have never heard of Jean Moulin, he was a hero of the French Resistance during the Occupation and met his death at the hands of the Nazis, so you would probably assume that the man who holds that chair, Bruno Gollnisch, would have an understanding of the horrors of the Third Reich. Think again.

The 'intellectual' of *Front National* reckons the Nazis were given a bad rap. According to Reuters, Gollnisch thinks 'serious historians no longer accepted that all the judgements of the post-war Nuremberg Trials of leading Nazis were fair' and 'he recognised that the gas chambers had existed but thought historians still had to decide whether they were actually used to kill Jews'.

Three years after that statement, Gollnisch was convicted for contesting the truth of the holocaust. He was given a suspended sentence and the conviction was overturned later by the *Cour de Cassation* (Supreme Court). He sits in both the National Assembly and EU Parliament and holds two other political positions. (French politicians can hold multiple jobs and a lot of them do – all the while collecting multiple salaries and accessing multiple expense accounts.)

Gollnisch fought for control of *Front National* but lost out to Marine Le Pen. Since then he's been on a roll. According to the *Guardian*, he recently 'dropped his trousers and mooned a regional council meeting in order to protest state subsidies being given to certain musical bands who sang about sex'. According to *Le Point* magazine, Gollnisch issued a statement on his party's website about the Muslim 'invasion of our homeland and the destruction of our culture and our values' which was being perpetrated 'with the blessing of the lodges (Freemasons) and the left'. But if Muslims get Gollnisch incensed, the Roma make him livid. When the Vatican came out with a statement condemning the French deportation of gypsies, Gollnisch was so furious he suggested they all be trucked to the Vatican City and left in St Peter's Square.

ALAN GRAYSON

**US HOUSE OF
REPRESENTATIVES**

POLYANDRY

Polygamy is so yesterday. Among the hipster set polyandry is the
new in thing and it really is a magnanimous thing for the new age
kind of guy to do. It's where the wife gets to enjoy the benefits of two husbands.

The Democratic Representative from Florida's 9th District, whose children are named
Skye, Star, Sage, Storm and Stone, was a little ahead of his time in 1990 when he tied the
knot with his wife Lolita. According to his lawyer's research, Lolita was actually married at
the time to another Floridian, Robert Carson.

According to *Fox News*, after she had initiated divorce proceedings in 2014 against
Grayson, who is worth about $30 million, 'Grayson claimed in a countersuit that Lolita
Grayson hoodwinked him into getting married even though she was secretly married to
another man at the time'. According to the *Orlando Sentinel*, Lolita claimed that she, 'was and
still am of the belief I divorced in 1981 (in Guam)'.

This all came to light after some fisticuffs at the Graysons' residence in March 2014.
According to the *New York Daily News*, 'she accused her husband of pushing her during a
fight at home, but Alan Grayson was never charged for any crime. According to divorce
papers, he is suing for $15,000 in defamation damages related to the incident.' She got a
restraining order against her husband after that.

Of course if you are a congressman you are going to have staffers that regularly shoot
videos of you, just as one staffer did when the altercation occurred at Grayson's house.
According to the *Huffington Post*, the video 'shows Lolita Grayson walking from a red
minivan parked in front of their home, pointing her finger and shouting. The video then cuts
to the congressman and his wife arguing at the front door to the house. It then shows Lolita
Grayson pushing her hand at her estranged husband's face.'

The congressman wants the court to force Lolita to pay back all the money he has given
her and give him exclusive use of their 1981 DeLorean. That's gotta hurt.

BEPPE GRILLO

ITALIAN PARTY LEADER

5 STAR POLITICS

From the country that has produced such great politicians as Sylvio Berlusconi and Alessandra Mussolini, it's refreshing to find someone in the Italian political arena who is smart, witty and isn't corrupt as hell.

Trouble is, anyone like Grillo has to be silenced because many of the outrageous claims he makes have a habit of turning out to be true. Trained as an accountant, he soon opted to become a stand-up comedian and concentrated on raw political satire. But Italian politicians — particularly the corrupt ones — are notoriously thin-skinned and they virtually banned him from the airwaves, so most of his performances have been live, in concert halls or other venues. He has, nevertheless, become very successful and very wealthy.

Grillo can't run for parliament because of a thirty-year-old conviction for manslaughter that resulted from a road accident, but he leads his own political party, *Movimento Cinque Stelle* (Five Star Movement), which runs on a platform of sustainability and environmental protection. It holds several seats in the Italian Senate, Chamber of Deputies and the European Parliament and has over 250,000 card-carrying members.

In 2007 Grillo launched an annual day of political activism which he called *Vaffanculo Day* (Fuck You Day). Before the 2013 elections, he held a political rally in Rome, attended by 800,000. The Five Star Movement garnered over 25% of the vote in that year making it the second largest political party in Italy. He writes an enormously successful blog (www.beppegrillo.it) in Italian, English and Japanese. He is regularly sued and had to settle a libel case for calling a Nobel Prize winner an 'old whore'. The German paper, *Der Spiegel* calls him Europe's 'most dangerous man', whereas *Time* magazine hailed him as a 'hero of Europe'.

FETHULLAH GULEN

LEADER OF THE HIZMET MOVEMENT

ERDOĞAN'S NEMESIS

Though he lives thousands of miles away from Ankara in Saylorsburg, Pennsylvania he's Turkey's second most powerful politician. Turkey's leader, Recep Tayyip Erdoğan, wants him back and behind bars and he fondly thinks the Americans will do his bidding. Speaking to the PBS in 2014, Erdoğan said he wanted America to be a 'model partner' and comply with Turkey's extradition order on Gülen.

The two bitter enemies used to be political allies. Gülen leads what many think is a religious cult that has millions of followers in dozens of countries. He teaches a moderate form of Sunni Islam that is tolerant, scientifically curious and open to dialogue with Jews and Christians. He emigrated to America in 1999, supposedly because he faced arrest after tapes emerged of him proposing the creation of an Islamic state. Either Erdoğan has become paranoid, or he's correct that the corruption investigations into senior members of his government is being directed afar by Gülen and his allies in the *Hizmet* movement in the police and judiciary.

Gülen has made no secret of the fact that he thinks Erdoğan and his cronies are siphoning off billions through corrupt deals and in 2013 it is believed his followers leaked either real or cleverly faked recorded telephone conversations between Erdoğan, his family and business associates in which talk of pay-offs and corruption were casually discussed. Erdoğan was furious and sacked hundreds of cops and judges. He is up against a formidable foe in Gülen who, although he lives a very Spartan life, is said to control a business, education and religious empire worth up to $25 billion. When speaking at the Council of Foreign Relations in New York in September 2014, Erdoğan said Turkey will issue a 'Red Notice' against Gülen and told President Barack Obama, 'just like we deliver the terrorists you request, you either deport [Gülen] or send him back to [Turkey].' With the West desperately needing Turkey in the fight against the IS, Erdoğan might just be granted his wish.

MEXICAN PARTY LEADER

WHOREMONGER

Gutiérrez is President of the Mexico City branch of the Institutional Revolutionary Party (PRI) and he's something of a sleazeball. His father, who made his fortune in the city's garbage dumps and was called the 'King of Rubbish', was a hotshot in the PRI before he was murdered.

It's common for the political parties in Mexico to have hostesses serve drinks or coffee during meetings and they are known for wearing high heels, short skirts, low cut tops and pounds of makeup. In short, Mexican politicians like to have slutty-looking women around them. Gutiérrez not only wanted them to look slutty but to play the part in full.

A story was broken by an intrepid reporter from MVS News, a very popular radio news program in Mexico's capital city. In April of 2014, the reporter answered one of the newspaper advertisements for a position as a hostess in Gutiérrez's office and secretly recorded the job interview. She was told by the interviewer that one of the requirements for the job was to 'take care' of her boss both 'orally and vaginally'. In turn, she would be paid 11,000 pesos ($840) tax free with more in tips, per month. The office employed between twelve and fifteen hostesses at any one time and they were mostly single moms, divorcees and students and were between the ages of 18 and 32.

When the PRI heard about the report on MVS News they suspended Gutiérrez from his job and conducted their own version of an investigation, which, to nobody's surprise, cleared him of any wrongdoing and reinstated him in the job. The Electoral Institute of the Federal District (IEDF) found that there was insufficient evidence to charge Gutiérrez in August of 2014.

JUSSI HALLA-AHO

EUROPEAN PARLIAMENT

THE WAGES OF SIN

If you think his name sounds like a mouthful, just imagine how difficult it would be to address his wife, Hilla Halla-aho. Halla-aho is just another European who is sick of immigration and multi-culturalism but, as opposed to all the others out there who mutter under their breath in their local bar as they get served their beer by a Romanian, he makes a good living out of his xenophobia.

While others complain quietly that foreigners are taking all the jobs, committing all the crime and driving up the cost of housing, Halla-aho takes home a cool €8,000 plus expenses a month by saying it all out loud. There are hundreds out there like him in Europe, cynically riding the tide of nationalist sentiment. Halla-aho is now an MEP for the Finns Party. He's also served on the Helsinki city council and the Finnish parliament.

He was arrested in 2009 on charges of breaching the sanctity of religion and ethnic agitation for remarks he made against Muslims which are frankly too monotonous to repeat. The case went all the way up to the Finnish Supreme Court and he was eventually found guilty and fined a whopping €400. Those are the cases that make careers and propel dozens like him into the European Parliament.

People like Halla-aho, Nigel Farage and Marine Le Pen are actually products of the liberal media, who feign outrage at the attention-getting stunts they pull, and the liberal politicians who try to sweep under the carpet the very real issues the xenophobes raise. They all have one issue and no solutions. If Halla-aho was brought into the process of providing ideas and solutions that halted the ghettoisation of the Muslim population in Europe and actually made them begin to feel a real Finnish, French or British identity then the business of hatred wouldn't pay so well. But Halla-aho is making his €8,000 a month by not doing that and he isn't about to kill the goose that lays the golden eggs.

KAZUYUKI HAMADA

JAPANESE HOUSE OF COUNCILLORS

THE MARRIAGE DOCTOR

It was the first state visit by a US president to the Land of the Rising Sun since Bill Clinton came in 1996. The April 2014 visit was meant to cement the sacrosanct US-Japanese relationship and reaffirm that the country was America's best friend in Asia.

Unfortunately, Kazuyuki Hamada, a member of the New Renaissance Party in Japan's upper house, was disappointed with Obama's stayover. It wasn't that the president snubbed Hamada, he was deeply let down that his wife, Michelle, didn't make the trip too. The lawmaker thinks he knows why Obama's approval ratings are in the tank and why his leadership has been questioned... he's cheating on his wife.

Hamada earned his PhD at George Washington University and worked for the Center for Strategic and International Studies, an American think tank. He's also published fifty books that have grown increasingly anti-American as the politician has aged and he has a blog, where he rambled on about the state of the president's marriage. His book published in 2009, Who is Obama? questioned whether or not the president was really born in the US.

Before the president touched down in Tokyo and shook the hand of Prime Minister Shinzo Abe, Hamada wrote on his blog that, 'it's an open secret that the president and first lady are negotiating a divorce and are waiting until Obama's presidency is over to separate' and he 'used the secret service to hide evidence that he's a cheater'. Hamada added sagely that, 'the biggest reason – of many – for the collapse of his reputation is his failed relationship with his wife.'

Hamada also claims that the first lady is a spendthrift and spent thousands on luxury items during her trip to China. He makes no mention of where he sources his unique knowledge about the president's marital relationships or the real birthplace of Obama, but he's clearly got a pipeline right into the White House that no American journalist can seem to match.

VICTORIA HAMAH

FORMER GHANIAN MINISTER

THE MILLION DOLLAR WOMAN

Ghanaians reckon she's a beauty, or at least some of them do. One publication calls her a 'Goddess of Beauty'.

The Former Deputy Minister of Communications may be down but not out. She got booted out of government by President John Dramani Mahama when a secretly recorded tape of her emerged in which she said she didn't want to squabble with her boss because she had yet to bag $1 million in her job.

The scandal has been dubbed 'Vikileaks' in the local media. The driver of the car that she was in when she made the statement – and who secretly recorded her – was also a cousin of the sacked *previous* Deputy Communications Minister.

In September of 2013 Victoria Hamah was interviewed by STARR 103.5FM and she said, 'politics has no end, I'm in politics, I'm a politician, I live for that'. She has stayed prominent in the media since her dismissal. She hosts *Real Talk* which is broadcast on *TV3* and *Chocolate Factory*, which is played on *Multi TV*. Both sometimes address salacious sexual issues.

There's also her own complicated love life. In September 2014, according to the *Daily Guide*, Hamah 'stormed the Dansoman Police Station in Accra and reported her boyfriend, Richard Frimpong Dardo, to the police after they had disagreed on an issue about sexual intercourse. Victoria was said to have told the police that Dardo had beaten her up and stolen [from] her [an] unspecified amount of money.' The paper further reported that Dardo claimed that Hamah wanted him to perform a specific sexual act he wasn't prepared to do and then berated him.

Five days later, the police issued a warrant for Dardo's arrest on fraud charges relating to the sale of six kilograms of gold, but by that time the late night spat over sex was forgotten – Hamah had a change of heart and stormed the police station demanding his release and proclaiming his innocence.

NEIL HAMILTON

VICE CHAIRMAN OF UKIP

CHRISTINE'S WHIPPING BOY

There's something about Christine Hamilton that got under the collars of a lot of middle-aged Brits in the 1990s.

Louis Theroux, son of the famous American travel writer Paul Theroux, summed it up best when interviewed by the *Telegraph* subsequent to a documentary he did on the couple after Neil Hamilton was implicated in the 'cash for questions' scandal that rocked parliament in the 1990s.

Theroux was quoted as saying, there's 'some mysterious dimension to their relationship ... possibly sexual in nature. I remember seeing them on the news', he added. 'I was struck by the way they looked — something about Neil's eyes and Christine's chin and the way they stood together. I thought there was something odd about them. She appeared the dominant partner and I wondered if ...'

Theroux wasn't the only one who has caught that vibe from Neil and Christine Hamilton and Christine did have the look that would attract any upstanding ex-public schoolboy who likes to be occasionally disciplined (there are a lot of those types in the UK).

Neil was accused of accepting money from Mohamed Al Fayed to ask questions in parliament. He was subsequently exiled from the Conservative Party and, for a decade or so, became something of a media celebrity with his wife. He has now decided that 'we want our country back, what our forefathers fought for; UKIP has a supporter in every street in the land, Labour or the Conservatives cannot say that.'

For readers outside of Britain, UKIP stands for the UK Independence Party and it is staunchly for getting the UK out of the EU. It has been described as a party full of loonies but they are not so crazy about having Neil Hamilton too closely associated with them. He has recently been demoted from European Campaign Director to Vice Chairman of the party, a largely ceremonial post.

Despite this, Hamilton seems to have his heart set on contesting the Boston and Skegness parliamentary seat for UKIP in the 2015 election.

MATT HANCOCK

UK HOUSE OF COMMONS

QUEER BAIT

A survey by the American Psychological Association of 64 white heterosexual males between the ages of 18 and 31 revealed some significant findings. They questioned the men beforehand about the level of comfort they felt when they were with gay men and they were subsequently grouped into homophobic and non-homophobic subjects and put in a room alone with sensors on their penis and shown three four-minute videos of straight sex, lesbian sex and hot man-on-man action.

Needless to say, the homophobic subjects were the ones who had raging boners when they watched two blokes chow down on a Brokeback breakfast. That seems to make sense. After all, a straight guy should be pleased to be in a bar with tons of straight attractive women and an equal number of gay men. It cuts down on the competition and just increases the odds of getting lucky on any given day.

None of this is to say that the Conservative Minister of State for Business and Enterprise, Matthew Hancock, is a closet cock-pipe cosmonaut. Far from it. But when he tweeted in September 2014 that the Labour party 'was quite full of queers', it does imply that there is something wrong with being 'full of queers', which might be a sign of homophobia. Hancock quickly tried to allay those concerns because everybody knows what kind of worries that might bring.

Some Labour MPs have called for his resignation or for the prime minister to sack him, but perhaps the best retribution would be to put Hancock into a dark room, strap some sensors on his pork sword, turn on a video of two cock jockeys having a go at each other and let the fun begin.

MICHAEL HARTMANN

GERMAN BUNDESTAG

CRACKERJACK

He's famously against the legalisation of marijuana, but the Social Democrat believes crystal meth improves his cognitive powers. In fact, according to him he snorts a couple of lines of 'ice' with the sole intent of helping his constituents and refused to resign his seat after a police raid on his home.

They didn't find any meth, but they were put on to Hartmann by his pusher, who was under surveillance. That being said, he was observed buying 100 grams of the magic powder which would certainly be enough to cover the needs of all of his constituents. His lawyer claims Hartmann only bought three grams and used it sparingly to help concentrate.

When it comes to the green stuff he takes a different line. When asked by a voter how he felt about legalising softer drugs in 2012, Hartmann famously said, 'cannabis is not a harmless drug.'

Hartmann is also president of the German Softball and Baseball Association and he also considers himself something of an expert on the terrorism threat from the far right saying, 'how horrifyingly high the level of violence is in the far-right scene is only now being realized', in 2012. He's advised the German security services to concentrate less on threats from Islamists and the 'left spectrum' and to focus more on neo-Nazi groups. Commenting on right wing moves to limit welfare benefits to immigrants, Hartmann again saw it as a far right plot saying, 'If you play that kind of melody, you're allowing the right-wing extremists to dance.'

SHEIKH HASINA & KHALEDA ZIA

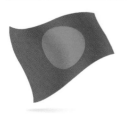

PRIME MINISTERS
OF BANGLADESH

THE BATTLING BEGUMS

Begum is an Urdu term for a woman of rank and Hasina and Zia are just that. Zia was Prime Minister from 2001 to 2006 and is the widow of the former president, Ziaur Rahman. Hasina is the widow of the country's first president, M A Wazed Miah. Not only do they detest each other, they've been battling for power between themselves for decades.

January 2014 saw yet another showdown: Hasina was the incumbent and Zia, once again, the challenger. Bangladesh's democracy is a fragile thing and it was really put to the test when Zia of the Bangladesh Nationalist Party (BNP) called for strikes and protests that brought a flood of violence. The rival parties battled on the streets with sticks and firebombs but Hasina of the Awami League won the election by a landslide. As soon as Hasina took power, Zia was charged with embezzling charitable funds to the tune of $670,000, which she claimed was a politically motivated charge.

There is an undercurrent of religious extremism in the country so the secular elite have tolerated Hasina's autocratic style as a means to counter it. The *Jamaat-e-Islami*, which represents the Islamic wing of politics, was banned from participating in the 2014 elections – many of its leaders were arrested on charges that they aided Pakistan during the War of Independence. Police killed hundreds of its members in protest marches during the election. Another Islamic party, *Hefazat-e-Islam*, also engaged in violent demonstration.

Both Zia and Hasina have political heirs living in the UK: Hasina's son, Sajeeb Wazed, went home to campaign on his mother's behalf in 2013; but Zia's son, Tarique Rahman, couldn't return because he is wanted on corruption charges that would have been overlooked had his mother won the election.

Rather than representing a rare instance where empowered women have made a positive difference in the world, the Battling Begums have probably done more to hold Bangladesh back than any two people in the world.

JORDAN HASKINS

CANDIDATE FOR MICHIGAN STATE ASSEMBLY

CRANK IT UP

Haskins has something of a past he'd like the voters in Saginaw, Michigan to forget. In a 2014 interview with the *Saginaw News*, Haskins said: 'we'll see what vision Saginaw wants in November. Me, the pro-life, traditional marriage, Judeo-Christian mindset versus the progressive mindset that Vanessa (Vanessa Guerra, his Democratic opponent) brings to the race.'

The Republican candidate for the Michigan's State House of Representatives had dropped out of the running before the primaries began, but he had left it too late and his name remained on the ballot. Since he was unopposed he won the Republican nomination anyway and re-entered the fray. Because of his unlikely past, his chances to win the election aren't spectacular. In his youth Haskins had an unusual sexual fetish he would like the voters to forget. He's done jail time in two states for breaking into cars and practising the strange art of 'cranking'. The sexual fetish involves disconnecting the ignition wires of a car and re-starting the engine whilst masturbating. The revving noise of the engine is what got Haskins off. He was arrested four times while he was in his teens for 'cranking'. Who knows how many times he got away with it.

When the news came out about his unusual past, he told *Mlive* that he's 'just trying to move on from that and do what I can.' On his Facebook page Haskins wrote: 'It seems the Democrats in this area cannot debate me on policy, ideas, constitution, morals, freedom, philosophy, etc. So, they have taken to the bandwagon of mudslinging and ad hominem attacks and questioning my capacity to represent the 95th District based on life as a teenager. They must be really desperate.'

Without wanting to encourage any deviant behaviour, you can find all you want to know about 'cranking' at PedalPumping.org.

JODY HICE

CANDIDATE FOR THE US
HOUSE OF REPRESENTATIVES

TRASH TALK

He's a Southern Baptist Preacher, has a radio talk show and is running for the US Congress from one of the most conservative districts in Georgia and perhaps the nation, and he's about as bat shit crazy as can be. No doubt he'll be elected and assume office in 2015.

To get a sense of what sort of Republicans the voters in Georgia's 10th District like, his predecessor, Paul Broun, proudly boasted he was the first member of Congress to call out Barack Obama for being 'a socialist who embraces Marxist-Leninist policies'.

Hice is of the opinion that a woman should only run for a political office if she has her husband's consent and he is renowned for making up quotes from the country's founding fathers to back up his arguments. In 2014 he cited a quotation from the sixth president of the United States, John Quincy Adams that was actually uttered by Dolly Parton. He self-published a book in 2012, *It's Now Or Never: A Call to Reclaim America*, which stated that 'the great American experiment is a distinctly Christian society' and wrote that gays have a secret plan to 'sodomise' America's children and Muslims should not be given First Amendment rights. He lost over $3,000 on the publishing venture.

He blames the Sandy Hook massacre, in which twenty school children and six teachers were gunned down in 2012, on America 'kicking God out of the public square'. He ventured into crazy territory on his radio show when he warned his listeners that 'blood moons' signify potential world-changing events. In his book he argued that the real reasons for the beginning of America's Civil War are still open to debate. He thinks people can simply walk away from the 'homosexual lifestyle' if they simply wake one morning and start acting like a man. But the absolute worst thing about Hice that should disqualify him from the ballot is that he has absolutely no sense of humour and takes himself very, very seriously. When he gets to Washington in 2015 he may be the only person in town who does.

KATE HOEY

UK HOUSE OF COMMONS

SOME NERVE

Kate Hoey is afflicted by a most peculiar psychosis: she seems to think it's her job to make up her own mind about stuff.

Sane politicians know how things are done: party whips and activists should be pandered to; you support the government when your party is in office and damn it to hell when it isn't; you never consort with 'the enemy' – even in a good cause; you weigh what support might be won or lost when taking a position. Hoey doesn't seem to get any of that.

The former Trotskyist is typically well to the left of the Labour party: she opposed the invasion of Iraq in 2003, the introduction of University tuition fees and the extension of detention without trial to combat terrorism. She always votes for left-wing candidates in Labour leadership elections. But then there's the other stuff. . .

She's a Eurosceptic – something typically associated with UKIP or the Conservative right – and she's most famous for her stand against Labour's ban on foxhunting in 2005, after which she accepted a job as Chairman of the Countryside Alliance, few of whose members are friends of her party – and it's not as if many of her electors in Clapham or Brixton regularly ride to hounds. She's a pin-up for Britain's gun lobby too, albeit in a country with some of the strictest firearm controls in the world.

She opposed her city's bid for the 2012 Olympics because she thought Paris had better facilities. Then, when London won out, she incurred Labour wrath by working with London's Conservative mayor, Boris Johnson, to make sure they were a success.

She upset London's cyclists by labelling them 'lycra louts that run red lights' and called for bikes to be taxed and registered like motor vehicles. (To the delight of the cycling lobby, she was fined £240 in October 2013 – for running a red light.)

One thing everybody agrees about is that she's got some nerve. It makes you wonder just who the hell she thinks she is – all this sticking-by-what-you-think-is-right business. What kind of state would the world be in if every politician went around behaving like that?

MIKE HUCKABEE

FORMER GOVERNOR
OF ARKANSAS

THE AYATOLLAH OF ARKANSAS

He's now retired and hosts a daily show on Fox 'News', but don't think for a second he isn't going to be a serious contender for the 2016 Republican Presidential Nomination.

He not only has an email newsletter that goes out each day to millions with messages like this: 'Does God still intervene with miracles to protect His own? An Israeli military hero says He does.'

He also has supporters raising funds, doing the groundwork to make sure he will be on the ballots in fifty states and paving the way for him to enter the Iowa Straw Poll, which is the first major step in the campaign.

The trouble with Huckabee is that he is disarmingly charming and genuinely charismatic and that somehow masks his religious and political agenda. If he were an Ayatollah in Iran he would have the world courting him. He's craziness with a smile. He's a former Baptist Minister who says things like, 'I got into politics because I knew government didn't have the real answers; that the real answers lie in accepting Jesus Christ into our lives.' There are millions of Americans in the Deep South who will respond to his call in 2016 when he says 'I hope we answer the alarm clock and take this nation back for Christ.'

According to *Politico*, 'Huckabee, the Fox News host and former Arkansas governor, has emerged as the best-liked member of the GOP (Republican) field, with a net favourability rating of 12 percentage points.' He has that populist edge that strikes a chord with voters and he's not afraid to say stuff like: 'I hear politicians who resent the fact that some single mom is getting assistance to put food on the table for her three children and those same people say it's perfectly OK to bail out to the tune of billions for big banks run by Ivy League people.' That's the sort of Republican message that might attract some Democratic voters who might be fed up with Hillary Clinton by 2016.

BRETT HULSEY

WISCONSIN STATE ASSEMBLY

BRETT THE BIZARRE

He drives a red convertible, which he bought with campaign contributions and the best you can say about him is that he is unpredictable.

The Wisconsin Democrat recently tried to grab his party's nomination for governor. One of his disastrous ploys was to hand out Ku Klux Klan hoods at the Republican State Convention. He called them 'Republican Party hats'. He also called on Civil War re-enactors to meet him outside the convention hall in full replica military uniforms. Nobody else showed up. In his press release he said: 'I have lived and worked in the South and would rather they (the Republicans) leave Wisconsin than continue to take us backward into Wississippi.' He pledged to end Governor, Scott Walker's 'racist Reign of Error' if he won the nomination. He didn't.

Hulsey has a long history and a lot of it isn't pretty. In 2012, he was arrested for disorderly conduct and fined $114 in 2012 for pushing a nine-year-old boy off his flotation device while he was playing at a beach. He was also asked to delete photographs he had taken of the youngster while he was supposedly taking pictures of the sunset. It was all a set-up, according to Hulsey; the child in question was the grandson of someone on the staff of the mayor of city of Madison and Hulsey thinks the arrest and publicity surrounding it was a bizarrely complex effort to discredit him before an important vote in the assembly.

One of his staff asked to be reassigned after he offered – or rather sort of insisted – that he teach her self-defence on the off chance that someone might attack her with a box cutter. She said she was worried by his erratic behaviour. According to the *Wisconsin State Journal*, Hulsey also made enquiries about bringing his muzzleloader rifle inside the capitol building.

He has since admitted that he is seeking counselling to deal with past child abuse and over his forthcoming divorce.

OLLANTA HUMALA

PRESIDENT OF PERU

BROTHERLY LOVE

All is not well in Peru. As the *Economist* reports, many Peruvians believe that President Ollanta Humala 'runs a parallel intelligence service for political purposes'. Suspicions about Humala stem from reports of around-the-clock police protection for Óscar López, 'who was given a suspended prison sentence for helping to run a vast espionage, extortion and embezzlement racket in the 1990s for Vladimiro Montesinos, intelligence chief under previous president, Alberto Fujimori.'

Humala and Montesinos have a history together. Back in 2000, when Humala was a colonel, he staged a bizarre rebellion that distracted Peru's attention while Montesinos fled the country on a yacht to escape arrest.

Humala is not at all popular in Peru right now; even his family thinks he's a disaster. 'People thought that Ollanta would be different,' said his brother, Ulises, to the *New York Times*, adding, 'Ollanta became a traditional politician, he lies like the rest of them.' The Humala bothers both contested Peru's presidential election in 2006 and Ulises intends to challenge again, warning that Ollanta 'could become a dictator'.

Of course, when things go bad on the home front for South American politicians, nothing distracts the voters better than a war. Humala just approved a new map of Peru that includes territory recognised as part of Chile – it's *desert*. The matter was supposed to be settled by the international court in the Hague but Humala didn't get what he wanted. The *Wall Street Journal* makes some interesting observations about this contentious piece of Chile / Peru. 'Estimates of how big the disputed piece of land is vary, with some saying it is 3.7 square kilometres and others saying it is five square kilometres'.

HUN SEN

PRIME MINISTER
OF CAMBODIA

COUNTRY FOR SALE

He has ruled Cambodia for three decades and, as the saying about power goes ...

According to *The Australian*, the country has, 'staggering levels of corruption, with Cambodia ranked 160th out of 175 countries by Transparency International. There are stories, unverifiable but plausible, that twenty or more of Hun Sen's closest associates have each amassed more than $1 billion through misappropriation of state assets, illegal economic activity, and favouritism in state procurement and contracting.'

According to the *Financial Times*, 'the former Khmer Rouge commander has consolidated his grip on power through a web of patronage and brute military strength.' He was once voted out of office but refused to leave and made himself Co-Prime Minister. According to *The Cambodian*, Hun Sen blames 'Cambodia's private sector, saying companies were equally responsible for the continuing corruption in Cambodia.' He recently spoke at an anti-corruption conference and said, 'if the private sector do not bribe, how could the government officials get the money.'

According to the *New York Times*, the Prime Minister also has some interesting ideas about how to deal with political opponents saying, 'I not only weaken the opposition, I'm going to make them dead... and if anyone is strong enough to try to hold a demonstration, I will beat all those dogs and put them in a cage.' The newspaper further reported that, 'though Hun Sen has worked only for the Cambodian government since 1979, he appears to be fabulously wealthy ... the US government estimated (in 1992) his personal wealth at $500 million.' This was in 1992. Every five years Cambodia goes through an election in which the results are guaranteed to reinstall the Prime Minister in power. He's well past 10,000 days and is still working on his big number.

GREG HUNT

AUSTRALIAN HOUSE
OF REPRESENTATIVES

WIKINUT

Hunt once won a prize for his plan to create an emissions trading market in Australia. That was before he was appointed Minister of the Environment under Prime Minister Tony Abbott.

Now that government policy seems to be that climate change is a myth he's turned right around and become an apologist for the government.

A graduate of Melbourne Law School and a Fulbright Scholar at Yale University, he's generally considered to be one of the nicer people in the world of Australian politics, but he knows it now pays to query anthropogenic climate change. As Minister of the Environment he helped repeal the carbon tax and instituted something called 'direct action' to reduce emissions which involves giving billions to businesses with no accounting for the results.

When questioned about whether climate change had any impact on the frequency of bush fires in Australia's outback his reply amused the whole country. Hunt said, 'I looked up what Wikipedia said just to see what the rest of the world thought' and found out 'bushfires in Australia are frequently occurring events during the hotter months of the year due to Australia's mostly hot, dry, climate.'

Perhaps his worst environmental sin was the approval of dredging at Abbot Point for a coal port, which put millions of tons of sediment in the sea near the Great Barrier Reef. He didn't attend the world climate discussions in Poland in 2013 because he said he was too busy repealing the carbon tax. Under Hunt, Australia's Climate Commission was abolished, the government continues to subsidise carbon fuels, it tried to open 74,000 hectares of Tasmania's virgin forest for exploitation and defunded the environmental defence office. Greg Hunt has proved to be the best Minister for the Environment Australia never had.

RENE RODRÍGUEZ HURTADO

**PRESIDENTIAL
CANDIDATE, EL SALVADOR**

WAR CRIMINAL

The Salvadoran Progressive Party chose Rodríguez as their presidential candidate in the 2014 elections. El Salvador has recovered from its nasty civil war that saw up to 70,000 killed on both sides of the divide. Rodríguez pitched himself as a simple guy who loved discipline and 'who had the opportunity to train with the United States Army'. He certainly did.

He is one of the notorious few that went through the US Army School of the Americas (SOA), which could be better described as a seminary for assassins. It used to be in Panama until that country lost its stomach for murder. Now it's at Fort Benning, Georgia. It teaches commando operations, sniper training and psychological warfare. It must have done a good job with Rodríguez because, in April 1995, a French court issued international arrest warrants for Lieutenant Colonel Rodríguez and three other SOA graduates for involvement in the torture, rape, and murder of 27-year-old French nurse, Madeleine Lagadec, in El Salvador in 1989. Her bullet-riddled body was found with its left hand severed.

Lagadec's murder wasn't unusual at the time. At the height of the hostilities, army death squads operated freely, often killing 50 people a night. In one village, El Mazote, the entire population of 900 was wiped out in one evening, including 131 children and infants. The twelve officers who oversaw the attack all graduated from the SOA.

Now Rodríguez has a Catholic radio talk show and brings communion to the sick and needy every week. He says he's a simple, disciplined guy and very much loves his countrymen: 'which is why I'm here wanting to serve our country from a political point of view'. Not many Salvadorians agreed with him. He garnered only 11,314 votes – less than 0.5% of the total. The man they chose to lead them, Salvador Sánchez Cerén, was once one of the guerrillas that Rodríguez was fighting.

ALTAF HUSSAIN

PARTY LEADER

SOMETHING'S ROTTEN IN LONDON

The leader of one of Pakistan's biggest political parties, the *Muttahida Quami Movement* (MQM) hasn't been to his native country for twenty years. He lives in London and is a naturalised British citizen. His party supports the Urdu-speaking descendents of the immigrants to Pakistan who moved there during the years directly following the partition of India.

Despite living a few thousand miles away from Islamabad, he feels compelled to stick his nose into the politics of Pakistan. He recently called on Imran Khan, the ex-cricketer turned politician, to cease his calls for civil disobedience to protest what he thinks were rigged national elections that put Nawaz Sharif into power (they might well have been rigged). He called Khan's movement a 'great joke with people'. Khan had already voiced his suspicions that Altaf was responsible for the murder of Khan's party vice president, Zahra Shahid Hussain, who was gunned down outside her Karachi home.

One of Altaf's political allies, Imran Farooq, was stabbed to death in North London in 2010 and British police have been searching for both a motive and a suspect ever since. It is thought that Altaf was seeking to build his own political profile, which might have irritated others in the MQM, but some think it might have been about money laundering.

According to the BBC, in 2013 police arrested Iftikhar Hussain, the nephew of Altaf Hussain, on 'suspicion of conspiracy to murder'. The BBC further reported in August, 2014, that, 'Iftikhar Hussain, the nephew of the Pakistani political party MQM, London-based leader Altaf Hussain, was arrested at Heathrow Airport and remains on bail until October.' In June of the same year, the BBC also noted that, 'Altaf Hussain – leader of Pakistan's third largest party the MQM – has been arrested on suspicion of money laundering.' He was released on bail after questioning.

JIM INHOFE

UNITED STATES SENATE

CULTURE VULTURE

He lives in an alternative universe where God will save the earth from global warming – if it's real. But Jim thinks all the talk about climate change is just a colossal joke. It's not only a 'hoax', it's 'laughable'.

How does he reach this conclusion? Jim says it still gets cold in the winter and it wouldn't be up and doing that if climate change was real. The ingenious Snr Senator from Oklahoma said, 'now they're trying to say this cold thing we're going through now is just a bump in the climate – that isn't true at all, it's a hoax.' The man who single-handedly figured out that the world's scientific community is guilty of a conspiracy to fool the public about climate change confidently predicted Mitt Romney would defeat Barack Obama by a 'substantial margin' in 2012 and that the Republicans would win control of the senate in the same year.

He's also a fundamentalist Christian who thinks that the secular forces of society are waging a 'War on Christmas'. In 2010 he refused to participate in Tulsa's annual Holiday Parade of Lights because the word *Christmas* was not used to describe the event. On a 2014 edition of *Washington Watch*, Inhofe said he couldn't figure if President Obama was a 'terrorist supporter' or a 'buffoon'. 'Never in my political career in my memory did it ever occur to me that we would have a President of the United States who would be doing things supporting the enemy,' said the senator.

You can imagine how Inhofe feels about the gay community. Speaking on the floor of the senate he said, 'I'm really proud to say that in the recorded history of our family, we've never had a divorce or any kind of homosexual relationship.'

BIDZINA IVANISHVILI

FORMER PRIME MINISTER OF GEORGIA

MONEY TALKS, SHIT WALKS

Ivanishvili, the leader of the Georgian Dream Party is the one person most responsible for turfing the increasingly authoritarian, Mikheil Saakashvili, out of power in Georgia. A billionaire many times over, he made his fortune in Russia, has a private zoo and lives in a $50 million 108,000 square foot house outside of the country's capital city, Tbilisi. He also has an art collection worth $1.3bn.

He's the ex-Prime Minister of Georgia who only wanted to stay in office for two years and he packed a lot of revenge into that period. In 2010, Saakashvili revoked Ivanishvili's Georgian citizenship for having the audacity to start an opposition political party. Ivanishvili had been granted French citizenship in 2010. Immediately after the Dream Party won a majority in parliament in 2011, he demanded that Saakashvili resign as president, although his term did not expire until 2013. Ivanishvili snapped at a *Bloomberg* correspondent when she asked if his new triumph reflected a return to organised crime in Georgia.

In 2014 the former Defence Minister, the former Chief of Staff for the army, and 15 other individuals who were closely aligned with Saakashvili's United National Movement had charges brought against them. The former Prime Minister has also been put under investigation and a number of charges have been made against Saakashvili, who now has a pre-trial detention order out on him.

Ivanishvili has professed that he wants to turn Georgia into the 'perfect European democracy' and the first step in that process was to install Georgy Margvelashvili as president. According to the *Economist* newspaper, Margvelashvili is 'a former education minister, whose most striking quality is a lack of political experience or ambition'. Meanwhile the economy is dire and any direct foreign investment into the country is a long forgotten dream. The neo-Nazi movement is flourishing and the anti-Muslim element has never been stronger. But, even though he's no longer Prime Minister, there's no question that Ivanishvili is behind every political move in Georgia.

JANEZ JANŠA

**FORMER PRIME MINISTER
OF SLOVENIA**

DOING TIME

The Slovenian Democratic Party might be looking for a new leader soon. Its current leader, Janez Janša, looks like spending a few years inside. His conviction was confirmed in 2014, as was his two-year prison sentence.

It's a sad ending for the colourful former Prime Minister who served two terms, from 2004 to 2008 and 2012 to 2013. According to the *Reuters* news agency, the 'centre-right government fell in February last year (2013), after an anti-corruption commission said Janša was unable to explain the origins of a significant part of his income over several years.'

It all had to do with the purchase of over 134 armoured vehicles from the Finnish defence manufacturer, Patria. *Reuters* further reports that 'six people in Finland are being prosecuted over the same arms deal and an Austrian court has convicted an Austrian citizen of corruption.' It was going to bring the partially government owned firm something in the range of $234M, so a lot of cash was being spread around to make sure the deal went through. Janša has still got his blog, proudly boasting of speaking to the United Nations General Assembly in 2012 and being interviewed by *Euronews*, but it might be difficult to keep it up while behind bars.

When in power he had the Eastern European habit of complaining bitterly about the threat of immigration, although Slovenia has no significant immigration problem (it has an emigration issue, though) and there are no real ethnic minorities to harp on about. However, the ultra-nationalist, xenophobic rhetoric worked on the voters who seemed to lap up his verbal attacks on foreigners. When a Finnish television documentary revealed the extent of corruption in the armoured car deal between Patria and the Slovenian government, Janša claimed it was all an elaborate left-wing media conspiracy to get him. That didn't work so well and now the former Prime Minister is cooling his heels in Dob Prison.

MAYOR OF LONDON

IT'S ALL ABOUT HIS JOHNSON

He's likeable and charming, but nobody really knows where the bullshit begins or ends with Boris.

You might not feel comfortable leaving your wife or daughter behind closed doors with the floppy-haired mayor. His marriage to Marina has lasted 17 years, although he has had at least three affairs and has fathered a love child. He's been described by Ian Hislop, editor of the satirical magazine *Private Eye*, as 'our Berlusconi, he's the only feel-good politician we have, everyone else is too busy being responsible'.

His affair with Petronella Wyatt, for whom he promised to leave his wife, ended badly for two reasons: he reneged on the promise and was sacked from the Shadow Cabinet – not for the affair, but for lying about it. In his early career, *The Times*, fired him for making up a quote. His former boss at the *Telegraph*, Conrad Black (no stranger to scandal himself) said he is 'a scoundrel – a sly fox disguised as a teddy bear'.

Boris seems to take nothing – including his politics – too seriously, and that's maybe how he's avoided much of the opprobrium hurled at his old Eton and Oxford chums: Prime Minister, David Cameron and Chancellor, George Osborne. At Oxford, all three were in the notorious Bullingdon Club together, a debauched drinking society for the spoilt sons of old money. But it's worth remembering that what also separates Boris from his pals is that he went to an Oxford college where only the smartest kids go. The buffoonery is an act; he's a very shrewd and intelligent guy.

As his sister, Rachel, said, 'does he want to be the prime minister? He's much more ambitious than that.' He has now announced plans to return to parliament in the 2015 elections and is already media favourite to become Conservative leader and prospective PM if Cameron becomes a cropper, which the way the 2015 elections are shaping up is a distinct possibility. Whatever happens we're certainly guaranteed to hear a lot more about Boris – and his Johnson.

JEFF JOHNSON

CANDIDATE FOR
GOVERNOR OF MINNESOTA

PARTY WITH ROSIE LEE

It's a pretty normal place – at least in the summer – but Minnesotans can elect some strange governors. Jessie Ventura, who thinks 9/11 was secretly planned by the US government and was a 'professional wrestler', served as governor of the state from 1999 to 2003.

Jeff Johnson hopes to follow in his footsteps. He ran for governor of Minnesota in 2014 on the Republican ticket, claiming to be a moderate who would bring about change. The Democrats painted him as a radical Tea Party advocate, a charge he strenuously denied although he seems to have spoken at every Tea Party event held in the state and actually asked for their endorsement, which they gave.

In a video taken at one of the Tea Party events he spoke at, Johnson said, 'there is this perception that the media has created that tea parties are kind of wacko. And we are not.' When asked if he was a Tea Party supporter he replied, saying, 'I'm not a member, but I don't know [if] you have membership, nor do they endorse by the way, I've been told that.' Shortly after he made that statement a video came out of Johnson asking for the endorsement of the Tea Party.

Minnesota is typically Democratic and has strongly backed President Barack Obama. Nevertheless, Johnson thinks he could bring some Tea Party beliefs into the Statehouse, but with eight weeks to go before the election he replaced his campaign manager. A poll conducted by the *Star Tribune* in September 2014 found that 33% of the voters had never heard of Johnson and 40% had formed no opinion of him. In sympathy, the *Pioneer Press* published an article about him in late September titled *His Name: is Jeff Johnson. He wants to be governor.*

PRESIDENT OF NIGERIA

GOOD LUCK?

He has a soccer club named after him, which should say something about his popularity. The *Nigerian Bulletin* says it was 'named after the initials of the Nigerian president, GEJ FC' (his middle name is Ebele). It's expected to start in the Nigeria Nationwide League with the intention of progressing to the top flight of Nigerian professional football.

But the mothers of the 200 schoolgirls kidnapped by *Boko Haram* in the north of the country, and never heard from since, might not feel like naming anything after the Nigerian president. Chances are that Lamido Sanusi isn't feeling the love for Jonathan either. He was sacked in 2014 as Governor of the Central Bank of Nigeria for keeping monetary policy tight and for being an outspoken critic of corruption.

Just when the rest of West Africa was suffering from an Ebola epidemic, Jonathan seemed shocked that someone disembarked from a plane in Lagos, breezed through a completely unprepared customs check and dropped dead from the disease, but not before making sure that he infected a few of the people he ran into. Jonathan assured the country that 'as a government, we promise that we will do everything humanly possible to contain the Ebola virus,' then made the decision to sack 16,000 resident doctors at the same time the country could potentially face a horrific epidemic.

Earlier in 2014 he signed into law the Same Sex Marriage Prohibition Act – as if people in homophobic Africa were dying to get hitched to their same sex lovers. Meanwhile, France, Britain and the United States worked out a deal to free the 200 kidnapped schools through a prisoner swap – and Jonathan cancelled it.

Nigeria reached the play-off rounds of the World Cup in 2014, but the team had threatened to stop training unless they were paid their promised bonus. They were on the verge of returning home until Jonathan assured them personally that cash was on the way. At least he had one success for the year.

ZELJKO JOVANOVIC

MEMBER OF THE CROATIAN PARLIAMENT

BLEEDING DOGTEETH

Zeljko Jovanovic seems like an admirable chap. According to the *Open Society* website, the Harvard-educated former journalist is now 'director of the Roma Initiatives Office for Open Societies Foundations'. He's not the sort of person that should be included in this book, and he isn't – because he's the wrong Zeljko Jovanovic.

The one we're going after is an entirely different man from an entirely different country. This Zeljko Jovanovic is a Croatian politician and a member of the *Socijaldemokratska partija Hrvatske* (Social Democratic Party). First of all, his car: it's an Audi A6 3.0 TDI Quattro, which is a snappy little number. It will set you back over £40,000 ($66,500), but Jovanovic, Croatia's Sport and Education Minister, had his provided by the government, free of charge. When asked by a journalist if he thought it was right to drive around in such an expensive car at the same time the government had to admit it didn't have enough money for flood relief, he angrily asked if he, 'should drive himself around in a horse-drawn carriage'.

Jovanovic gets a lot of flak in Croatia because he is an ethnic Serb. The director of Zagreb Dinamo Football Club, Zdravko Mamic, was once arrested for making 'racist' comments about Jovanovic. According to the *Balkan Insider,* Mamic said that 'Jovanovic is an insult for the Croatian brain; he hates everything that is Croatian; you cannot see a laugh on this man, you just see bleeding dogteeth.'

It's not his Serbian background that bothers some Croatians, it's his reckless mouth. According to the *Croatian Times,* in 2011 Prime Minister, Jadranka Kosor, 'lodged a private lawsuit against Social Democratic Party representative, Zeljko Jovanovic, for calling her party, the Croatian Democratic Union, a criminal organisation'. Jovanovic responded: 'in case I am invited to court, I will have an opportunity to support with much evidence my statement in the Parliament that the Croatian Democratic Union is a criminal organisation, which planned, implemented and organized a criminal enterprise with a goal to rob the state budget and destroy the life of Croatian citizens, whose salaries and pension are not enough for a normal living.'

ERIC JOYCE

UK HOUSE OF COMMONS

STONE COLD SOBER

There are eight places in the British Houses of Parliament where you can get shit-faced. That's not bad: it means that if you were banned from seven, there would still be one where you could fill your skin to the brim. According to the *Guardian* newspaper, the Sports and Social Club is 'located next to the bins in the basement, it is the only bar most voters would recognise as a normal pub, with darts results and welcoming scruffiness.' That's where Scottish MP, Eric Joyce, says he didn't get hammered on the 14th of March, 2013.

That said, the *Guardian* noted in 2013 that, 'he was arrested on suspicion of assault… after an altercation at the Sports and Social Club, apparently over taking a glass out to a smoking area.' They also note that, 'Joyce resigned from the Labour Party last year (2012) after being fined and handed a three-month pub and bar ban for punching and head-butting fellow MPs.'

Joyce has vigorously defended himself, saying he doesn't have a drinking problem – might have had a little problem with the booze in the past, but that's all over with – and put the matter firmly to rest when he said, 'nor do I inject alcohol right into my eyeballs while crying'. That's that then, except for the fact that he was found guilty of assault, fined £3,000 and had to pay £1,400 in compensation.

The Labour MP from Falkirk, Joyce was once a Major in the British Army and he's either got a drinking problem or bad anger management issues. He's been fined £1,500 for being abusive to a worker at Edinburgh airport. In 2010 he was done for drunk driving and the *Daily Mail* noted that 'Senior Labour officials said Eric Joyce, 51, should stand down following claims of a two-year relationship with teenager Meg Lauder, which is said to have started when she was only 17.' In September 2014 the *Falkirk Herald* reported that Joyce did something that he should have done a long time ago: he took the ice bucket challenge.

WAHAB JUNAID

ASPIRING PARLIAMENTARIAN

FUNDRAISER

Junaid wants to run for the House of Representatives for the Lagos State in the 2015 elections in Nigeria but to do that requires funding and not many Nigerians are inclined to contribute to his campaign. He's been nominated but the party told him to go out and raise funds.

He's not into begging for campaign donations, but Junaid is a resourceful guy and found a way to raise the money in order to run: tapping illegally into a Nigerian National Petroleum Corporation pipeline, loading it into his tanker and selling it on the black market. With each haul he makes he can net 3 million naira ($18,000). That buys a lot of campaign posters and a few radio commercials. There's one hitch, though: Junaid keeps getting caught.

He was first nabbed for stealing oil in 2008 but somehow got off on the charge, as he did on two other occasions. He was arrested again for the fourth time in October of 2014 and contritely told the *Daily Post* that 'in the course of looking for funds, a friend of mine, Oloje, who is also a vandal, informed me that the area was calm, and that I could come and lift some fuel and get money for my political ambition.' Junaid may not be the most believable of political aspirants but he says he is a trained veterinarian and his local nickname is 'doctor'.

He felt hard done by the last arrest because he thinks it was orchestrated by his political opponents who are out to get him. He further told the *Post*: 'I was waiting with my tankers to lift the product when policemen arrested me. My enemies, who are bitter that I was anointed for the political position, betrayed me. Please forgive me and give me another chance. I am sorry and I promise that as soon as I am elected, I will assist the police in the war against pipeline vandalism.'

JEAN-CLAUDE JUNCKER

PRESIDENT OF THE EUROPEAN COMMISSION

PINBALL WIZARD

Perhaps it's because he spent eighteen years as prime minister of the most boring place on the continent of Europe that he drinks like a fish and smokes like a chimney. There are dusty African capitals where there is absolutely nothing to do but watch the flies cluster around a dead dog, but when it comes to Europe there is no place more mundane, humdrum or monotonous than Luxembourg.

That's probably why the EU chose Juncker to be the new President of the European Commission in 2014. The catchphrase, 'there's nothing drunker than Juncker', fits the man to a T. He's rumoured to belt back a couple of cognacs with his breakfast and he's got a famous weakness for the single malt whisky, Glenfarclas. He keeps a bottle of the stuff within reach in his office. He's also said to be a master pinball player.

Juncker has blown some serious money on white elephants in Luxembourg and there have been some scandals – notably the internal spying that his security department conducted – but the real and undeniable scandal about him is plain for everyone to see. Luxembourg exists mainly as a tax haven, not only for rich, corrupt African dictators, but for the multinationals who use it as their base to avoid paying taxes in the countries where they do business. It's state where $3.75 trillion is hidden away in countless banks.

Companies like Amazon, Vodafone, Caterpillar and 40,000 other holding companies 'headquarter' themselves in Luxembourg, do business in the rest of Europe and pay a pittance in tax. It's ironic that the man who will be running the EU up until 2019 is the same guy who helped enable some of the world's largest companies to screw the rest of Europe.

JOSEPH KABILA

PRESIDENT OF THE DEMOCRATIC REPUBLIC OF THE CONGO

WAR BUS

Africa is generally ill-served by its politicians and the Congo is very much a case in point. Politics in Africa is rarely a battle between those advocating a greater, positive role for government and those wanting government off our backs. Things rarely get that sophisticated; it is all about power and power alone. Perhaps the continent should collectively think about hiring city managers, provincial managers and country managers who would only develop policy to drive growth, provide social care and assure the rule of law.

The last thing the Congo needs is Joseph Kabila. On his visit to Washington in 2014 the *Daily Mail* newspaper quoted a senior congressional aide as saying, 'Kabila is everything that's wrong with Africa rolled up into one evil package.' The newspaper also named *Forbes* magazine as a source when it stated that 'Kabila has himself looted $15 billion from his country and stashed it in offshore accounts, and that his brother Soulemane has pilfered another $300 million.'

You could overlook the fact that the president once ran an army made up of abducted children, that he's been accused of ordering the murder of a human rights crusader or that he's thought to have bribed his political allies to oust the Parliamentary Speaker. But, since he took power at the age of 29, over 5.4 million people are estimated to have died in the Congo because of internal conflicts and there remains a UN peacekeeping force of some 20,000 in the country. Its capital, Kinshasa, was once nicknamed *Kin la Belle*, Kinshasa the Beautiful. Now it's known as *Kin la Poubelle*, Kinshasa the dustbin.

The son of a former president who took over in a coup and was assassinated, Kibala didn't even grow up in the Congo; he grew up in Tanzania, where he earned the nickname 'War Bus' because of his love of military action movies. As soon as he graduated school there, he raised an army of *kadogos* (child soldiers) and marched them to the capital where he overthrew President Mobuto and has remained in power ever since.

JAROSLAW KACZYŃSKI

FORMER PRIME MINISTER OF POLAND

CRAZY AS A DUCK

He's the twin brother of the former Polish president, Lech Kaczyński, the one who made the unfortunate decision to board a Polish Air Force Tu-154 for a flight to Russia. As you might recall, the Soviet era aircraft didn't quite make it to its destination – like 39 other Tu-154s since they came into operation.

Jaroslaw's simply called 'the duck' because his surname means duck in Polish. He's also really, really Catholic and the leader of the Law and Justice Party, which was quick to politicise the 2010 death of the duck's brother.

Lech Kaczyński had to step down as Prime Minister in 2007 after his party lost a brutal election to Civic Platform, a moderate, centrist party that wanted Polish troops out of Iraq and stronger relations with the European Union. It's led by Donald Tusk and has opted for a moderate policy with Russia and even pushed the EU to allow residents of the Russian enclave of Kaliningrad to enter the country without visas.

Meanwhile, the duck's Law and Justice Party has been playing on Russia's refusal to return the remnants of the Polish plane and Putin's decision to invade the Ukraine. 'In our relations with Russia you need to be patient and avoid provocations, but if events like the recent ones take place, you have to tell the truth: cowardice is only an encouragement,' said Kaczyński recently.

He's never married and lives alone with his mother and their many cats. Although he's not a popular figure, the opposition has been doing a splendid job of putting their feet in their mouths and providing him with a chance to revive his party's fortunes. As Bloomberg recently reported, '*Wprost* magazine published secretly recorded conversations of central bank Governor Marek Belka discussing with Interior Minister Bartlomiej Sienkiewicz steps to boost the economy and help the government win elections.' They further reported that Kaczyński said, 'this scandal showed the truth about this government and we'll keep bringing it up until elections.'

POONAM KANGRA

PARTY STALWART

UNDER HER THUMB

She demands loyalty, and if she doesn't get it the punishment can be cruel. It looks like Poonam Kangra's husband, Darshan, will be making his own tea in the morning, fetching his own bottle of beer from the fridge at night and boiling his own rice.

It's not like he cheated on her with another woman. Kangra, the president of the District Youth Congress in Sangrur, in the Punjab district of India, judged her husband to be disloyal to her political party and filed for divorce in October of 2010.

According to *India Today*, 'she could not tolerate her councillor husband, Darshan Kangra's anti-party activities. Darshan had voted against Congress leader Harbans Lal in a no-confidence motion. Consequently, Lal was removed from the post of the Sangrur Municipal Council's president.' The newspaper further reported that, 'The Congress has already expelled Poonam's husband from its primary membership for six years for voting against a party nominee. Denying that it was a political gimmick to regain the party's confidence, Poonam said she had filed the application for divorce in a Sangrur court on Wednesday (6 October 2010).'

Darshan claimed the divorce proceedings were edged on by various members of the Congress Party and, to be fair, Poonam said she would have reconsidered the divorce if the party had let her husband back in. It can't have made Darshan confident that love always wins out when his soon to be ex-wife told *India Today*, 'the party is supreme. The Congress is more important than my husband. I can sacrifice any relationship to prove my loyalty to the Congress.'

Darshan said in reply that, 'I am sure she will be convinced about my conjugal faithfulness as well as my sincerity towards the party. She will be back with me.'

**PRESIDENT OF
UZBEKISTAN**

FAMILY FEUD

In September of 2014, Vladimir Putin 'congratulated Islam Karimov on Uzbekistan's Independence Day and 'noted Uzbekistan's success in economic and social development, as well as the nation's current role on the global arena'. What role? The country of 30 million has basically stagnated under Karimov's rule with a GDP of $3,500 per capita and an inflation rate of 12%.

According to the Heritage Foundation, 'Uzbekistan remains economically repressed. Pervasive state controls persist in many areas, stifling progress in the development of a modern diversified economy. Corruption is widespread, and contract enforcement and protection of property rights are seriously deficient.' That might have something to do with the country's president who runs a state almost as secretive as North Korea and has a family life that could only be called bizarre.

His relationship with his eldest daughter and formerly speculated successor, Gulnara Karimova, is both bizarre and troubling. Gulnara was once a jewelry designer, fashionista, pop singer, ambassador and diplomat. She has performed with Julio Inglesias, Sting and Gerard Depardieu, but now she is under house arrest in Tashkent, a sentence imposed by her father after he beat her in a fit of rage (and surreptitiously released the details to the press).

She had enough money stashed away in Europe to launch a 'Free Gulnara NOW' campaign. The campaign's website claimed that she is facing starvation and abuse and has demanded that all local charges against her be brought to an international criminal court.

Knowing her father, that is something that's not likely to happen and the blonde beauty will likely languish for years until her Daddy's health gives out.

MUTHUVEL KARUNANIDHI

A MAN OF MANY TALENTS

Suffice it to say, Hinduism is rich and complex, and if you aren't born into it, you'll never be a part of it. Unless you have an academic interest in the world's oldest religion, then the deities that are important to the various denominations will be irrelevant to you.

That said, of all the Hindu figures the most paramount is Lord Rama who represents all that's good in the world: devotion, courage and compassion. About 80% of Indians are Hindu, with the rest being Muslim, Christian and other religions, so some 20% of the population couldn't care less about Lord Rama.

You can count on Muthuvel Karunanidhi being one of those. He even questioned the existence of Rama, which is a sacrilege to Hindus. He specifically questioned the myth that Rama and his army of *Vanara* (ape men) built a bridge from India to Sri Lanka some 1.7 million years ago, specifically asking, 'From which engineering college did he graduate? Is there any proof for this?' Karunanidhi is an unabashed Dravidian rationalist and seems to relish mocking those who aren't.

The former Chief Minister of Tamil Nadu and the head of the *Dravida Munnetra Kazhagam* (DMK) political party has won every election he has contested in the last 60 years. He's also a writer, poet, amateur historian, essayist, composer, lyricist, former journalist and cartoonist. No longer Chief Minister, he is still a Member of the Legislative Assembly representing Tiruvarur. He's also an award winning screenwriter having penned over 75 scripts that have gone into production.

Perhaps his prolific activities outside politics have generated a sufficient income to keep him largely free of charges of corruption. He even donated his house to be turned into a hospital after his wife, Padmavathy, died. The only charges against him that have stuck to any extent are that he has embraced nepotism and is trying to create a political dynasty. (India has a few of those.)

**PARTY LEADER
AND ACTIVIST**

CHECKMATE

The former World Chess Champion formed his own opposition political party in Russia in 2005, the United Civil Front which wanted to bring about democratic reform. He tried to run for president in 2008 on the party ticket but could not meet the requirements and now he's joined the Other Russia group (very diverse coalition of Putin opponents) and aligned himself with the political oddball, Eduard Limonov.

As opposed to Limonov, Kasparov remains steadfastly pro-American and often has far more liberal views. He was arrested at a 'Pussy Riot' protest and threatened with prison and he has been a thorn in the side of Vladimir Putin for years. And, unlike Limonov, he has been one of the strongest political critics of Russia's annexation of the Crimea and its covert invasion of the Ukraine. He has described Washington and Berlin's response to the crisis as 'cowardly'.

In *Time* magazine he wrote in August 2014 that the, 'Western rhetoric of appeasement creates a self-reinforcing loop of mental and moral corruption' and 'strong sanctions and a clear demonstration of support for Ukrainian territorial integrity would have had real impact'. In the *Wall Street Journal* he wrote that Putin belonged in an 'exclusive club along with Saddam Hussein and Slobodan Milošević'. Kasparov has been so vitriolic in his criticism of President Barack Obama that he could easily fit into the ranks of the American neo-conservatives who also vilify the president as weak and waffling. The former chess champ also seems intent on egging on the US into a state of conflict with Russia as a means to turf out Putin from the Kremlin. He has compared Obama to Neville Chamberlain and called him 'weak' and a 'disaster' and has given backhanded praise to Putin for 'outplaying him'. All this makes him the darling of the American right but increases his unpopularity in his own country. He is seen as a viable opponent to Putin in the West and as a spent power in the East.

ARVIND KEJRIWAL

FORMER CHIEF MINISTER OF DELHI

INDIA'S JIMMY CARTER

The leader of Aam Aadmi Party (AAP) is a magnanimous kind of dude.

In October 2014 he even offered to allocate funds to build a bio-digestible, four-unit toilet for women on the premises of the Delhi office of another political party, the Bharatiya Janata Party (BJP). He wrote that, 'though it is the office of the BJP, it falls under my constituency. I want to rise above politics and offer funds (to build the toilet)'.

He was Chief Minister of Delhi between 2013 and 2014 but resigned after forty-nine days when he couldn't push through anti-corruption legislation.

He started his party in 2012 to end the bribe taking culture of politics in India and since then he has been a leading figure in the anti-corruption movement in the country. Needless to say, his work is cut out for him.

The fact that he couldn't get the power to appoint a Citizens' Ombudsman to hear complaints about demands for bribes says a lot about the official pervasive corruption in the region

Kejriwal is a vegetarian and a practitioner of the *Vipassan¯a* form of meditation. He's also launched a drive to clean up Delhi by photographing piles of rubbish and sending them to the three mayors of the three municipal corporations that run the city and he's even personally pitched in to help unblock the drains near the Prime Minister's residence.

He is also under investigation for overspending in his election campaign for the legislative assembly, he's alleged to have spent 1.4 million rupees ($227,000). He took on Prime Minister Narendra Modi for the seat representing the sacred Hindu city of Varanasi, but lost.

SALLY KERN

OKLAHOMA HOUSE OF
REPRESENTATIVES

BRAVELY FACING DOWN THE DEVIANTS

Oklahoma state Representative Sally Kern has gone well beyond saying things like 'blacks don't work as hard as white people' and has now aimed her cross-hairs against what she sees as the scourge of the 21st century: homosexuality.

In fact, she thinks homosexuality is now a greater threat to America than any potential terrorist attack. In her view it's even worse than Islamism. Kern thinks homosexuality is like a cancer spreading rapidly from shore-to-shore in the US and it 'will destroy our young people'. Like a lot of people of her ilk, she's developed a persecution complex, which is reflected in the book she wrote, *The Stoning of Sally Kern*. The tome allegedly 'speaks the truth about homosexuality'.

Talking recently about her favourite subject, Kern stated that 'every day our young people . . . they're bombarded with "homosexuality is normal and natural". It's something they have to deal with every day. Fortunately we don't have to deal with a terrorist attack every day.' She went on to add: 'I think that it's also more dangerous because it will tear down the moral fibre of this nation.' Some unkind critics of *The Stoning of Sally Kern* have suggested that it might be best if Sally Kern take a trip to Colorado and get really stoned.

Kern started her mission to prevent a homosexual takeover of America in 2005 when she sought to get Oklahoma's libraries to ban all books with homosexual themes. After reading some history, Kern stated that 'studies show that no society that has totally embraced homosexuality has lasted more than, you know, a few decades.' The super-patriot warns that 'this stuff is deadly, and it's spreading, and it will destroy our young people, it will destroy this nation!'

SERETSE KHAMA IAN KHAMA

PRESIDENT OF BOTSWANA

CONFIRMED BACHELOR

Sometimes when somebody is described as a 'confirmed bachelor' it has other connotations and there is no evidence that Ian Khama is anything else from what he says he is, but he's also a decent looking guy in his prime, the president of a country and he's single. Like Barack Obama, he's of mixed race. He is also the Paramount Chief of the Bamangwato tribe, although he can barely speak their native language of Setswana.

He didn't really have to try to be president; he sort of inherited the job. His father, Seretse Khama, was the first president of the country. Much as Botswana is touted as the one true democracy in Africa, it's really a one party state where the Botswana Democratic Party (BDP) basically calls the shots. There's a reason for that: whilst the country has a bizarrely vibrant media, its one government paper, the *Daily News*, is the only publication that reaches the entire nation. The other newspapers are read mainly in the capital, Gaborone, which is the one city that consistently votes against the BDP.

Khama hates drinking and has raised the duty on booze considerably, although it just pushed the brewers of the local *chibuku* beer underground. Khama is BFFs with Morgan Tsvangarai, who heads the opposition party in Zimbabwe and he's a mortal enemy of Robert Mugabe. In order to 'connect' with the people, Khama has set up his own Facebook page, which was instantly filled with bizarre and insulting comments.

Khama was in a car accident in 2014 and gave the driver whose jeep was destroyed a brand new one. This was reported in the *Sunday Standard* and the journalist who wrote the story was arrested for sedition. The US embassy complained about the arrest. That provoked a reaction from Jeff Ramsey, the president's spokesperson (he's also American by birth) who said, the US 'might wish to put its own house in order before rushing to hastily comment on the judicial affairs of others.' If you can get a charge of sedition against you for writing about a car accident, what would happen to a journalist who speculated why Khama's been a confirmed bachelor his entire life?

MIKHAIL KHODORKOVSKY

PARTY LEADER AND ACTIVIST

OPEN RUSSIA

He spent a decade in the clink and was let
out at the end of 2013 on the promise that he
wouldn't stick his nose in Russian politics again.
The former head of Yukos was the 16th richest man in
the world in 2003, with an estimated net worth of $15 billion. That was also the year he
was arrested for fraud and his company virtually collapsed taking away much of his wealth.

He was sent to prison in May 2005 and, while locked up, he was found guilty on further
charges of money laundering and embezzlement, which further extended his sentence. Most
believed the prosecution of Khodorkovsky was politically motivated. Amnesty International
worked for his release and the European Court of Human Rights stated that the basis for
the charges was suspicious.

In December of 2013, in a gesture that was meant to demonstrate his magnanimous
nature, Vladimir Putin signed Khodorkovsky's pardon and he was released from prison. Now
that he's out of the country, he's going back on his word and re-entering Russian politics,
albeit at a distance. It's his intention on starting a pro-European movement in Russia in
2014 to counter Putin's nationalist United Russia party. He's only worth an estimated $170
million now but he's considered the most trusted man in Russia. Khodorkovsky's Open
Russia initiative is being conducted online and the millionaire has admitted he would be
open to running for president. When asked how Putin would react to his initiative, he said,
'I expect him to be upset.' There are others, though, who see a darker side to the Open
Russia movement and think that it's really being directed by the Kremlin as a public relations
gimmick. There is a significant minority who think it's part of the deal arranged by Putin and
Khodorkovsky to present a limited but legitimate opposition to United Russia in order to
create an illusion that democracy still exists in Russia.

KIM JONG UN

SUPREME LEADER OF THE DEMOCRATIC PEOPLE'S REPUBLIC OF KOREA

THE FAT BOY WITH THE BOMB

Kim Jong Un thinks long hair is bad for people because it deprives the brain of energy and therefore harms intelligence, and that's about as sane and rational as North Korea's leader gets.

This is the guy who reportedly fed his living uncle, Jang Song Thaek, and five of his aides to a pack of 120 starving dogs and had his former girlfriend executed for making a pornographic film. Obviously, it doesn't pay to be on Kim's bad side.

Running a country where executions are routinely carried by flamethrowers has got to be a fun job. You can be 'best friends' with ex-basketball stars like Dennis Rodman, explore your addiction to bondage porn and watch endless military exercises and parades in your honour.

But the most fun thing of all is getting to threaten to launch a nuclear war, particularly if a Hollywood studio wants to release a film about your assassination. To make matters worse, the film in question is meant to be a comedy and Kim isn't the type to laugh at himself. According to a North Korean spokesman, 'making and releasing a movie on a plot to hurt our top-level leadership is the most blatant act of terrorism and war and will absolutely not be tolerated.' The spokesman went on to say, 'if the US administration allows and defends the showing of the film, a merciless counter-measure will be taken.' The so-called 'gangster filmmakers' themselves were nonplussed by the threats and even have reportedly invited Kim to the premier of the film but have declined the offer of a one way ticket to Pyongyang to meet Kim's collection of hungry dogs.

PRESIDENT OF ARGENTINA

QUEEN CRISTINA

'Our society needs women to be more numerous in decision-making positions and in entrepreneurial areas' said Argentinean President, Cristina de Kirchner. 'We always have to pass a twofold test: first to prove that, though women, we are no idiots, and second, the test anybody has to pass.' This is an interesting comment because, unfortunately for Argentina, their president still seems to be struggling with the first part of the test.

Known as 'Queen Cristina' or, in some circles, the 'She-Devil', she can at least take comfort in the fact that she has got a few Hollywood celebrities as BFFs, including Sean Penn who supports her in her hyped-up dispute with Britain over the Falkland Islands – or the *Islas Malvinas* as they are known in Argentina.

It's hardly a new political trick in Argentina to divert attention away from economic issues when things aren't looking too bright for the country. Argentina has the highest rate of inflation in Latin America, it defaulted on its international debt in 2014 and thousands of soccer fans who travelled to Brazil to see their country compete simply decided to stay rather than come back to a ruined economy. Rather than confront the difficult economic issues Argentina faces, de Kirchner bought a full page in the *Guardian* newspaper in 2013 and published an open letter to the British Prime Minister, David Cameron, appealing for the return of the islands that the country fought a disastrous war over in 1982.

The economy was growing strongly when de Kirchner took over the presidency but she has almost single-handedly ruined the future for a generation of the country. She did this by printing pesos and ramping up inflation, meddling with leading businesses, nationalising an oil company, an airline and pension funds. The economy hasn't hit de Kirchner yet. She still manages to live the life of the rich and famous.

PIA KJAERSGAARD

DANISH PARLIAMENT

DEMAGOGUE

She's principally a one-issue politician and it's an issue that seems to have some appeal in Denmark. Not all of the outwardly-friendly, easy going Danes are so comfortable having a significant Muslim immigrant population in their midst and when they close the voting booth door that sentiment gets expressed, which is what feathers the nests of people like Pia Kjaersgaard.

It's not so much that her beliefs are so nativist, it's that lingering suspicion that a growing number of European politicos sow the seeds of xenophobia for their own benefit. There's an industry in Europe that's been built on the fear that each country's unique culture is being destroyed by droves of wild-eyed Islamic fundamentalists whose evil intent is to turn Western Europe into a Muslim caliphate.

It's arguably true that European cities have been ghettoised to an extent and their Islamic neighbourhoods are increasingly isolated from the greater culture in which they live, and the fault for that often lies with immigrants who make little effort to integrate into the greater society. But, when Kjaersgaard says things like, 'not in their wildest imagination would anyone have imagined, that large parts of Copenhagen and other Danish towns would be populated by people who are at a lower stage of civilisation, with their own primitive and cruel customs like honour killings, forced marriages, Halal slaughtering and blood-feuds', is she saying that just to generate votes and jobs for the Danish People's Party, or is she trying to make some sort of constructive criticism of the immigrant community in Copenhagen?

As the MP said to *Weekly Commentary*, 'thousands upon thousands of persons, who apparently, civilisationally, culturally and spiritually, live in the year of 1005 instead of 2005, have come to a country that left the dark ages hundreds of years ago.' Those aren't the words that will solve any problem but it's troubling that they seem to be the ones that will get you re-elected again and again.

VÁCLAV KLAUS

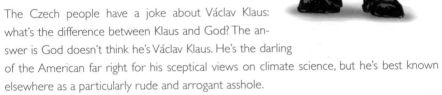

**FORMER PRESIDENT OF
THE CZECH REPUBLIC**

TOO RUDE FOR OBAMA

The Czech people have a joke about Václav Klaus: what's the difference between Klaus and God? The answer is God doesn't think he's Václav Klaus. He's the darling of the American far right for his sceptical views on climate science, but he's best known elsewhere as a particularly rude and arrogant asshole.

New Republic magazine says he is 'legendary for his lack of manners', and notes that his predecessor, Václav Havel, found him 'utterly unbearable'. During a recent trip to Prague, President Obama chose to spend the evening having dinner alone with his wife, Michelle, rather than listening to Klaus talk about himself.

Klaus has held high office in the Czech Republic, serving as Prime Minister and President. The British *Daily Telegraph* admires him for his views on climate change and free markets. Writing in the *Financial Times* newspaper, Klaus said, 'As someone who lived under communism for most of his life, I feel obliged to say that I see the biggest threat to freedom, democracy, the market economy and prosperity now in ambitious environmentalism, not in communism.' In 2007, Klaus wrote an article in the Czech newspaper, *Hospodarske Noviny*, saying 'global warming is a myth and every serious person and scientist says so.' He even wrote a book for the right-wing American think tank, the Competitive Enterprise Institute, *Blue Planet in Green Shackles*, that pounded what Klaus thinks are the phonies who are spinning the climate change myth.

Like so many other right-wing European political nuts, he's got the hots for Vladimir Putin and calls his behaviour 'rational'. He blames the United States and the European Union for Russia's annexation of the Crimea. In 2013 the upper house of the Czech legislature voted to charge Klaus with treason because of a widespread pardon he had given to various people under investigation and for his refusal to ratify European Union treaties. This was a largely symbolic act as Klaus retired from office shortly thereafter – although he has yet to shut his mouth.

JOEL KLEEFISCH

WISCONSIN STATE ASSEMBLY

STONE COLD CRAZY

He's Republican, an evangelical Christian, a gun lover and he's about as loony as you get in Wisconsin. One of his big legislative initiatives Joel Kleefisch proposed was to open a hunting season for the Sandhill Crane, a majestic bird that has been carefully brought back from near extinction. The reason he wants to bag one of the birds is simple and only Kleefisch could express it so elegantly: 'they're the rib eye of the sky'.

Kleefisch was actually a radio journalist and won an award for 'best investigative report or series' in 1999 from the Milwaukee Press Club. That was before he entered politics and put his crazy hat on. *Milwaukee Magazine* actually keeps a 'blooper page' specifically for Kleefisch and details some of the more inane utterances that come from his mouth.

In 2007 Kleefisch introduced legislation that would have required former sex offenders to have fluorescent green licence plates for their cars on the premise 'child sex predators have been watching our children and this gives us an opportunity to watch them back'. Speaking about the matter on the Assembly floor, Kleefisch said, 'sexuality among youth isn't a right, in fact, it's a crime.'

He's been accused of plagiarising the wording on a legislative initiative but he passed the blame on to one of his staffers. When it became clear that the reason he proposed a bill to reduce child support payments for the wealthy was because one individual who would greatly benefit from the passage of the legislation was a big contributor to Kleefisch's campaign, he sort of apologised during a WTMJ radio interview. 'I should've realized that this would have the perception of him having undue influence ... and for that I apologize,' said Kleefisch. 'I learned a lesson here today.'

CHARLES AND DAVID KOCH

POLITICAL SPONSORS

THE BROTHERS

Much in the way the Speaker of the US House of Rep-resentatives, John Boehner, says his name should be pronounced 'baner' instead of 'boner', the Koch brothers are equally sensitive and say the correct way to say their name is 'coke', not 'cock'.

They aren't politicians but they are kingmakers nonetheless. They're each worth $40 billion and they earned their wealth the old-fashioned way: they inherited it. They own the second largest private company in America: Koch Industries. Charles and David sunk $400 million into the unsuccessful bid to put Mitt Romney and his magic underwear into the White House. For the 2014 mid-term election, in which they hoped to bring about a Republican majority in the United States Senate, they laid out $290 million and bought 44,000 political advertisements.

Based in Wichita, Kansas, Koch Industries does not have to go through the transparent financial reporting that a publicly held company does but it is estimated that it turns over $155 billion a year. The company has the unique distinction of being the 13th biggest air polluter in the nation, and the Koch brothers want to keep it that way, so they finance the climate change deniers and those politicians who see the Environmental Protection Agency as an impediment to business. The company owns such a large portion of the US energy market and trades in a range of derivative products that there are worries that any misstep the company could make could cause a systemic risk to the US economy.

The brothers support a series of conservative 'think tanks' that do their best to contest climate change and they've spent millions trying to prevent implementation of the Affordable Care Act (Obamacare). Their image and reputation has, in fact, begun to undermine whatever influence they have. All the Democrats have to do now is point out that one of their opponents is backed by the Koch brothers and they become toxic.

JANUSZ KORWIN-MIKKE

MEMBER OF THE EUROPEAN PARLIAMENT

WHICH 'N' WORD?

According to the Brussels-based magazine, *The Parliament*, there's a bit of an uproar about Korwin-Mikke's colourful use of language during a debate on youth unemployment. Many in the audience are sure they heard the word, 'nigger', while the Polish MEP insists he said 'negro'. He blames a leftist media plot for what he says is a misunderstanding, but either 'n' would be right in character.

Korwin-Mikke thinks the government should do away with all subsidies to the unemployed, arguing that 'hunger is the best teacher'. The self-described 'libertarian conservative' has a number of controversial beliefs. He wants to bring back the monarchy and thinks democracy is the 'stupidest form of government ever conceived' because someone else's vote is worth just as much as his. He's also not big on women's rights and doesn't think they should have the right to vote and they should concentrate on staying 'at home bringing up families'.

When *The Parliament* asked why no party was interested in having Korwin-Mikke join them, he blamed it all on a plot by the Polish intelligence services. He's not a Holocaust denier but he thinks Hitler had no knowledge of the attempted extermination of Jews and other minorities between 1939 and 1945. Like a lot of other far right Europeans, Korwin-Mikke has a serious man crush on the Russian president, Vladimir Putin. 'He is a good president for Russia and there's no reason to insult him,' he said, after Russia invaded and occupied the Crimea. 'There is no reason to be anti-Russian in Poland, anti-Russian action is contrary to the interests of the Polish,' Korwin-Mikke added. In fact, he takes crazy one step further than anyone else when it comes to Putin. He said that Putin would make a great president of Poland, better than the one they currently have.

MARIÁN KOTLEBA

GOVERNOR OF BANSKÁ BYSTRICA

THE BANE OF THE ROMA

One out of every eleven Slovaks are 'parasites', at least according to the newly elected neo-Nazi, Marián Kotleba. He is now Governor of the Banská Bystrica Region of Slovakia, which ironically was once the centre of anti-fascist resistance. The 'parasites' Kotleba refers to belong to Slovakia's minority Roma population.

Once a proud wearer of Nazi style uniforms and an admirer of the country's former collaborationist government, which cooperated closely with its Nazi masters during the Second World War, Kotleba has now begun to try to hide his far right past and is putting on a cloak of respectability.

He founded the *Slovenská Pospolitost* (Slovak Togetherness) party which has since been banned by the government. He's been arrested numerous times for his participation in anti-Roma demonstrations. The problem in Slovakia is that, behind closed doors, both the Roma population and the Hungarian minority are deeply hated and Kotleba is able to capitalise on that. As *The Economist* reports, 'since 2008 no fewer than 14 segregation walls have gone up throughout Slovakia, isolating Roma from their neighbours'. The newspaper further states that 'the walls differ in size and scope, but all are designed to segregate the poorer Roma communities.'

In the summer of 2014 a celebration of the Slovak National Uprising against the Nazis was held in the Banská Bystrica Region. Governor, Kotleba, who openly was not invited to the ceremony. As reported in the *Slovak Spectator*, the organiser of the celebration, Stanislav Mičev, said, 'I won't invite a fascist to celebrate an anti-fascist uprising'. The turnout for the election that Kotleba won was remarkably low; only 17% of eligible voters turned out, making his victory a shock to many of the region's inhabitants.

Kotleba also considers NATO a 'terrorist organisation'.

DENNIS KUCINICH

US HOUSE OF REPRESENTATIVES

LITTLE GREEN MEN

It would have to have been with Shirley MacLaine (she believes in reincarnation), wouldn't it? It was 1982, near Mt Ranier in Washington State that Kucinich saw his first flying saucer. He could have just kept it between himself and the actress, but he had to talk about it in public and mention that he felt, 'a connection in his heart and heard directions in his mind'.

The left-leaning journal, *American Prospect*, describes the Democrat Kucinich as, 'a favourite among lefty college kids and Birkenstock-wearers around the country' and 'among the wackiest members of Congress', but that was before he lost his primary challenge in 2013 and retired from Congress (for the moment). In an amazing turnaround, he was hired shortly after his political defeat by the conservative broadcaster, Fox News, presumably as an object of ridicule.

Although Kucinich refuses to adopt the orthodoxy of either major political party in the United States, he stands with Rand Paul in his concerns about the threat of drone strikes to American citizens in the 'War on Terror'. He's also got a much younger and very hot wife, so something is working there. In September of 2014 Kucinich and his wife launched a 'From Terror to Peace' tour of the country to 'change the present paradigm of fear, endless war and destruction of liberty'. According to the *Plain Dealer*, 'they said they'd like to redefine national security to be truly reflective of our practical aspirations and human security needs, such as food security, water security, economic security, job security, health security, education security, environmental security and peace'. Amazing how the left the world over have such a merry talent for stripping a word of all tangible meaning simply by applying it to everything.

Just as he did in 2008, Kucinich is most likely to launch a presidential primary run against the presumed Democratic nominee, Hillary Clinton, and he's just as likely to galvanise the far left wing of the party in his favour.

BRENDA KUPCHICK

CONNECTICUT STATE CONGRESS

SIBLINGS

Brenda Kupchick has a lot going for her. She lives in Fairfield, a prosperous commuter town on the coast of Long Island Sound. She is a rare Republican lawmaker in a deeply Democratic state. On her own website she explains that, she 'and her husband, Peter have owned and operated Peter Kupchick Heating & Cooling for the past twenty years'.

In an interview with the *Fairfield Patch* in 2012, she pointed out that she has 'worked with both parties and supported and passed stronger anti-bullying legislation for our students and strengthened Domestic Violence laws to protect victims' and she is working with constituents to build 'a justice centre for victims of domestic violence'. These are all laudable goals, which is why it sort of jars the perfect picture to find out that in August of 2013 she was arrested for laying into her sister, Lisa Fabrizi.

According to the *Stamford Advocate*, 'a law and order state representative from Fairfield was ordered to turn over her gun Monday following her arrest on charges of assaulting her younger sister.' The paper further reported that, 'the perfectly coiffed Kupchick, 48, earlier stood out among the sea of prostitutes and drug addicts in the main arraignment court. She was the only one there wearing pearls' and further relayed that, 'police said Kupchick attacked her sister, scratching Fabrizi's face, following a family picnic at Kupchick's Farist Road, Fairfield, home Saturday night.' The *Fairfield Citizen* later reported that, 'police sources said Kupchick believed her sister was intoxicated and about to drive home with her children in her car.' The paper reported that the charges were later dismissed on the condition that she could be 'prosecuted again on the charges if she is arrested a second time within the year'.

ARLETTE LAGUILLER

PRESIDENTIAL CANDIDATE
AND PARTY
SPOKESPERSON

ARLETTE THE STARLETTE

The leader of the *Lutte Ouvrière* (Workers' Struggle) party, Arlette, as she is referred to in France, is an unabashed Trotskyist politician who believes 'the organisation of production should be according to the needs of men and not for individual profit'. Being a Trotskyist in the modern world is a bit difficult, but Arlette has been preaching about the communist revolution since 1973 and has since run in every French presidential election – not very successfully. During her first campaign for president – she was the first woman in France to run – she said her party should 'destroy the apparatus of the bourgeois state, its government and its parliament, its courts, its police and its army, and seize power directly because ballots do not change lives'.

The Socialist Party of President François Holland is about as socialist as you'll get in mainstream Western European politics, and the problem with *Lutte Ouvrière* is, like all good communists, they are constantly involved in internecine warfare while splinter groups like the *Ligue Communiste Révolutionnaire* break off and draw away support. The communists used to garner a big chunk of the votes in French national elections but Arlette now only gets under 2%. But she's regarded affectionately by the public for her eccentrically frugal lifestyle and her bluntness.

Of Marine Le Pen of the *Front National*, she said: 'Marine Le Pen's campaign is just like Hitler's except they simply replaced the Jews with Arabs and Negroes'. That statement is essentially true, but not something that is normally said in public. Her son, Nicholas, got in trouble with the police for calling Le Pen a 'fascist bitch'.

Arlette remains optimistic about the future for the far left in France: 'I am convinced that capitalism will not be the last form of society that we know. The revolution will be violent, but doubtless much less murderous than any war. 'So . . . it will come.'

WILLIE LANTIGUA

FORMER MAYOR OF
LAWRENCE, MASSACHUSETTS

TOTALLY UNTRUE

Lawrence, Massachusetts doesn't have a lot going for it. Massachusetts does have something going for it. It is the fourth richest state in America in terms of per capita income, with each resident earning about $35,485 per year. Lawrence, on the other hand, has a per capita income of $11,360, making it the most impoverished city in the state and the 18th poorest in the country.

Now imagine if a visionary like Willie Lantigua was the mayor of the town of 70,000 people. According to *Vice* magazine, in 2012, the mayor was under investigation for 'alleged bid rigging, suspicious out-of-state travel, illegal swapping of city-owned cars, and corruption and campaign finance violations' and to top it off he dumped his wife and married his mistress – who was perhaps privy to his undertakings because, 'luckily for Willie under Massachusetts law the new Mrs Lantigua doesn't have to testify against him if he's formally charged with anything'.

According to the *Boston Globe*, in 2011, 'recent disclosure that the mayor is under federal investigation has prompted a recall campaign launched by local residents'. When asked by the newspaper if certain allegations against him were true, Lantigua replied, 'this is totally, totally, totally untrue. There's nothing to the allegations. I'm just going to continue standing tall.' He lost his 2013 re-election campaign for mayor to Daniel Rivera by a narrow margin of 81 votes and has now decided to run for the Massachusetts House of Representatives in 2014, despite federal and state corruption investigations against him.

The *Valley Patriot* newspaper reported in August of 2014 that, 'the state's Inspector General [has opened a probe] as part of a multi-agency criminal investigation against former Mayor William Lantigua over a paving scam Lantigua was involved in while he was running for re-election.'

ENRIQUE FLORES LANZA

MINISTER OF THE PRESIDENCY

EL CARRETILLAZO

He's supposedly a human rights lawyer and he's Minister of the Presidency in Honduras. The *Huffington Post* calls him a 'liar and a crook', but that may be because stealing $2.5 million from the government's coffers is considered small change in Tegucigalpa, where politicians regularly fleece the government out of hundreds of millions.

How do we know that Flores took the money? He admitted it in August of 2014 and just brushed off any criticism for the theft. The fact of the matter is that if Flores was arrested for the crime the country would undergo renewed turmoil with potential rioting and instability that nobody wants.

So, Lanza walks free and still collects his ministerial salary. Well, not quite. The Honduran Supreme Court finally found some backbone and arrested the minister and put him on trial.

The press refers to it as the *El Carretillazo* scandal. *La Prensa* newspaper even revealed video footage of large amounts of money being taken away from the Central Bank of Honduras in wheelbarrows. The total theft was over $300 million and Flores revealed exactly how and to whom it was distributed among various Ministers and politicians – including, of course, himself. According to *La Prensa*, Flores 'argued that the money was taken out in compliance with legal procedures promoted by Government House and approved by the Cabinet', which says something about how governments work in Central America. *Honduprensa* reports that 'the prosecution has enough evidence for the court to make an order for formal prosecution'.

WAYNE LAPIERRE

NATIONAL RIFLE ASSOCIATION
OF AMERICA

MERCHANT OF DEATH

He gets paid $970,000 to say the best way to prevent another school massacre is not to take away the God given right to own an assault rifle but to monitor every person in the country who has mental problems and put armed guards on the gates of every school. He once described Federal gun control agents as 'jack booted government thugs' in 'Nazi bucket helmets and black storm trooper uniforms' in a letter that sufficiently angered former President George H.W. Bush to resign his NRA membership.

The head of the NRA is the 'go to' guy for every US politician who wants his organisation's endorsement and considerable support. The NRA is essentially an adjunct political party, which faced its greatest crisis after John Hinckley opened fire on President Ronald Reagan and his entourage in Washington DC, in 1981. James Brady, Reagan's Press Secretary, was one of four people shot, including the president, and Brady never fully recovered. His wife set up the 'Brady Campaign to Prevent Gun Violence', the NRA's first and last formidable foe that lobbied successfully for the passage of the Federal Assault Weapons Ban, which, had it still been in effect, might have prevented Adam Lanza from bringing an M4 carbine to a Connecticut school in 2012 and murdering 26 people.

Lapierre has spoken about the fear a mass murder 'will be the pretext to unleash a tsunami of gun control' and said, 'it's not paranoia to buy a gun. It's survival. It's responsible behaviour, and it's time we encouraged law-abiding Americans to do just that'. Some NRA members even believe the Sandy Hook school massacre was an event fabricated to bring gun control laws into effect. The organisation has nothing to do with Americans who like to hunt; it's a political movement for gun obsessives who can have their paranoia exploited by people like Lapierre for profit. In an era where the NRA is stronger than ever, the percentage of Americans owning guns is at its lowest, and falling.

MARK LATHAM

FORMER LEADER OF THE OPPOSITION: AUSTRALIAN HOUSE OF REPRESENTATIVES

FILLING IN THE SUCKHOLES

He once broke a taxi drivers arm because he thought he was being screwed on the fare. The Australian former Labour MP and onetime opposition leader certainly had a colourful style to him. Calling one of his disabled opponents 'a deformed character' and referring to a female journalist as 'skanky ho' are just two examples. He even said that if he was using a urinal next to a political opposite he just might piss on them.

'Howard is an arse-licker,' he said of the Australian Prime Minister, John Howard when he made a trip to the US in 2005. 'He went over there, kissed some bums, and got patted on the head.' He added that Howard had 'forgotten how to be a good Australian, not some yes-man to a flaky and dangerous American president.'

During the 2004 election he called a political satirist a 'fucking idiot'. A newspaper photographer took a snap of him while he was at a restaurant with his children and he grabbed the camera and smashed it on the floor. But it was after he retired from politics in 2005 that his political life got even more interesting. One of his political memoirs, A Conga Line of Suckholes, recounted in vivid detail what political life in Canberra was really like. The book refers directly to a quote of his describing his political opponents: 'There they are, a conga line of suckholes on the conservative side of politics.'

His book, The Political Bubble: Why Australians Don't Trust Politics, published in 2014, considers how to deal with the growing contempt that normal Australians have for politicians. He writes that what he calls 'the cycle of apathocracy' can be partly eliminated by doing away with what he calls the 'partisan bickering of manufactured outrage'. Clearly there's been some sort of epiphany since his boast of 2002: 'I'm a hater. Part of the tribalness of politics is to really dislike the other side with intensity. And the more I see of them, the more I hate them.'

LARISA LEE

NORTHERN TERRITORY
LEGISLATIVE ASSEMBLY

YOUR CHEATIN' HEART

'It happens all the time in families, my family is larger than most,' Lee told a reporter for NT News in April, 2014.

The Australian politician represents Arnhem in the Northern Territory Legislative Assembly for the Palmer United Party. What she was talking about with NT News is not an everyday occurrence in most families. Not everybody scraps with their niece in broad daylight because she is sleeping with their boyfriend.

According to the *Guardian*, 'on 24 April (2014), the Palmer United party MLA found out her niece Sherese Dooley, 18, was having an affair with her partner, Benjamin Ulamari, after finding photos on his phone. She tracked her niece to the Katherine Centrelink and called her outside to discuss the affair before assaulting her.'

Magistrate Elisabeth Armitage admonished Lee, telling the burly MLA, 'you got out of the car when you saw her, you went up to her, grabbed her by the hair and dragged her across a concrete driveway. You didn't stop there, but then proceeded to punch her a number of times to the head with a closed fist. You swore at her and threatened her.' Because Lee had no prior convictions, the magistrate let her off lightly. She was fined $300 and had to post a $1,000 'good behaviour bond'.

It wasn't the first time Lee had to pay damages. She had a 'garlic bread nightmare' just weeks before she had a punch up with her niece. According to NT News, 'Larisa Lee, just days before trying to bring down her own Government, nearly brought down a Darwin hotel in a poorly executed attempt to heat a loaf of garlic bread. A letter from Darwin Central hotel management, seen by NT News, described a situation in which Ms Lee heated a loaf of garlic bread in her room's microwave for an excessive amount of time, resulting in burning and [a] large amount of smoke.' Lee had to pay $2,000 to clean up that mess. There was also the investigation into the misuse of Lee's government fuel card in 2013. According to ABC News, Lee had run up a fuel bill of more than $17,000 in just six months.

SOMSAVAT LENGSAVAD

DEPUTY PRIME MINISTER OF LAOS

COUNTRY FOR SALE

Lengsavad is the guy you go to if you want to get a huge swath of land in Laos. Being ethnically Chinese helps him cut deals with entrepreneurs who want to build a casino, a golf course or a rubber plantation. It doesn't matter if people are living on the land, even if they are veterans who fought against the Americans. They're easily displaced, given a few kips and told to fuck off.

Lengsavad has set up a whole patronage network that has earned him millions, in real money. He's in charge of a 7.2 billion dollar railway project that will link Kunming in southern China to the Laotian capital of Vientiane. The country is borrowing the total amount from the Chinese government, assuring it stays in Beijing's pocket as opposed to Vietnam and Myanmar who are both inching closer to American influence.

The average yearly income for the 6.6m Laotians is $1,130. Except for the country's communist elite who shop across the border in Thailand, things are pretty bleak. There is no political opposition allowed, no free press, the internet is monitored and it is illegal to view any anti-government content and everyone has to undergo ideological training. Not so for Lengsavad. He's rubbing shoulders every year in Davos at the World Economic Forum and promoting his 'land for capital' program. That involves primarily Chinese companies building infrastructure in return for receiving vast tracks of land.

The money Lengsavad is borrowing to build the railway project amounts to 90% of Laos's GDP, which means a lot of land for the Chinese to exploit and a lot more displaced Laotians. Lengsavad has already given away 30% of Laos to foreigners and he's just getting started.

PAUL LEPAGE

GOVERNOR OF MAINE

THE BRAIN DRAIN FROM MAINE

Paul LePage is likely to be the craziest of the fifty governors who run the fifty United States. For a state that normally fields some pretty sane politicians, rural Maine really went to town when they elected hog crazy LePage as governor in 2010. That being said, he had three opponents and came far from garnering a majority of the votes.

There's a long list of things LePage would like to do but, to his frustration, the state legislature prevents the enactment of most of his proposed laws. For one thing, he would like to lower the working age from 16 to 12, which is unlikely to happen, although he naturally managed to lower taxes for the rich, which is always a winner for the Tea Party.

He denounced one Democrat state senator by saying 'he always wants to give it to people without the Vaseline'. He compares the Internal Revenue Service to the Gestapo and predicted that Obamacare would bring on the holocaust. He said that President Obama hates white people and famously told him he could 'go to hell' in a campaign speech. He thinks wind energy is basically a con and thinks they have little electric motors inside to spin them around to make it look like they are generating power.

He prefers private education over state funded education, famously saying: 'if you want a good education, go to private schools. If you can't afford it, tough luck: you can go to the public school'. He told the NAACP to kiss his butt when they invited him to breakfast for Martin Luther King Day. LePage has reportedly had meetings with the Sovereign Citizens, a right-wing hyper extremist group that believes the federal government is secretly conspiring to bring about a Christian holocaust and has inferred that his Democratic opponents are guilty of treason. When it comes to crazy governors, Mainers can be proud to have a hands down winner.

JEAN-MARIE LE PEN

EUROPEAN PARLIAMENT

FAMILY FEUD

More Europeans probably know his name and cause than know who François Hollande is and what sort of job he has. If you are in the majority, here's a hint: Hollande has the same job that Le Pen has been trying to get for decades. The former leader of the *Front National* is a polarising figure in France; the kind of person you vote for only when you've made sure the curtain in the polling booth is tightly closed.

He's the godfather of the far right in Europe and now has acolytes all over the continent. He's also a well-known anti-Semite and thinks the Holocaust was a 'detail in history'. That's just for starters.

He's a Eurosceptic, against immigration, for law and order and wants to see a return to traditional values. He actually campaigned for the British National Party (BNP) in 2004. For those unfamiliar with the BNP, in its heyday it was more of a violent neo-Nazi gang than a real political party and it attracted young white thugs who liked nothing better than a riot. He turned over leadership of the *Front National* to his daughter, Marine Le Pen in 2011 and she's done much to varnish and polish the image of the party. This brings us to the latest feud between the father and daughter: the 'matter of the *fournée*'.

According to the *New York Times*, in June of 2014, Jean-Marie Le Pen made a reference to a French Jewish singer, Patrick Bruel, on his video blog on the party website saying that 'we'll include him in the next batch' and then referring to the *fournée* (batch of bread to be baked) which many interpreted as a reference to a crematorium. Daughter Marine quickly pulled the offending video off the site, saying her father had made a 'political error'. According to the *Times*, the father then told a radio interviewer that 'if there are people in my camp that have interpreted it in this way, they are nothing but imbeciles'. Rumours persist that the relationship between father and daughter has been rancorous, but Jean-Marie Le Pen spends his days far away in Brussels now, collecting his €8,000 a month serving as an MEP.

MARINE LE PEN

EUROPEAN PARLIAMENT

DAUGHTER OF DARKNESS

The embodiment of much that is troubling France and the daughter of *Front National* founder, Jean-Marie Le Pen, is on a roll. Marine Le Pen now leads the party, which has become the third largest in France. Brigitte Bardot has even called her 'the Joan of Arc of the 21st century' in a recent interview in *Paris Match*.

The party itself is about economic protectionism, anti-immigration and law and order. The problem for France is that Le Pen has made the *Front National* almost respectable and the Union for a Popular Movement and the Socialist Party are floundering and the economy is in the toilet. It's unlikely she will ever be elected president but there is a good chance she will come in first in a three way race. (Unless a contender gets more than half the vote, there is a runoff between the two top contenders.)

But she has her father to deal with first. Speaking about immigration from West Africa to journalists, Jean-Marie Le Pen said, 'Monseigneur Ebola could sort that out in three months'. It's such outbursts that remind voters of what *Front National* used to be. In contrast to her father, she claims she wants to limit but not end immigration. She wants France out of the EU and to readopt the franc. She is against gay marriage and is 'pro-life'. According to recent polls, she would win 26% of the vote if a presidential election were held in 2014.

Things are not great in the father/daughter relationship. After she removed his rant about baking a Jewish singer in an oven from the party's website, Jean-Marie Le Pen said his daughter had stabbed him in the back. After that little spat, according to the ever-reliable *Daily Mail*, the authorities began looking into all donations to the party of over €1 million. In a fit of paranoia, the senior Le Pen went on to tell *Les Inrocks* magazine, 'if I get on their nerves, the only thing for them to do is to kill me.'

YARON LERMAN

ISRAELI PARTY LEADER

STONED AS A WALL

Yaron Lerman is out to 'out' politicians but not in the way that immediately comes to mind.

The libertarian leader of Israel's *Green Leaf* party says he has pictures of eighteen leading politicians with a joint between their lips and he's threatening to expose them if the country doesn't legalise pot. He's not doing it because he thinks the world would be a better place if Israelis could get stoned when and where they wish, he's doing it for a much more sensible reason.

The Beqaa Valley lies about 30 miles east of Beirut and the one major cash crop grown there is marijuana which is processed into hashish and sold around the world, including inside Israel. That cash crop is controlled by Israel's archenemy, *Hezbollah*, the 'Party of God'. Lerman is convinced that the 700,000 pot smoking Israelis unwittingly contribute ILS 500,000,000 ($134 million) to the coffers of *Hezbollah* every year.

Lerman also wants to change the structure of the Israeli Defence Force which he views as lacking in professionalism and questions whether it can deal with the threats facing the state. He thinks the 2014 action in the Gaza Strip, Operation Protective Edge, 'was one of the most unsuccessful wars of attrition waged by the State of Israel'.

He wants to do away with compulsory enlistment and build a professional army that doesn't have to put 18,000 of its soldiers in jail every year. Lerman is also the chairman of the Movement for a Volunteer Army. He also supports the institutionalisation of prostitution and legalised gambling.

AUSTRALIAN SENATE

TOBACCONIST

Leyonhjelm is a 'libertarian purist' who makes the US senator, Rand Paul, look like a social meddler. In one of his first speeches in the Australian Senate he praised the country's smokers, saying, 'ladies and gentlemen, thank you for smoking'. He later admitted that his party, the Liberal Democrats, took funding from the tobacco giant, Philip Morris.

That's not the first party to which Leyonhjelm has belonged. First of all he was a socialist, then he joined the Shooters Party, which promotes gun rights, and then he joined the Outdoor Recreation Party. Many think he was elected to the senate, in the complex preference voting system because many confused the Liberal Democrats with the governing Liberal party. Whatever the reason, he began his six-year term in 2013.

He wants to decriminalise marijuana, allow same sex marriage and charge a fee for permanent residency in Australia as a means to discourage people smuggling. He opposed Australia's involvement in the coalition that was formed to counter ISIS and voted against anti-terrorist legislation because he believed it would encourage torture.

He hired the controversial writer, Helen Dale, as his advisor. Dale once went under the name of Helen Demidenko and claimed she was of Ukrainian descent. She wrote an award-winning book about Ukrainian collaborators in the Second World War. It turned out later that the claim of Ukrainian heritage was simply a ruse. It was discovered that she was essentially a Brit, which shocked the literary world but amused the new libertarian senator. Leyonhjelm is against all efforts to fight global warming claiming that they are a waste of money. In terms of narcotics, though, the new senator thinks pot should be available in supermarkets and all hard drugs should be available to addicts. He sees full drug legalisation as a means to destroy organised crime.

AVIGDOR LIEBERMAN

ISRAELI KNESSET

YVETTE

The belligerent, far right, ex-nightclub bouncer with the girly nickname has never been known for being conciliatory, but now there's just a hint that he may be contemplating peace with his Palestinian neighbours.

According to *Haaretz* newspaper, the Soviet-born Israeli Foreign Minister spoke about implementing the 'Arab Plan' in September of 2014. This is a proposal formulated by Saudi Arabia that would establish a Palestinian state in the West Bank. Either that was a slip of the tongue spoken in a cabinet meeting or the super-nationalist founder of the *Yisrael Beiteinu* party has had a major change of heart. Many think that after his acquittal on fraud charges in 2013, the firebrand politician has softened. Before his legal troubles began he wanted Arab Israelis to be subject to a loyalty oath. Lieberman had to resign his ministerial position before the trial but was able to return as minister in December 2013 and, according to the *New York Times*, 'he is not just picking up where he left off. Mr. Lieberman sent a memo to the prime minister's office saying that, unlike in his first term, he intended to be intimately involved in the Palestinian issue, managing relations with the United States, and Iran.'

His party mainly represents Russian émigrés and has also always taken an ultra-hard line in any negotiations with the Palestinians. Prime Minister Ariel Sharon tossed him out of the cabinet because of his opposition to the pullout from Gaza in 2004. In 2009 he was quoted by *Haaretz* newspaper as saying, 'nothing is going to come out of this Peace Industry except for conferences in five star Hotels and a waste of money.' As an example of his notorious temper, he was convicted of assault in 2001 for punching up a 12-year-old boy his son claimed had hit him.

According to *The Algemeiner*, Lieberman clarified his position on the Arab Plan recently by saying, 'The reality has changed, but for us it is as if nothing has changed … The diagnosis was wrong. Our conflict is not with the Palestinians. The conflict is three-dimensional – with the Arab states, the Palestinians, and Israeli Arabs.'

EDUARD LIMONOV

PARTY LEADER AND ACTIVIST

OUT PUTIN PUTIN

He was a petty thief and criminal before he turned
to poetry and moved to Moscow during the old days
of the Soviet Union. Then he somehow came to
New York, working as a journalist and becoming a
young punk rebel who frequented Studio 54, before
writing an explicit homosexual novel and moving to
Paris.

After the collapse of the Iron Curtain, Limonov moved back to Moscow, founded a
newspaper and got really weird. He also founded the National Bolshevik Party, which has,
as its platform, the creation of a grand empire stretching throughout Europe and Asia and
under the rule of Moscow. Even in ultra-nationalist circles it was considered too extreme
and has since been banned. In 2001 he was nabbed for terrorism, possession of illegal
weapons and acts that undermined the constitution and put in the clink for two years.

Now Limonov has created another movement, the Other Russia party that has come out
in strong support for the annexation of the Crimea and continued military intervention in
the Ukraine. He previously argued for intervention in the wars that followed the splintering
of the former Yugoslavia and he used a machine gun to fire at Croatian Army headquarters.
Members of Other Russia form part of the militias that are fighting the government forces
in the Ukraine. In his book, *Outlines for the Future*, he wrote that it would be a great idea to
force 'every woman between 25 and 35 to have four children'.

He told the *Guardian* newspaper that, 'Europeans are so timid they remind me of sick
and elderly people' and 'in Russia, fortunately, the people still have some barbarian spirit'.
Limonov wants to run in the next presidential elections on the Other Russia ticket and,
while he may be an anathema in the West, he has a sliver of a chance in Russia.

SYLVI LISTHAUG

NORWEGIAN STORTING

ALASKAN SILVI

She's not a favourite of Norway's environmentalists but the camera likes her. She was raised on a farm and became politicised at the tender age of 16 when she discovered the joys of the Progress Party.

She once described Norway's agricultural policy as communist, so what better post to appoint her to than Minister of Agriculture and Food. Considering that food is costlier in Norway than in any other European country, perhaps Sylvi was the right choice for the job. She sounds a bit less normal, though, when she claims that she's discovered hidden propaganda in the nation's schoolbooks. Targeting one textbook, Kosmos 10, she said: 'textbook Kosmos is randomly selected, but much of what it says is totally outrageous. It is full of statements, scare tactics and sometimes downright misinformation.'

'It's almost like reading the Red Party platform,' she added. What the textbook publishers and school administrators argued was that the selected portions that Listhaug took out of the book were put there to generate debate. She wasn't having any of that, though: 'this book is nothing more than brainwashing, if I had children who were reading this book I would put my foot down.'

Meanwhile, the farmers she is supposed to helping naturally want more money. In fact, they'd like something like $250 million more a year and a more protectionist import policy. Considering it currently costs something like $80 simply for a deboned leg of lamb in Norway, the farmers aren't generating lots of sympathy with the public. The farmers have a secret weapon in the negotiations: when things don't go their way they typically dump tons of cow manure on the streets of Oslo and in front of government offices.

Listhaug loves the United States and wants everyone to know it. In fact, she compares herself to a Midwest Republican but many on Norway's left liken her more to somebody we all know from just a skip over the polar ice.

NORMAN LOWELL

PARTY FOUNDER

THE LIGHTNING AND THE SUN

He is a banker, a writer, a martial arts expert, an artist and head of a Maltese political party, *Imperium Europa* (Empire of Europe).

According to the party's website, the aim of the party is to make Malta the first liberated white nation in the world. The thought process that went into the party manifesto is so deliriously convoluted it's difficult to make much sense of it but the gist of it seems that, if the party achieves power, then 250,000 of the 'elite' in Europe will unite to rule the continent in the style of the Roman Empire. Naturally, no non-white people need apply for the inclusion in the elite. The *Imperium Europa* would be a homeland for the white race or those of European ethnic background.

Lowell is trying to spread his message by gaining a seat in the European Parliament in Brussels. In the 2014 elections the party fielded two candidates and got 7,000 votes. He has written a book, *Imperium Europa*, that has the ambitious agenda of 'changing the world' by uniting the 'Europid race'.

A self-described 'racialist', Lowell spews an interesting line of anti-Semitic conspiracies and, predictably, has no great love for the African continent or its inhabitants, particularly those that have made it to the shores of Malta.

When asked about rescuing migrants who are stranded at sea, Lowell told *Malta Today* that, 'by saving them at sea, Malta is encouraging migration'. Lowell sees *Imperium Europa* aligning itself on the European stage with the banned Greek neo-Nazi party, Golden Dawn.

Malta has a policy of granting citizenship to wealthy investors who are willing to sink €1.15 million into the country. Lowell is convinced this will attract 'Jewish oligarchs' to Malta who would take over the island state. He thinks that all Jews should be relocated to New Caledonia in the far off Pacific.

ALEXANDER LUKASHENKO

PRESIDENT OF BELARUS

DADDY

He leads a fascinating life and you can follow his every step on his own presidential blog. One day he's in an orphanage, the next he's congratulating the people of Belarus on their 'day of knowledge', then he's sending a special message to the people of Moldova on their day of independence, then it's off to Kazakhstan for a face-to-face with their lovely leader, Nursultan Nazarbayev.

Being President of Belarus has got to be an interesting job. It's a pretty safe one too because the elections are a farce and everybody knows it. Lukashenko and his senior aides have been banned from travelling to any European Union countries after the government violently suppressed opposition demonstrators in 2010, but who's complaining when a holiday in the lovely Polesky State Radioecological Reserve beckons. It's just a stone's throw from Chernobyl and the wildlife is plentiful.

Lukashenko has been in his job for over twenty years and doesn't get upset when he's called 'Europe's last dictator'. The last elections in 2012 were a clear win for the government since two of the opposition parties withdrew from the contest saying the results were already determined before the vote took place. According to the BBC, 'opposition leaders called on voters to do something else – go fishing, visit relatives, pick mushrooms or make soup – rather than vote.' Lukashenko had earlier told the BBC: 'my position and the state will never allow me to become a dictator, but an authoritarian style of rule is characteristic of me, and I have always admitted it.'

His followers call him *Batka* (Daddy) but his opponents call him 'Fuhrer'. According to the *Moscow Times*, after his third presidential election, 'Lukashenko went so far as to admit that he had forged previous election results'. They have quoted him as saying, 'yes, we falsified the last election. I have already told this to Westerners. In fact, 93.5% for President Lukashenko. People said this was not a European result, so we changed it to 86%. This truly happened.'

OLEH LYASHKO

UKRAINIAN SUPREME COUNCIL

VIGILANTE

If you want bare-knuckle politics, then you should go to Kiev, the capital of the Ukraine and watch Oleh Lyashko, the leader of the Radical Party conduct a 'debate' with an opponent. 'Look at this pot-bellied fatty!' Lyashko said recently to Oleksandr Shevchenko, a political opponent with the Independent Party, according to the *Washington Post*. 'Instead of going to the Donbass and helping our guys, people like him go to parliament and raise their hands. Shevchenko decided a 'non-verbal' response was best and took a roundhouse swing at Lyashko, knocking him to the floor and starting another one of the frequent brawls that enliven Ukraine's Parliament.

There are a lot of questions swirling around about Lyashko's background but nobody questions that the convicted fraudster is a staunch nationalist and very anti-Russian. But there are also rumours that he may also bat for both sides, which he countered in a statement to the *Kiev Post*. 'Personally, I have a traditional sexual orientation,' he told the newspaper, but he didn't specify if that was a traditionally Spartan sexual orientation or some other tradition. He did some time inside for embezzlement but was later pardoned. The Kiev based Centre for Social and Economic Research (CASE) told the progressive organisation, *Think Progress*, that they expected Lyashko's party to become the second largest political block in the country. They were wrong; his party came in third.

CASE told *Think Progress* that 'Lyashko has gained a cult following of anti-Russia, pro-Ukraine young males by lambasting members of the political opposition as traitors'. *The Los Angeles Daily News* reports that Lyashko 'built a following by staging vigilante safaris during which he captures and abuses suspected rebels and sympathetic officials on film'. *Amnesty International* is also concerned about Lyashko's illegal abductions and alleged torture. They have reported on what they call 'Lyashko's continuing campaign of violence, intimidation and abduction against individuals'.

MA YING-JEOU

PRESIDENT OF TAIWAN

MR UNPOPULARITY

He's got an approval rating of just 9% and over 62% of the people don't trust the guy at all and it's only getting worse by the day. Ma is the most unpopular president of Taiwan, ever. When asked to grade his performance in office on a scale of 1 to 100, the voters rated him a 44. Even supporters of the president's political party, Chinese Nationalist Party (KMT) only grade him a 59, which would be a flunking score at any school.

It shouldn't have turned out this bad for Ma, who went to law school at Harvard, worked on Wall Street and did a stint as a banker in Massachusetts before returning to Taiwan. When he was the Mayor of Taipei he had approval rating in the mid-60s, but near the end of his term, he was indicted by the Taiwan High Prosecutors Office for embezzlement of $339,000 – though eventually found not guilty.

He announced his bid for the presidency in 2007 and was elected in 2008 on the basis that he would engage with Beijing and improve trade relations. But the voters think he has gone too far and the economy isn't exactly outperforming the rest of the world. He has signed 21 agreements with mainland China but, at the same time, the Taiwan-centric 'sunflower' movement has been growing in strength leading to student demonstrations.

As the Taiwanese see promises broken and political independence taken away from Hong Kong, they have grown increasingly distrustful of the People's Republic of China. It's also been alleged that one of Ma's negotiators leaked information to the mainland, allowing the PRC to gain better terms on some of the trade agreements negotiated between the two countries. The students are particularly upset that the trade in services will be liberalised and thousands of jobs will go. Ma's term expires in 2016 and many think it is either going down the drain or is being flushed down the toilet.

VANCE MCALLISTER

US HOUSE OF
REPRESENTATIVES

DUCK SOUP

When the Duck Dynasty dumps you it's time to hang up your hat and call it quits. If you're outside of America and you've never encountered the reality TV show, *Duck Dynasty*: try sticking the Kardashians' mansion in the Louisiana swamps, deck out the male members of the family in *ZZ Top* beards and call them the Robertsons, a family that made a fortune from making and selling duck calls to hunters. Really. *Duck Dynasty* is quite influential in Republican circles because the Robertsons are supposed to be God-lovin' rednecks that speak their minds. The admittedly Democrat weblog, *Daily Kos* claims the show is 'fake yuppies in a redneck drag con job'. But with over 8 million regular viewers they can still sway opinion.

The New Orleans *Times-Picayune*, claims that, 'ever since Louisiana Congressman Vance McAllister was caught on video kissing a married staffer in April, the reaction from the reality TV family that endorsed him last year has been quieter than the early-morning opening hours of duck season.' The *Kos*, further reported that 'McAllister, who campaigned for office last fall as a devout Christian and devoted husband and father, was caught in video surveillance two days before Christmas (2013) passionately embracing and kissing one of his congressional aides. The aide, identified as Melissa Anne Hixon Peacock, is married to one Heath Peacock, long-time friend of McAllister as well as a big ol' campaign donor, to the tune of $5,200.' McAllister told *Vanity Fair* magazine: 'I'm asking for forgiveness from God, my wife, my kids, my staff, and my constituents who elected me to serve.' In true gentlemanly fashion, McAllister apologised all round and said he wouldn't run again in 2014 – but he naturally changed his mind.

Perhaps he'll recycle the ad he used in his first campaign when he said, 'it's here in this house that Kelly (McAllister's wife) and I worked to instil the values of faith, family, and country in our five children. If you will trust me with your vote, you can count on me to take those values to Washington.'

JOAN MCALPINE

SCOTTISH PARLIAMENT

PICTURE PERFECT

It was a nice gesture for the flame-haired Scottish Nationalist to make. After all, her lover had lost his job and was short of a few quid and his wife was a photographer of sorts, so why not use some public money to help them out?

Jane McLachlan was none the wiser when the MSP used her to take some publicity shots and put about £1,750 her way, but then she had to go and explore her husband's computer one day and found out that her spouse was bonking her latest client. Then all hell broke out.

According to the *Express* newspaper, 'in October 2012, mother-of-two Ms McLachlan discovered her husband of 30 years had been seeing Ms McAlpine when she found secret messages on his Facebook account'. The paper went on to report that, 'shocked, she posted a message on Twitter in her husband's name, which read: "I f****d Joan McAlpine." A distraught Ms McLachlan deleted the message ten minutes later, but by that time, the cat was out of the bag.'

The *Daily Mail* newspaper reported that, 'parliamentary records show that Miss McAlpine paid back the full sum of £1,750 from her own pocket on October 18, 2012, only five days after Mrs McLachlan discovered the MSP's sexual relationship with her husband – and after she threatened to expose the affair.' The newspaper further reported that McAlpine issued a statement regarding the incident saying, 'it is entirely permissible to hire photographers for producing work for constituency publications. Equally, I was perfectly entitled to decide in October 2012 to finance the work undertaken myself.' McAlpine was also banned from driving in 2012 for repeated speeding offences although she had been a staunch supporter of 20 mph speeding zones on safety grounds.

HAZEL MCCALLION

MAYOR OF MISSISSAUGA

HURRICANE HAZEL

The mayor of Mississauga, Ontario, has survived nine Canadian prime ministers and eight Ontario premiers. When she entered politics in 1970 Mississauga was a conglomeration of towns and settlements with a population of about 250,000. Now it is Canada's sixth biggest city with 750,000 inhabitants, governed by what could be the oldest mayor in the world.

At 93 years old, she is thinking of retiring next year. A former professional ice hockey player, she was re-elected with 91% of the votes in 2006 and 76% in 2010. She is outspoken, to say the least, which is why she has earned the nickname 'Hurricane'. She is so popular that she doesn't bother campaigning for office and refuses political donations, suggesting instead that voters donate to charity.

In 2006 she intervened in a police standoff with an armed man that had gone on for five hours. She told the man he was wasting the town's resources and, meekly and to everyone's surprise, he agreed with her and surrendered himself into police custody.

In 2013 she went on a fishing trip with the notorious Toronto mayor, Rob Ford, and pulled in a 16 pound salmon while he held her to prevent her falling off the boat. She later kissed him. She doesn't use a computer or own a smart phone but she has a son, Peter McCallion, who fancies himself something of a cowboy and a property developer and he's not against accepting a little help from his mother to put together some property deals. She recently lost the support of the *Mississauga News* who accused her of 'influence peddling', calling her 'a lame duck mayor who won't work with anyone who challenges her authority', but during her tenure the city has not accumulated any debt and has been run like a business.

She is the only politician in Canada, to date, to endorse the idea of a Palestinian State.

MATTIE MCGRATH

IRISH DÁIL

'TITS ON A BULL'

They make €92,672 per year, represent only 25,000 constituents, and there are 166 of them in the *Dáil Éireann* (the lower house of the Irish Parliament). In comparison, a British MP makes the €84,292 per year and represents about 70,000 voters and a congressman in the US makes €134,642 per year and has about 700,000. That means it costs almost €4 per voter in Ireland to get representation in the lower house, just over a euro in the UK and about 25 cents in America.

Maybe the Irish should pocket that €4 rather than pay the likes of Mattie McGrath his hard-earned lucre. According to the Irish *Journal*, the Irish Communications Minister, Pat Rabbitte, says of McGrath: 'Mattie himself, parliamentary-wise, is about as useful as tits on a bull.' McGrath is a *Teachta Dála* representing Tipperary South and, among other things, was against lowering the legal limit of alcohol for drivers because some people drive better with a few drinks in them. According to the *Independent*, he told a radio interviewer that, 'I know people for whom drink is a relaxant and they might be more nervous without it' and 'people say that after one drink it lessens your concentration, you're not as good a driver, or you're not able to drive. I don't accept that.' In 2011 he left the *Fianna Fáil* party and ran as an independent.

In 2014 he took the 'ice bucket' challenge but did it with a JCB digger.

McGrath also thinks 'we cannot open the floodgates in regard to abortion', even after the tragedy of Savita Halappanavar, who died in 2012 in a hospital in Galway after not being allowed to have one.

SANDRA MCLEOD DE ZACARIAS

MAYOR OF CIUDAD DEL ESTE

A DISTINCTION OF SORTS

Corruption, smuggling, and tax evasion are endemic in Paraguay. Transparency International ranks Paraguay 150th worst out of 176 countries and the US government says corruption there 'is a major impediment to consolidating democratic institutions.

WikiLeaks published a State Department cable (2010) that labelled the new president of the country, Horacio Cartes, as 'the head of a money laundering and drug trafficking operation'. That just gives some perspective into the Mayor of Ciudad del Este, Sandra McLeod. *Foreign Policy News* has named McLeod as 'Paraguay's wealthiest and most corrupt mayor'.

In a country where the poverty rate is 39%, McLeod, who followed her husband into mayoral post when he resigned, allocated a budget out of municipal funds of $570,000 for public relations to trumpet her accomplishments in office. Ciudad del Este is one of the wealthier cities in the country and is the capital of the Alto Parana department. *FPN* further states that, 'abuses of power are nothing new in Paraguay's largest city; where corruption, impunity, waives of contraband cargoes in the local airport as well as juicy briberies for the judges and district attorneys have been a daily routine in Ciudad del Este.'

According to *Index on Censorship*, 'Sandra McLeod, mayor of Ciudad del Este was recently accused of attempting to bribe another Radio Corpus journalist to favour her party on air. He refused and was later forced to resign'. According to Juan Pio Balbuena, writing in *Primera Plana* newspaper, 'the Auditor General's Office of the Republic of Paraguay, since 2001, has been unable to intervene and have access and review the accounting books and exert a candid investigation in the city hall of Ciudad del Este because, years ago, Javier Zacarías Irun (McLeod's husband) bribed a Supreme Court judge, Manuel Seifildin, who issued an order that prohibited the intervention of the Auditor General in the local government offices of Ciudad del Este.'

On the 26th of May, 2014, 25,000 protestors filled the streets of Ciudad del Este to call for the resignation of McLeod. She didn't heed their advice.

NICOLAS MADURO

PRESIDENT OF VENEZUELA

THE GHOST OF CHAVEZ

Hugo Chavez thought Halloween was an American conspiracy and his successor, Nicolas Maduro Moros, is even crazier.

Claiming that Chavez recently came back from the dead and appeared to him as a small bird and chirped messages in his ear is only indicative of how mentally unstable the Venezuelan president is. 'Today the battle starts – go to victory – you have our blessings,' was the message the late, great president whispered into Maduro's ear, or at least that's what he claims he heard. He also claims that Chavez ascended to heaven and had a 'face-to-face with Christ', during which time he instructed Christ to instruct the College of Cardinals to choose Francis as the next Pope.

Regarding his political nemesis, Henrique Capriles, he thinks 'the first thing we have to do is shoot (Capriles) legally'. Maduro's grasp of economics is also a little suspect. He describes the public's desire for US dollars as 'a nymphomania [sic] that is impossible to satisfy'. He's also taken to sleeping on Chavez's tomb to gain inspiration. 'I come at night, sometimes I sleep here often,' he says.

Maduro is all for population growth. 'We must multiply ourselves,' he said, 'like Christ multiplied the penises,' although that was a slip of the tongue. He has some simple common sense advice about the food shortages that are plaguing the country: 'Eat less' – a solution that will surely go down well with the population. Maduro also convinced that Chavez was intentionally given cancer by the dark forces of the United States. 'Chavez was poisoned by dark forces that wanted him out of the way,' claims Maduro. In terms of his political opponents, Maduro is dismissive, calling them 'snobs, faggots and facists' and promised to bring 'a curse' on those who voted against him. He won the last election, but by the narrowest of margins.

JULIUS MALEMA

SOUTH AFRICAN NATIONAL ASSEMBLY

AFRICA'S WORST NIGHTMARE

Thanks to Nelson Mandela and the first wave of ANC politicians the path from apartheid to freedom went fairly smoothly in South Africa. Then along came Julius Malema. He's not just your run of the mill demagogue, he spouts a unique kind of hate and there's no need to guess who it's directed at: white people in general and white farmers in particular. Mugabe gave the world a lesson in what happens when you kick white farmers off the land in Zimbabwe and no rational person would want to replicate that experience in South Africa, no matter what colour they are. Malema was convicted of 'hate speech' in 2010 and 2011 leading the ANC to expel him from membership. He has subsequently been charged with money laundering, fraud and racketeering. In Zimbabwe's election he endorsed Mugabe and on his return to South Africa infamously sang the song *Shoot the Boer*.

Malema has also done a good job of irritating the people of neighbouring Botswana saying, 'the ANC Youth League will also establish a Botswana command team, which will work towards uniting all oppositional forces in Botswana to oppose the puppet regime of Botswana.' Botswana has been a stable and prosperous democracy since its independence in 1966 and has the highest standard of living in sub-Saharan Africa.

In terms of his opinion of the opposite sex, Malema has a refreshingly old-fashioned attitude saying: 'when a woman doesn't enjoy it, she leaves early in the morning. Those who had a nice time will wait until the sun comes out, request breakfast and taxi money.' Malema doesn't just alarm the whites and Indians in South Africa, he terrifies the new African middle class who would rather have good government than a revolution.

ROSAURO MARTINEZ

CHILEAN NATIONAL CONGRESS

MURDERER IN OUR MIDST?

History has a way of catching up with people. The former army captain and *Renovacion Nacional* member of the Chilean National Congress has been stripped of his parliamentary immunity and charged with the premeditated murder of three Revolutionary Left Movement (RLM) supporters in 1981.

The part-time farmer and rodeo enthusiast professes his innocence and has been freed on bond. Although he has represented District 41 in the national legislature since 1993 and was Mayor of Chillan before that, Martinez has never tried to hide his activities while he was in the military. As part of the army's 'Operation Machete', the gun battle that ensued that saw 11 RLM and army soldiers killed was simply conducted under standard protocol, according to Martinez, but five others who worked with him at the time say he used excessive brutality.

He was arrested in the city of Valdivia in September of 2014. The arrest comes at the same time Michelle Bachelet's government is seeking to repeal the Amnesty Law, a legacy of the dictatorship of General Augusto Pinochet, which prevents prosecution for politically related acts between September 1973 and April 1978. Up to 40,000 Chileans were killed or tortured during the rule of Pinochet, including the president herself who was locked away for a while.

Martinez told the local media that he 'will continue to work with the courts to clarify what happened in 1981' and that he reiterated his innocence. Martinez's real adversary is the Chilean journalist and historian, Cristian Alarcón, who has devoted years to finding out, step by step, what happened in the town of Alto Remeco on September 20th 1981. His published research in the *Centre for Investigative Journalism* is what may really sink the former commander of the 8th Commando Company.

JOE MATURO

MAYOR OF EAST HAVEN, CONNECTICUT

TACO BELL

In a WPIX radio interview in 2012, Republican Mayor, Joe Maturo, was asked what he would do for the Latino community in his city, Maturo replied, 'I might have tacos when I go home. I'm not quite sure yet.'

According to the *Huffington Post*, 'an immigrants' rights group in East Haven delivered thousands of tacos to Mayor Joseph Maturo's office the day after he made comments that many are calling him insensitive.'

Maturo issued a press statement after the tacos were delivered that said, 'recognising that there are many in need in our State, we have arranged for all of the tacos to be donated to local soup kitchens and pantries.'

One person who should know him best is his secretary. According to WTNH Television, in July of 2014, 'East Haven's Mayor Joe Maturo's secretary said she was sexually harassed by him. Filed Monday with the State's Commission on Human Rights and Opportunities, the woman said Maturo would look at her chest and ask, "seriously, how much do those weigh?" She said oftentimes he grabbed his crotch and said, "this is for you".' According to CBS Connecticut, the woman said Maturo exposed himself to her in October of 2013. The Mayor claims that he was going to fire his secretary anyway and the allegations she made were vindictive and spurious.

He's got a lot on his mind anyway. According to the *East Haven Patch*, 'Mayor Joseph Maturo Jr. believes the only thing standing between him and collecting an additional $43,000 is the fact he is a Republican in a Democratically-controlled State Capitol.' According to the *New Haven Register*, 'Maturo makes $75,000 a year as mayor of East Haven. He stopped collecting his $43,000-a-year pension in 2011, when he was first elected mayor, and has been fighting to get it reinstated ever since.'

CLINTON MEAD

AUSTRALIAN PARTY FOUNDER

WTF

In the past decade anti-smoking legislation has forced those of us who enjoy tobacco out in the cold and effectively ostracised a significant portion of the population. Second hand smoke is repulsive to non-smokers but the harmfulness of it has yet to be proven. Banning smoking in bars and restaurants has probably led to the closure of hundreds of pubs in Britain, Australia, Ireland and the Netherlands. The stigmatised few huddle in their own homes at night drinking supermarket lager and furtively puffing away. You would think someone would start a backlash.

It took an obstinate Australian to lead the counterattack. Clinton Mead founded the Australian Smokers' Rights Party in 2011, in time for the general election of 2013. The irony of it is that Mead isn't a smoker. He's running for the rights of smokers on an anti-organised crime platform.

The Australian government has jacked up the taxes on cigarettes so much that Mead reckons that 13% of sales are now on the black market, generating $1 billion in profit for criminal syndicates. According to Mead, the 50% rise in taxes on cigarettes is creating a situation where, 'people who have never committed a crime in their lives are now dealing with organised criminals.'

Mead also thinks that the legislation forcing cigarettes to be sold in plain packaging 'won't achieve much except support organised crime, by removing legal products brand recognition. It will be a race to the bottom for the cheapest, dirtiest cigarettes.' As opposed to other politicians that want rights for smokers restored, Mead and his party do not accept any donations from tobacco companies. Mead didn't expect the party to win any seats in 2013 but hopes to pick up a senate seat at the next election.

FORMER PRIME MINISTER
OF SLOVAKIA

MR NASTY

The *Economist* called him 'a nasty, authoritarian populist who plainly had little love . . . for real democracy, for a market economy, or for human rights, especially for Gypsies and ethnic Hungarians'. It's been twelve years since that judgment was made but has time softened the Slovakian? Not really.

The *Economist* noted that, in 2000, Meciar was 'charged with paying illegal bonuses worth $350,000 to his cabinet ministers during his time in office' after 'masked commandos from a special unit that is supposed to stamp out organised crime dynamited Mr Meciar's back door and took him away at gunpoint.'

Elected three times as Prime Minister, Meciar now leads the People's Party – Movement for a Democratic Slovakia. Considered the 'Father of Slovakia', it was he who engineered his country's divorce from the Czech Republic. According to the BBC, Meciar's 'manipulation of parliament, the electoral law, the media and the secret police were cited by European Union officials as the reasons for putting off Slovakia's application to join the EU while Mr Meciar was in office.' In other words, he was known as an authoritarian thug.

The ex-boxer has taken a few lunges at impertinent journalists while on television. The US and the EU have described him as being both corrupt and xenophobic but he claims to have changed and now supports Slovakia's entry into the European Union. While Prime Minister, he drove up the national debt and scared away direct foreign investment, making many long for the old days of Czechoslovakia. He had a major issue about the Roma people and ethnic Hungarians, who have lived for generations in Slovakia. According to Meciar, the Roma, 'are antisocial, mentally backward, inassimilable and socially unacceptable.' He also outlawed the official use of Hungarian and had Hungarian language road signs torn down.

JEAN-LUC MÉLENCHON

EUROPEAN PARLIAMENT

REBEL WITHOUT A CLUE

There's nothing quite as fanatical as a recent convert. Jean-Luc Mélenchon, a junior minister for vocational education in the early 2000s, had long been on the left of the French Socialist Party, and campaigned for a 'No' vote in the EU constitutional treaty referendum alongside far-left politicians like Olivier Besancenot and José Bové. However, he was always seen as a team player and a loyal socialist party member – until he left the party in a huff in 2008 to found his own embryonic 'Party of the Left', taking a few green and socialist politicians with him.

The firebrand orator and provocateur quickly became a national figure – and his beliefs became more stridently left wing. As a presidential candidate in 2012, he called for a massive wave of nationalisation and a *maximum* wage of €250,000 per year. Since then, he has been perhaps the fiercest opponent of centre-left president François Hollande, whom he considers, rather predictably, a traitor to the cause.

A strong admirer of Fidel and Raul Castro, he stated in 2011 that the Castro régime was 'not a dictatorship' and walked out of the European Parliament chamber when the Sakharov Prize for Human Rights was given to Cuban dissident Guillermo Farinas. Mélenchon is a big fan of Belarusian strong man Aleksander Lukashenko, opposing sanctions against his régime. He also supports China in its occupation of Tibet, which he says is a 'theocracy'.

But his dearest love is reserved for Russian president Vladimir Putin, especially since the start of the Ukraine conflict: Mélenchon called French president François Hollande a 'traitor' for refusing to continue with the deal to sell two amphibious warships to Russia, saying that the decision made France a 'vassal state' of NATO and Washington, and that Putin had 'no choice' but to invade Crimea in the face of NATO expansionism.

ROBERT MÉNARD

MAYOR OF BÉZIERS

WHAT HAPPENED?

In America it would be the equivalent of President Barack Obama leaving the Democratic Party and joining the tea baggers, repealing his own healthcare legislation and developing a man crush on Ted Cruz.

Robert Ménard was one of the founders of Reporters Sans Frontières, an NGO set up in 1985 to support freedom of the press. It has crusaded on behalf of jailed and persecuted journalists around the world, oftentimes embarrassing reluctant governments into releasing reporters from custody.

He also created a pirate radio station, *Radio Pomarède* in the 1970s and became president of *l'Association pour la libération des ondes* (the Association for the liberation of the airwaves). Despite being a former activist in the Revolutionary Communist League, in 2008 he tried to disrupt the opening ceremonies for the Olympics in Beijing in protest to the Chinese government's persecution of Tibetan civil rights.

But something has changed Robert Ménard since then. Now he is mayor of the French town of Béziers. He captured the job in 2013 when he ran with the support of the far-right *Debout la République* (Arise the Republic) party and the even-crazier *Front National*, which are both anti-immigrant and anti-EU.

Ménard has banned the hanging of laundry outside citizens' homes, has displaced the homeless and now he want to stop the children of the unemployed from participating in extra-curricular activities after school. The advisors he has hired to help him in his current job have some strange neo-Nazi leanings. According to *Le Figaro,* he only wants children of the employed to have access to early morning 'supervised study' – because, he reasons, the children of the unemployed don't need the supervision. He has also established a curfew in the town for children under thirteen.

MORTEN MESSERSCHMIDT

EUROPEAN PARLIAMENT

TOY BOY MORTEN

He likes older women, he sings and he's been convicted for publishing material that linked multi-racial societies to such things as violence, rape and forced marriages. Oh, and he's been overwhelmingly elected twice by the Danish people to the European Parliament.

He and his current babe, Dot Wessman (who is old enough to be his mother), recently released a Christmas album where they both crooned such hits as *Do We Cut Our Christmas Hearts Together?* The pair of lovebirds live in Bakken, just north of Copenhagen.

Morten is a big fan of Gert Wilders, the Dutch far right politician. The *Dansk Folkepartei* (DF), of which Morten is a member, wants to ban satellite televisions from Denmark that carry Arabic stations. In 2007, Messerschmidt was charged with singing Nazi marching songs and giving the Hitler salute in a bar. He was sensible enough to take a two-year break from politics after that.

In *Frontpage* magazine, Morten stated that 'I think we need three sets of rules of immigration. One for Europeans, who will be regulated by EU-law. One for people from the rest of the Western World, including parts of East Asia, South America, etc. And then a third set of rules for the third world, who in general do not really offer anything we can benefit from, speaking of education, labour craft and knowledge. And as for the second initiative we must stop paying welfare to people without Danish citizenship – and make much harsher regulations for those only coming for economic reasons.' Regarding the citizenship granted to Afghan and Iraqi refugees, the *Dansk Folkepartei* suggested that 'they should be sent home to help build their country up. DF votes for those reasons against the bill.'

Despite the arrest for the Nazi salute and for publishing racist materials, Morten insists it's all a misunderstanding and he isn't racist.

ASSEMBLY OF ST PETERSBURG

EVIL DOERS

It would be wonderful if Vitaly Milonov was caught with his pants down in a gay bar one day or to be seen cruising the streets of Paris with a rent boy. He's out to protect Mother Russia from the evils of modernism, by which he means the tide, or torrent, of homosexuality that is sweeping through the West.

Speaking in Sevastopol, after the Russian 'liberation' of the Crimea, he said, 'St Petersburg and Moscow should take a cue from Sevastopol and eradicate the experimental practice of sodomy.' He further added, 'we must no longer have gay parades, gay shows and clubs. All social media pages for homosexuals should be removed, if we do not, it will destroy the unity of the nation.' He told a French journalist that homosexuals 'rape kids' and that allegations that they have been targeted by neo-Nazi groups and beaten on the streets of Moscow is 'fake information'.

A member of the Legislative Assembly of Saint Petersburg for the far right United Russia faction he said in 2013 that gay athletes could be arrested at the Sochi Olympics if they were promoting homosexuality to young people. He also thinks the *Eurovision Song Contest* is one big 'Europe-wide gay parade' and he's called it a 'Sodom show'. He's the lawmaker behind St Petersburg's anti-gay propaganda bill.

It's got to be a disappointment to Milonov that the 'Annual Queer Fest' opened in St Petersburg in September 2014. The organisers, 'Coming Out', expect thousands of visitors, although Vitaly Milonov probably won't be one of them. Another thing that really gets under Milonov's skin is Jews because he reckons that they 'killed the Saviour'. Two more bizarre thoughts that are bouncing around in his head are proposals to grant full citizenship to embryos and to make women who haven't had a baby by the age of 23 join the army.

NARENDRA MODI

PRIME MINISTER OF INDIA

VOW OF CELIBACY

The US had to overlook his alleged involvement in the 2002 riots in Gujarat in which 1,000 people were killed in sectarian riots and, in turn, he had to overlook the arrest, strip-search and indictment of the Indian diplomat, Devyani Khobragade, in December 2013. That brilliant diplomatic coup was pulled off by the Indian-American Attorney for the Southern District of New York, Preet Bharara, and it succeeded in one thing only: pissing off almost every Indian in the world. But in September 2014, Barack Obama and Narendra Modi were able to bury their hatchets, but one wonders if Obama knows just how strange his Indian counterpart is.

Before he met Obama, Modi addressed thousands from a rotating platform in Madison Square Garden and told the crowd that, 'our country used to play with a snake, now we play with the mouse.' At least he was there in person; in India he has addressed crowds via holograms. At the state dinner, Modi didn't eat anything because he was in the midst of a religious fast.

Modi scuttled India's deal with the WTO, which would have ended the most ineffective food security program in the world. It guarantees prices for farmers while the poor get subsidised food. In a country with little cold storage, 70% of perishables are lost before they get to market – so farmers get paid but consumers get little. A crazy policy, but the weirdest thing about Modi is the wife he kept secret for fifty years. In February of 2014 he told a crowd that he wasn't liable to be corrupt because, 'I am single, who will I be corrupt for?' Modi was only with his wife for three years before he ambled off to the Himalayas. While there he succumbed to the charms of the *Rashtriya Swayamsevak Sangh*, an organisation that requires adherents to take a vow of celibacy.

BUNG MOKTAR

MALAYSIAN HOUSE OF REPRESENTATIVES

LONG LIVE HITLER

He failed at running a grocery store and never went to university – though he once claimed to have graduated from 'Boxton University' in the UK – so he did what came naturally and entered Malaysian politics and now serves as an MP. He was convicted for polygamy in 2010.

After Germany pounded Brazil in the 2014 World Cup, he sent out a tweet saying, 'WELL DONE... BRAVO... LONG LIVE HITLER.' When the back-lash came, Bung said he was only, 'referring to the strength of Germany's football team as Hitler's time' – whatever that means.

The Singapore paper *Straits Times*, lists the top 'Bung-les' of his chequered career, including the time he referred to the menstrual cycle of an MP when she criticised the leaking roof in Parliament. Bung quipped, 'Where is the leak? Batu Gajah leaks every month too.' He's been caught on camera making obscene hand gestures to opposition MPs, he asked a wheelchair-bound MP to 'stand up and show respect', he claimed that female drivers don't know what they are doing on the road and he's tweeted that those who disagree with him are 'losers' and 'brainless'. Nevertheless his voters have elected him four times by substantial margins.

In 2013, he raised the subject of notorious sex bloggers, Alvin Tan and Vivian Lee who were widely read widely by young Malaysians. According to *Singapore Press Holdings*, 'Alvin and Vivian, better known as Alvivi, rose to infamy after a blog containing entries about their sexual exploits was revealed. They are also currently facing trial in Malaysia over an offensive Ramadan greeting.' Alvin ditched Vivian in 2014 after he caught her in bed with his best friend. Bung is quoted by *ABN News*, as saying, 'this couple used to make sex videos in Singapore and now they are doing this (insulting Islam) in Malaysia. Maybe Bandar Kuching (a region controlled by an opposition politician) is also involved.' He had to apologise for that.

ANDREAS MÖLZER

FORMER MEMBER OF THE
EUROPEAN PARLIAMENT

A SLIP OF THE TONGUE

It's interesting to see that old-fashioned racism is coming back into vogue – particularly in a country with such an interesting history as Austria.

According to the BBC, the previously sitting Austrian MEP, Andreas Mölzer of the *Freiheitliche Partei Österreichs* (Austrian Freedom Party), was forced to pull out of the 2014 Euro elections after calling the twenty-eight-nation European Union 'a conglomerate of Negroes'. So it's been a tough year for Mölzer, although he's still got his job as editor of the right-wing rag, *Zur Zeit* (For Now) and he continues to write fantastical novels where the Aryan race survives against all odds.

The BBC further reported that Mölzer 'had also said the EU made Hitler's Third Reich look informal and liberal' – although for years he'd cheerfully accepted his €8,000 a month salary and the generous perks that go with sitting in the European Parliament.

Despite Mölzer pulling out of the race, the *Freedom Party* did better than ever in the 2014 elections, coming in third place and picking up four seats, twice what they'd won in the previous election.

Like any good Eurosceptic, Mölzer believes Turkey has no place in the European Union. Writing in his own blog, he said, 'the Freedom Party have always made clear that Turkey is anchored in a cultural history and mentality moderately deep in the East, thus is not a part of Europe and there never will be' (though given the changes Recep Erdoğan has brought about, he may be now be right).

Mölzer has also caught the European far right love bug for Vladimir Putin, calling him a hero who 'has managed to steer the post-Communist, crisis-ridden Russia into calmer waters.' He further states in his own blog that 'Russia is again a factor in international affairs, an authority and a support for many peoples and states that just do not fit with the Americans.'

NADINE MORANO

FORMER DEPARTMENTAL MINISTER

GET 'EM OFF!

There's no compromise when it comes to cultural sensitivity. In July of 2014 the UK was shocked when the *Metro* ran a story about a British party girl giving oral sex to 24 men in Magaluf for a £2 bottle of cava. Not one word was heard from the British Prime Minister, David Cameron, either praising her for her entrepreneurship or criticising her lack of deportment.

A month later, the *Independent* reported that French politician, Nadine Morano, was shocked when she reported on her Facebook page that she had gone to an unnamed beach resort and had seen 'a Muslim woman sitting on a French beach in headscarf, long-sleeved tunic and trousers while her husband stripped off and bathed in the sea.'

Just 20 miles separate France from Britain but it seems like the countries are thousands of miles apart when it comes down to cultural norms. Would Morano have been equally shocked if the Muslim woman in question had performed oral sex on twenty blokes for a €5 bottle of Burgundy while her husband frolicked in the waves?

Anyway, Morano's was unabated. The *Independent* further reported that the former Minister for Apprenticeship and Professional Formation wrote that 'when you choose to come to a country of secular laws, like France, you have an obligation to respect our culture and the liberty of women. Or you go somewhere else.' Perhaps Magaluf beckons for the Muslim holidaymaker?

In the past, Morano has criticised gay pride parades as events 'filled with guys in garter belts' and has praised the far right nut, Marine Le Pen, for having 'talent'. She's also previously advised young Muslims to not 'put their caps on back to front' – as if they would listen to her sound advice.

The fervent supporter of former president, Nicolas Sarkozy, obviously misses the media spotlight now that he's out of power and will say anything to get in the news.

KRISZTINA MORVAI

EUROPEAN PARLIAMENT

NAZI BARBIE

Her marriage to the left-wing television host, György Baló, is now over, leaving the Hungarian MEP free to make remarks like this: 'I would be glad if those who call themselves proud Hungarian Jews would go and play with their own little circumcised pricks instead of slurring me.' It would have been pretty hard for the blonde psycho to say that when she was married to Baló. Her ex-husband and father of her children is Jewish, which is not such an easy thing to be in today's Hungary.

According to Tijn Sadée, a journalist with Radio Netherlands, the party that Morvai represents in Brussels, Jobbik (Movement for a Better Hungary), wants to 'take Hungary back from the Western capitalists who looted the country after the fall of the communist regime in 1989'. Sadée also says that many think Morvai is a 'monstrous psychiatric case' who is a 'noisy product of a rotten political climate' in Hungary.

Morvai isn't alone in getting into a lather about imagined Jewish conspiracies; the country now has a sizable paramilitary group, the 'Hungarian Guard' that parades around in Nazi style uniforms and has close links to Morvai's political party. She gets their attention and votes with comments like this about those same proud Hungarian Jews: 'We have raised our heads up high and we shall no longer tolerate your kind of terror. We shall take back our country.' In one of the US diplomatic cables released by WikiLeaks, Morvai was described as a 'Nazi Barbie'. For those Jews who are getting a bit worried about people like Morvai and her followers in Hungary, they can take heart in the fact that Jobbik and their ilk are equal opportunity haters: they dislike Muslims and immigrants too. Oh, and they're also homophobic and racist – although they vehemently deny that. Jobbik have already declared Morvai as their candidate for the Hungarian Presidency.

ROBERT MUGABE

PRESIDENT OF ZIMBABWE

HE'LL DIE EVENTUALLY

The man who coined the catchy phrase, 'the only man you can trust is a dead white man', has single-handedly taken a prosperous country, once known as 'the bread basket of Africa and devastated it, not only for just the white farmers, but for everyone.

Zimbabwe's biggest export is people and all the neighbouring countries dread the upcoming death of Mugabe, because that's when the hardest working, best educated Africans will return home. If you cross the border into Zimbabwe from Botswana or South Africa you recognise immediately that something is very wrong.

He has led his political party, Zimbabwe African National Union – Patriotic Front and the country since 1980 and oversaw ethnic cleansing that killed thousands of his political rivals. He has occasional elections – they're rigged – and one political opponent: Morgan Tsvangirai of the Movement for Democratic Change, who lost his wife prior to one election in very suspicious circumstances. His crimes are too numerous to list and his arrogance and incompetence have bred a mentality of hopelessness in the country.

As an international pariah, there aren't many countries for Mugabe to visit and do the Head of State thing, so he just goes to the same few places lots of times. Unusually for an African leader – and a Marxist – he's a devout catholic, so he pops up to the Vatican whenever there's a major gig. Three popes have now welcomed him on numerous occasions and, shamefully, there's no evidence of any of them suggesting he atone for his sins much less of them telling him he could kiss their ring. President Xi of China thinks he's the bee's knees and in August 2014 hailed him as a 'renowned liberation leader and an old friend' of the country, when the ageing despot made his thirteenth pilgrimage to the communist paradise.

For those wondering when he is going to leave the scene, he has an answer: 'only God, who appointed me, will remove me – not the MDC, not the British, only God will remove me.'

JOSE MUJICA

PRESIDENT OF URUGUAY

SANTO MUJICA

On a continent that has historically had some of the most autocratic, repressive and clinically insane leaders in the world a question has to be asked: where the fuck did they find Jose Mujica?

Uruguay is often referred to as the 'Switzerland of South America' but it wasn't always that way. The military took over the government from the early 1970s to 1985 ostensibly because of the threat a left-wing guerrilla group, the *Tupamaros*, posed to the country.

The *Tupamaros* aspired to a Cuban style state and one of their fighters, Jose Mujica, was shot six times in battles with the government and spent 14 years as a political prisoner.

The country is now a peaceful democracy that has a thriving middle class and the poorest president in the world. Mujica has been president of Uruguay since 2009 and is enormously popular. He refuses to live in the government mansion and donates the bulk of his salary to charity. He resides in his wife's dilapidated farmhouse with his three-legged dog, Manuela, and drives a clapped out Volkswagen Beetle. He has signed legislative initiatives that have allowed abortion up to 12 weeks of pregnancy – a bold move in a devoutly catholic South America – and legalised marijuana. Mujica also signed into law a bill that allows gay marriage saying 'not to legalize it would be unnecessary torture for some people'.

Though he's a pretty mild mannered guy, in 2014 he got particularly pissed off when FIFA banned his fellow Uruguayan, Luis Suarez, for biting Giorgio Chiellini during a game at the World Cup. He said of FIFA's management committee: 'those at FIFA are a gang of old sons of bitches' and 'not even a criminal would receive this penalty', and said he didn't see the player bite the Italian. Everybody else in the world did.

NAMIBIAN PARTY FOUNDER

WHAT THE EFF?

There's something going on down in southern
Africa and it isn't good. The relatively prosperous countries of South
Africa, Namibia and Botswana are dealing with some restive young people who feel shut
out of political life and have a radical agenda they want to implement.

It started after the South African, Julius Malema, was booted out as leader of the African
National Congress Youth League for being a racist prat. He got his own back by founding a
new party, the Economic Freedom Fighters (EFF). Malema doesn't call himself something
mundane like the party leader: he is the self-described 'Commander in Chief' who heads a
'Central Command Team'. It's all very Che Guevara, replete with uniforms, insignia and
command hats. It sure beats studying accounting, or at least that must be what Epafras
Mukwiilongo thinks because he founded the Namibian Economic Freedom Fighters (NEFF) in
2014.

You can forget about joining the NEFF if you are one of three things: white, gay or Chinese.
But if you are for emancipating the working classes, nationalising the mines, taking white
farmer's lands away and you're a radical left winger, you'll love Mukwiilongo and his gang of
merry men.

One requirement is you have to look good in red, because the party uniform is the same
red as the EFF uniform right down to the beret. Don't mention gay rights to Mukwiilongo. He
sees that as an international conspiracy, saying, 'the NEFF is committed to uniting all Namibians
to root out this evil practice'. He told reporters at a press conference at Windhoek airport
that he had travelled to Uganda to raise money from 'anti-homosexuality organisations'.
Actually, despite being a racist, Mukwiilongo's mentor, Julius Malema, isn't a homophobe. He
released a statement in 2014 saying, 'the criminalisation of same-sex love is a relic from
Western colonisation.'

GERI MÜLLER

SWISS FEDERAL
ASSEMBLY

AWESOMELY GOOD TASTE

Britain's Brooks Newmark wasn't the first European politician to get into trouble for taking pics of his pecker. Geri Müller has been suspended from his job as Mayor of Baden, a town northwest of Zurich, by the Swiss Parliament of which he remains a member.

In August of 2014 Müller's ex-wife was being harassed by a 33-year-old woman, identified mysteriously only as 'NW' – presumably to protect her privacy, who was threatening to kill herself and publish nude pictures of Müller that he had taken of himself while in his office at city hall.

The photos haven't been published but they have been shown to journalists, as well as the messages that go with them. In one tasteful shot of Müller's penis the accompanying message invites the woman to 'make use' of it, and to another is added: 'At the office. I am already excited. Wearing only a T-shirt.' Fascinated locals have started calling the developments 'Geri-gate.' It turns out that the sexting is more complicated than it sounds and it's not just all about a middle-aged man doing something stupid.

Müller is a big supporter of the Palestinian cause and has travelled to the Gaza Strip, on one occasion meeting and being photographed with *Hamas* Prime Minister Ismail Haniyeh. He has also invited various *Hamas* members to Switzerland. This has not gone down well with the local Jewish population in Switzerland. According to the *Times of Israel*, certain prominent Jewish figures were in contact with 'NW'. They referred her to a local lawyer and gave her the names of a few newspaper editors who would gobble up the salacious story, all as a means to discredit Müller.

The left-leaning Green Party politician is said to be banned from travelling to Israel because of his relations with *Hamas*. He is also a Swiss Federal MP representing the Canton of Aargau in the lower house of parliament. Müller has refused to resign and says he did nothing wrong, and 300 Green Party members have staged a demonstration in support of him.

PRESIDENT OF UGANDA

SCIENCE IN UGANDA

'They're disgusting. What sort of people are they?' Museveni asked a CNN reporter in February of 2014, adding, 'I never knew what they were doing. I've been told recently that what they do is terrible. Disgusting. But I was ready to ignore that if there was proof that that's how he is born, abnormal. But now the proof is not there.'

The President of Uganda is not alone in Africa in his opinion of homosexuality. The continent only has one country that has legalised gay marriage: South Africa. In the interview with CNN, Museveni said further: 'I was regarding it as an inborn problem. Genetic distortion, that was my argument. But now our scientists have knocked this one out.'

Of course Museveni ought to have known there was going to be an international backlash after the country instituted harsh anti-homosexuality legislation, but he seemed taken aback by the extent of the reaction. According to the *Independent* newspaper: 'the Ugandan President has said that it is unreligious and sinful for other countries to provide aid on the condition that his people are given the freedom to express their sexuality'. The newspaper further reported that the President, while attending a religious conference, said, 'Uganda does not need aid. Uganda is so rich; we should be the ones to give aid. The only thing we need from the world is trade, if they can buy our products. Aid becomes important only when people are asleep.'

According to the BBC, the legislation Museveni enacted, 'includes life sentences for gay sex and same-sex marriage, but a proposed sentence of up to 14 years for first-time offenders has been removed.' It includes penalties for 'aggravated homosexuality' and 'promotion of homosexuality.' Mercifully, the death penalty for homosexuality was not imposed.

ALESSANDRA MUSSOLINI

ITALIAN SENATE AND EUROPEAN PARLIAMENT

PLAYGIRL

She is the granddaughter of Il Duce, the niece of Sofia Loren, an ex-Playboy model and, although a self-confessed neo-fascist, a complex woman whose political belief spectrum is very wide and falls in areas that often seem to contradict each other.

With her sultry, centrefold looks, it's easy to attribute her success to the triviality of the Italian electorate, but women typically vote for her more than men and her support is stronger among older people. She feels no shame in describing herself as a fascist, saying: 'Until recently the word fascist was considered shameful. Fortunately, that period has passed. In fact, there is now a reassessment of how much Grandpa Benito did for Italy.' (The relatives of the 7,000 Jews 'Grandpa' sent to extermination camps might not entirely agree.) Although she can make such statements, she can turn around the next day and campaign for women's rights and protest against the release of suspected rapists. The day after, though, she can tell Vladimir Luxuria, a transgendered politician, that, 'it is better to be a fascist than a faggot'.

Right now, though, she has problems on the home front: her husband, Mauro Floriani, may have been a bad boy of late. ANSA news agency reported in March 2014 that he 'is one of 20 alleged clients of the teenage girls from Parioli (a wealthy neighbourhood in Rome) authorities say were prostituting themselves to earn money for designer clothes and cell-phones.' Of course, it's denials all around from Mauro but, according to the Independent, the 'police have been screening hundreds of phone calls made to the girls from those apparently soliciting prostitution – which allegedly included Ms Mussolini's husband.'

Just a month earlier, she bridled when someone in a TV audience criticised her grandfather. 'Do I have to stay here and listen to this shit?' she said before storming off the set.

SECRETARY-GENERAL
OF HEZBOLLAH

LET THE GOOD TIMES ROLL

'There is no legal or legitimate state called Israel,' claims
Nasrallah. He also adheres to the belief that, 'Beirut
was destroyed by (Ariel) Sharon and protected by
Hafez Assad', current President of Syria, and to back up
that belief he has committed the armed wing of *Hezbollah* to Assad's defence in the mess
that is the Syrian Civil War.

Based in south Beirut, the 'Party of God' or the 'Party of Allah' has been led by Nasrallah
since 1992, after the Israelis assassinated the previous leader, Abbas al-Musawi. It is strangely
assimilated into both Lebanese society and the government and, on the ground, seems
much less radical than it does at a distance.

Nasrallah is viewed as something of a hero in the country for ending the Israeli occupation
of southern Lebanon in 2000, defeating the South Lebanese Army and arranging a prisoner
swap with the Israelis. Israel bombed the *Hezbollah* controlled areas of south Beirut in 2006
and inflicted severe damage. When speaking in public his most common phrases are 'death
to Israel' and 'death to America'.

He seemed particularly prescient in 2012 when he said in an interview with Julian
Assange: 'the only solution to the Israeli-Palestinian conflict is to establish a democratic
state on Palestinian land where Muslims, Jews and Christians live in peace.' Given the state
of Israeli politics and the reluctance to retreat from the settlements on the West Bank
many Palestinians have given up the dream of a two state solution and now wish to be
incorporated into a greater Israel where they can turn their efforts from war to something
more akin to an anti-apartheid movement.

They have to find their own Nelson Mandela first because Nasrallah isn't ever going to
fill that role.

NURSULTAN NAZARBAYEV

PRESIDENT OF KAZAKHSTAN

MAN OF THE YEAR

You know you've been truly honoured when you join the ranks of such great humanitarians as Vladimir Putin and the President of Belarus, Alexander Lukashenko, and are celebrated as the 'Man of the Year'. The honour is bestowed by the Russian Biographical Institute and the Institute for Economic Strategies, both of which are based in Moscow.

Another sure sign that you are a winner is if you hire former British Prime Minister Tony Blair as your consultant. According to the *Telegraph*, Blair 'gave Kazakhstan's autocratic president advice on how to manage his image after the slaughter of unarmed civilians protesting against his regime'. Thankfully, not all the protestors were killed, according to the *Telegraph*, 'other protesters, mainly striking oil workers, were rounded up and allegedly tortured'.

Despite all the carnage, Nazarbayev somehow still manages to win elections with 96% of the vote. Perhaps that's because he is just a fountain of good ideas – like the one the *Independent* noted: 'Nazarbayev said dropping the stan and renaming the country Kazakh Eli, which stands for The Land of Kazakhs, will make it stand out and encourage investment in the mineral-rich nation.' The newspaper quoted the sage as saying, 'foreigners show interest in Mongolia, whose population is just two million people, but whose name lacks the stan ending.'

Perhaps being in charge of a country for over 25 years eventually atrophies the brain but at least it's been good for Nazarbayev's wallet. According to the *Telegraph*, Rakhat Aliyev, in his book *The Godfather-in-Law*, claimed that Nazarbayev, Aliyev's former father-in-law, 'has had children with a flight attendant and a model, that he has a collection of over 5,000 designer watches and that he pocketed bribes for oil concessions granted to US companies.'

JAIME NEBOT

MAYOR OF GUAYAQUIL

GOLDEN SHOWER

Nebot is the Social Christian Party's mayor of Ecuador's largest city. Guayaquil is the principle port for the country and has a population of a little over 2 million. He has been mayor since the millennium and he has done much to regenerate the city by bringing power and telephone lines underground, building sidewalks, creating parks and improving the tourist trade. Nebot has also run twice for the presidency but wasn't successful.

Before Nebot was mayor he was elected to parliament and that's where he made his real mark on the country. During a televised session, Nebot grew angry with one of his colleagues. 'Come here so I can urinate on you', he shouted, 'I can't just hit you. I have to urinate on you.'

In 2012 he reluctantly placed a bust of Che Guevara in the Cerro Santa Ana and, in the run up to the election he told the *Ecuador Times* that, 'people vote for what I do and for what I don't do, do you believe that people vote for me because of my moustache?' He has described the left-leaning president of Ecuador, Rafael Correa, as 'friends [with] Fidel Castro, who has 55 years in power, and Daniel Ortega with 30 years.'

He launched a new campaign to attract tourists to the city, which was branded 'Guayaquil is my destiny', although why some would go there on a holiday beggars belief.

In 2013 he announced he was running for re-election as mayor, humbly stating, 'someday there will be a Guayaquil without Nebot, as there was a Guayaquil without Olmedo, and one without Febres-Cordero. I worry about who will be the replacement.' He shouldn't have bothered campaigning. Nebot was re-elected easily in 2014 with over 60% of the vote.

BROOKS NEWMARK

UK HOUSE OF COMMONS

MEAT TWEAT

The British press loves a scandal and, if they can't uncover one, they'll create something, which is why it's handy to have an idiot like Brooks Newmark in government. The American-born Newmark went to Harvard and Oxford and had a career in merchant banking before he became an MP and eventually Minister for Civil Society, but don't let that fool you, he's as dumb as a board.

First of all he got stitched up by a male freelancer for the *Sunday Mirror* who used pictures of Malin Sahlen, a contestant on *Sweden's Next Top Model*, which he downloaded to a Twitter account in the name of 'Sophie Wittam' and passed himself off as an ingénue PR girl for the Conservative party.

'Sophie' then approached the MP ostensibly but flirtatiously for career advice. Newmark bought the ruse and went the whole hog. After explicit tweets back and forth the married father of four got down to business and sent 'Sophie' a crotch shot. He had to resign his post as minister the next day. Although the other newspapers did get sanctimonious about the *Mirror's* tactics, the sex scandal, which was at this stage really a dumb scandal, brought a few other things wriggling out of the woodwork.

Newmark had already been getting it on with a single mother to whom he had reportedly sent forty pictures of his love muscle over two years. She was naturally unimpressed to learn that the two-timer was trying to two-time her. When the news of the affair broke it was time for his wife to move on and for Newmark to announce he wouldn't run in the next election and apologise to the public for his 'bizarre and abhorrent' behaviour. It was all down to the pressures of work of course and he went off to a psychiatric institution for some cockupational therapy. Meanwhile every Nigerian conman must have Newmark in their sights. If he's dumb enough to send off a cock-shot to someone he never met then surely he'd swallow some story about a rich West African widow who wants him to look after $10 million for her.

BRIAN NIEVES

MISSOURI STATE SENATE

PIECE OF FUCK

In the world of politics there's a special place that
Brian Nieves occupies. He's not only one of the
nastiest pieces of work on the planet, he's by far the most entertaining nut case who holds
public office. One opposition campaign worker, Shawn Bell, claimed Nieves pulled a gun on
him after Bell congratulated him on a primary win in 2010.

The Missouri state senator is not an unknown figure, given the vitriol that spills from his
mouth. Calling a retired teacher a 'fucking pussy' and a 'piece of fuck' isn't a spontaneous
thing with Nieves. He does it on purpose to generate as much press as possible. The salary
for a state senator in Missouri is around $36,000 per year with $104 per day in expenses
when the legislature is in session. It's a part-time job that doesn't pay well enough to
support a wife and three children. So Nieves plays the game of right-wing partisan politics
much in the same way as Rush Limbaugh – just on a smaller, more regional scale. It's a scam
that works and makes money, but only if he can generate sufficient press coverage to keep
the racket going. That means sneeringly calling an assault rifle a 'Nancy Pelosi Special' or
calling torture by water boarding a 'little water in the face'. Nieves knows that kind of talk
gins up the crazy Tea Party base, and they are suckers when it comes to buying conservative
books and listening for hours to right-wing shock-jock radio, which is another of Nieves'
specialities.

Nieves hosts an early morning talk show called *The Patriot Enclave* on KWMO out of
Washington, Missouri. He also has a company called Nieves Enterprises that generates
sales of over $1 million. Calling one of his more liberal constituents a 'sub-Human and,
in my humble opinion, a very dangerous man who must be shown for what he is' might
be something a normal person *might* say in private, but Nieves purposely puts it on his
Facebook page, knowing full well it will become newspaper copy the next day. That's how a
humble state senator can turn $36,000 a year into many multiples of that.

NIKOS NIKOPOULOS

HELLENIC PARLIAMENT

A EUROPE OF FAGGOTS

The world – or at least a lot of it – has now more or less got its head around gay politicians, so when the Luxembourg Prime Minister, Xavier Bettel, announced that he and his partner were going to get hitched when the law allowing gay marriages comes into effect in the tiny Grand Duchy in 2015, most of Europe just yawned.

Not so with the Greek politician and president of the conservative Christian-Democratic party. He had a Twitter outrage. According to the *EU Observer*, Nikopoulos tweeted, 'from a Europe of nation states to a Europe of... faggots!! The prime minister of Luxembourg is engaged with his darling!'

The former deputy labour minister has basically had it with Europe and he resigned from government over objections about the massive bailout Greece received and the austerity terms they had to accept.

Bettel actually politely responded to the tweet from the Greek, writing, 'hello, I heard you want to tell me something, but I don't speak Greek. Sorry.' Nikopoulos faced a torrent of abuse over the tweet on social media (don't they all have something better to do?), which only seemed to push him over the edge. He tweeted another insult, writing, 'after the sleazy attacks and barrage of insults I respond: From a Europe of nations to a Europe of fags... In other words those who provoke shame.'

The *Observer* further reports that 'the MP is currently campaigning against an anti-hate crime bill which is set to include tougher sentences for those who commit homophobic or racist acts' and is quoted as saying the legislation, 'will be the end for the institution of the family'. According to *Kathimerini* newspaper, Nikopoulos later sent a letter to Bettel apologising for his behaviour and said it was not his 'usual manners.' But he told the newspaper that, 'I will not apologise for my solid and straightforward views which triggered my electronic message.'

HYOGO PREFECTURAL ASSEMBLY

THE POLITICIAN WITH CONTRITION

Nonomura-san was an obscure Hyogo Prefectural assemblyman until he shot to instant global fame for his spectacularly insane crying fit during a three hour press conference in Kobe, Japan in July 2014.

The laughing stock from Hyogo was accused of misusing about 3 million yen, or about $30,000, in expenses he claimed were used for 'business trips,' which reportedly included more than a hundred visits to a hot springs resort.

During the press conference he made various random statements claiming he 'became an assembly member to change society', 'I want to change this society', 'I staked my life on changing this society', and 'don't you understand?' In between the gasps he howled loudly, screamed, wept and banged his feet on a desk. The video of the spectacle hit the internet in seconds and quickly went around the world. The following day, Nonomura sent faxes to media organisations saying he had 'answered all possible questions' at the news conference and asked reporters to 'refrain from any attempts' to interview him.

At a meeting July 7, the prefectural assembly decided to re-examine Nonomura's spending over the past three years. Representatives from various parties called on Nonomura to fulfil his responsibility to prefectural residents and return the unaccounted-for funds or resign from the assembly. Nonomura, who used a freight elevator to elude reporters, said at the meeting, 'I will talk with the assembly chairman with resignation in mind.' Hyogo prefectural assembly members are each provided with 6 million yen in political activity funds a year. Nonomura used up the entire amount last fiscal year.

Since the July 1st news conference, the assemblyman has not answered any calls or other inquiries.

DAVID NORRIS

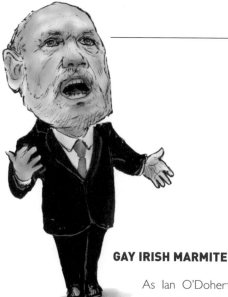

SEANAD EIREANN
(IRISH SENATE)

GAY IRISH MARMITE

As Ian O'Doherty wrote in the Irish Independent, Norris is 'Ireland's most famous gay man and someone who is the walking, talking equivalent of Marmite – people either love him or hate him.' Nobody epitomises the sanctimonious strain of Irishman better than Norris. Ireland is a country that is hesitant to actually do anything assertive in the world, preferring to hide behind a cloak of 'neutrality' while still reserving the right to have its opinions taken seriously.

Think of Ireland as 'Manchester or Liverpool West'. What surprises many Americans in particular is that there is little discernible difference between the UK and Ireland. The Irish watch British television, read British newspapers, root for British soccer clubs and, when things get bad on the home front, they hop on a ferry and move to Britain (they don't even need a passport).

Norris is a senator. This really doesn't mean much but he think it gives him the right to pontificate, perhaps more so since he has 'come out of the closet', which really isn't that big a deal. His latest wheeze is outrage about Israel's actions in Gaza in 2014. He demanded that the Israeli ambassador to Ireland resign. The call for resignation happened during a senate debate on the situation in Gaza, as if that would make any difference in the world. The Israeli ambassador, Boaz Modai, told Norris that he was sorry to disappoint him, but he was 'going to be in Ireland for another year'.

Norris ran for the presidency in 2011 but pulled out when he was caught by a blogger, John Connolly. What Connolly found out was that Norris's former partner, Ezra Nawi, had been done for the statutory rape of a Palestinian teenager and Norris had written a letter in 1992 asking for clemency, claiming that Nawi had been lured into a trap. It wasn't so much the letter that did Norris in but the fact that he used official senate letterhead in his plea. His support collapsed and he withdrew from the election.

PAUL NUTTALL

EUROPEAN PARLIAMENT

THIN-SKINNED HEAD

He had a sense of humour failure in March, 2014. As opposed to his boss, Nigel Farage, who voluntarily had the piss taken out of him on the BBC comedy quiz show, *Have I Got News For You*, the Deputy Head of the UK Independence Party (UKIP) wasn't having it when the musical duo, *Johnny and the Baptists*, launched their Stop UKIP tour.

According to the *Daily Mail*, 'Paul Nuttall has condemned the distasteful satire, calling on the British Arts Council to investigate funding given to theatres hosting the act.' He further added on the UKIP website, 'it does, of course, show just how much left wing supporters are getting extremely worried about the growing success of UKIP. We wouldn't be under attack from these musical comedians unless we were proving a threat to the established order.'

UKIP is a one-issue political party and its avowed purpose is to get the UK out of the European Union, which must irritate Nuttall all to hell when he collects his €8,000 cheque each month for his work as an MEP. His attendance record in the European Parliament is almost rock bottom, although there are 20 out of the 756 MEPs who actually attend less than he does. He is a leading light in the UKIP *Save The Pub Campaign* and the *Campaign Against Political Correctness*. He opposes abortion and the ban on smoking in pubs – he thinks the landlord should decide whether to allow smoking. He wants to ban burqas, wants nuclear power to replace renewable energy sources and wants to bring back the death penalty for certain crimes.

But mostly he's against freeloading immigrants, saying, 'there is a growing underclass in this country… you've got the family next door on benefits who still have the flatscreen tv, still have the car and can afford to go on holiday'. He doesn't explain how getting Britain out of the EU will change that.

TEODORO OBIANG NGUEMA MBASOGO

PRESIDENT OF
EQUATORIAL NEW GUINEA

OMNIPOTENT IMPOTENT

As a common rule of thumb, you are usually thoroughly stuffed if you are unlucky enough to be born in a country that has a 'president for life'. That's what the people of Equatorial Guinea have to look forward to until their president meets his maker.

Obiang showed unique family loyalty by ousting his uncle from power in 1979 in a military coup. He had him quickly tried and shot by firing squad within weeks of overthrowing him. Prior to taking over the reins of power Obiang was warden at Black Beach Prison, a particularly hellish lock-up that's known for the torture that is routinely meted out to the prisoners.

Presidential elections are held every seven years in Equatorial Guinea but, with some precincts reporting that he received 103% of the vote, they are pretty much just a formality. As head of the aptly named 'Democratic' Party of Equatorial Guinea, Obiang can do pretty much anything he wants as president of the country and, with a parliament where 99 out of the 100 members are in the same political party, it's not like anybody is going to stop him no matter how bat-shit-crazy he is.

The list of high crimes and misdemeanours he has committed to date include torture, kidnapping, solitary detention, murder and arbitrary arrest. But those aren't the fun things. The really good part is the wholesale theft of the country's oil wealth and that runs into the billions that fund ever more lavish presidential palaces. It doesn't help to tamper his ego when the nation's radio network refers to Obiang as the 'country's god'. Unfortunately, the president takes that kind of talk seriously and has decided he 'can decide to kill without anyone calling him to account and without going to hell'. The only hope for the country's citizens is that the rumours that Obiang has prostate cancer turn out to be true and the only comfort they can take is that the treatment probably made him impotent.

LARS OHLY

SWEDISH RIKSDAG

LARS HAS BALLS AND HE'S PROUD OF THEM

Lars Ohly recently flashed a picture of his balls around the world. Granted it was accidental, but nevertheless, Lars' gonads have attracted considerable attention and comment in the world press. It happened when the Swedish politician snapped a selfie on the beach to show his classy new Liverpool Football Club tattoo which tastefully adorns his lower left leg. Before he posted the photo to his Instagram account he failed to notice that his family jewels were on display as well.

The former party chairman of the *Vänsterpartiet* (Swedish Left party) is no stranger to controversy. He was famously caught out when he claimed to have played Nacka Skoglund, a famous Swedish soccer star, in a friendly match which, in retrospect, never happened.

He also conveniently seems to have forgotten he was once a communist. In fact, he was a Leninist up until 1999, and during the Cold War he was a staunch defender of the super-good governance of Eastern Europe. He was a member of the Swedish-Cuban Association that upheld the view that Fidel Castro was anything but a dictator. He later recanted that belief and resigned from the association.

In 2006 he gave Marie Söderqvist the finger on national television, but later blamed it on 'a blackout'.

Although his children attend private schools, he's against them. He's also against privatised medicine and hospitals but had an operation at a private hospital. He's against property speculation but has made a small fortune on a condominium in Stockholm. Oh, and he cried when the Berlin Wall was torn down. Naturally, he denied those tears years later. Lars seems not so much of a leftie as he is a fantasist and hypocrite.

TOMIO OKAMURA

PARTY LEADER

DAWN OF DESTRUCTION

He wasn't even born in the Czech Republic and now he wants to expel a sizable portion of the population that were. The son of a Japanese-Korean father and a Czech mother, Okamura was born in Tokyo and only arrived in Prague when he was six years old. He's a sort of Czech version of Donald Trump or Alan Sugar and rose to fame as a judge on *Den D*, the Czech version of *Dragons' Den*.

There's a lot of opacity around his business dealings. According to the *Prague Monitor*, 'Okamura's own finances remain something of a mystery — for starters, he isn't the owner of the business he's mostly closely associated with.' Like Trump, he's also written a business book with a title very similar to *The Art of the Deal*. Okamura's book, *Umění Vládnout* (The Art of Ruling), was also a best seller.

Nevertheless, he made a successful run for the Czech Senate in 2012 on a platform that stated: 'Czech Romanies (Gypsies) should be sent to India to live in a newly created homeland' and that 'if someone comes (to the Czech Republic) to work, then they should work if they find a job. But if they don't have work, they'll just have to return home and not leech off our system.' He is now reckoned to be the third most popular politician in the Czech Republic, although the standings of the political party he created, *Dawn of Direct Democracy*, have taken a hit of late due to some financial scandals.

Okamura recently got into trouble by denying that the Nazis attempted to exterminate the Romany population of the country, instead saying the concentration camps they were kept in until they were executed were labour camps for those who were too lazy to work. Historians estimate that between 1939 and 1945 the Nazis murdered about 25% of the one million Romanies living in Europe.

JERRY O'NEIL

MONTANA HOUSE OF REPRESENTATIVES

BASE METAL IN MONTANA

He'd like to arrest any federal official who wants to implement the Affordable Care Act (Obamacare) in Montana. Jerry O'Neil, a lawmaker in the Montana Legislature, is known for his bizarre beliefs and paranoid fantasies.

Although it would be unconstitutional to nullify a federal law, O'Neil is for it, while still saying he wants to uphold the US Constitution.

Oh, and he wants to be paid in gold and silver coins for his work because he's convinced the US dollar is going to collapse. He's made a special request that he be paid with 'unadulterated' coinage. In his letter to the Montana Office of Legislative Services he said, 'It is very likely the bottom will fall out from under the US dollar. If and when that happens, how can we in the Montana Legislature protect our constituents? The only answer I can come up with is to honor my oath to the US Constitution and request that your debt to me be paid in gold and silver coins that will still have value when the US dollar is reduced to junk status. I therefore request my legislative pay to be in gold and silver coins that are unadulterated with base metals.'

He has a unique policy that will save the state money on its prisons: the public beating of criminals. In 2013 he introduced a bill that would allow corporal punishment as an option for those convicted of misdemeanours and felonies. The whippings would be conducted either by county sheriffs or officials with the state Department of Corrections. O'Neil is quoted as saying in the *Billings Gazette*: 'ten years in prison or you could take 20 lashes, perhaps two lashes a year? What would you choose?'

VIKTOR ORBAN

PRIME MINISTER OF HUNGARY

PRO PROCREATION

Viktor is concerned that the great civilisations of Western Europe may disappear because they aren't 'getting it on' (in a Christian way) as much as they should. 'Civilisations which can't keep up their levels (of getting it on) naturally are going to disappear', Orban said recently during a speech he gave in Berlin.

According to the *Financial Times*, he said 'it was acceptable for people of the same sex to live together but "the basic solution is that we have a form of society where men and women live together".' He's hoping his recommendations work because the last thing he wants is for immigrants to fill the ranks of the disappearing Europeans.

'The goal is to cease immigration whatsoever,' said Orban in August of 2014 –although it really isn't much of a problem in his own country. 75,000 people immigrated to Hungary in 2012 compared to 900,000 Europeans that moved to the UK – including 50,000 Hungarians. 120,000 Hungarians live in Germany. The former president of France, Nicolas Sarkozy, was the son of a Hungarian immigrant to France. There are 1.5 million Americans who claim Hungarian ancestry. 70,000 Hungarians have packed up and moved to Sweden and there are 55,000 of them in Austria.

The Hungarian PM told the *Wall Street Journal* that other European countries oppose his promotion of procreation 'because they've failed to turn around demographic trends with family politics; have kept social tension at bay by subsidising the jobless; and aren't fazed if the ethnic basis of a nation state is broken.'

He's got some other strange ideas. According to *Bloomberg*, 'Hungarian Prime Minister Viktor Orban said he wants to abandon liberal democracy in favour of an illiberal state, citing Russia and Turkey as examples.' 'I don't think that our European Union membership precludes us from building an illiberal new state based on national foundations', *Bloomberg* quoted Orban as saying. The news agency further stated: 'Orban listed Russia, Turkey and China as examples of successful nations, "none of which is liberal and some of which aren't even democracies."'

GIORGIO ORSONI

FORMER MAYOR
OF VENICE

THE MOSE SCANDAL

As the head of the centre-left coalition, Orsoni was elected as mayor of Venice in 2010. Four years later and he's resigned in a plea agreement that saw him previously under house arrest.

He lost the confidence of his party over charges of corruption in the awarding of contracts to construct underwater barriers to protect the city from the relentless threat of the sea. He was one of thirty people arrested after it was revealed that the company that was awarded the contract had a special $25 million pool of cash to bribe officials.

According to the *Financial Times*, 'the Modulo Sperimentale Elettromeccanico, or Mose, has been more than a decade in the making. The project, which will put 78 gates across three inlets that feed into the lagoon, has been contentious from the outset, not only due to the soaring cost but also the potential impact on the lagoon ecosystem. Its latest completion date is 2016, although that is widely expected to be put back.'

It's estimated that the entire construction project will cost Venice $5.5 billion. Orsoni should have known better. According to the city's own website, which still claims he's the mayor, 'the father of three is not only a lawyer but President of the Venice Bar Association and President of the Triveneto Union for Bar Association councils.'

Orsoni is accused of using $500,000 in donations from the consortium building the project for campaign expenses, although it has never been proved that he knew of the donations or where they came from. Orsoni negotiated a suspended jail sentence of four months in the plea bargain. Also implicated in the corruption scandal was Giancarlo Galan, a former minister, and Emilio Spaziante, an ex-police general.

DANIEL ORTEGA

PRESIDENT OF NICARAGUA

GOD COMPLEX

He is Nicaragua and Nicaragua is him, or he'd like to think so. He has his detractors who think he's become the dictator he deposed but most Nicaraguans think of him as a revolutionary hero who has given his all to improve the life of ordinary people. He isn't giving as much grief to America that many thought he would, but he's not a great friend of the USA.

He joined the Sandinista National Liberation Front that overthrew the brutal dictator, Anastasio Somoza (guess which side America was on). Ronald Reagan funded the *Contras*, the opposing force to the *Sandinistas*, which resulted in a long and bitter civil war that was finally settled in 1990.

Since that time, America provided millions in economic aid to the country, but that was cut off when the US found that Nicaragua was supplying military equipment to the rebel forces in El Salvador. Ortega was finally elected President of Nicaragua in 2007, promising to be a 'thorn in the side of America, along with Venezuela and Cuba'. He's no longer a Marxist and now considers himself a 'democratic socialist'.

According to the *Global Post*, a 'retired army general Hugo Torres, a Sandinista dissident who was a member of the revolutionary council of state in the 1980s claims that,'"Ortega is a messianic *caudillo* (leader) with fascist tendencies". He thinks he is illuminated and predestined to rule the country. He's become crazy with power.' The publication also says that his critics 'claim Ortega is pushing the country toward a retro-tropical dictatorship with a God complex.'

One of Ortega's visions will begin (or not begin) in 2014. He wants to build a second link between the Caribbean and the Pacific Ocean, thereby breaking the monopoly of the Panama Canal. He's signed a deal with a Chinese outfit costing upwards of $40 billion – a lot of money for a poor Central American country that really hasn't justified the fact that a second canal is viable.

GARY PAINTER

SHERIFF OF MIDLAND COUNTY, TEXAS

THEM QURAN BOOKS

We can find out a lot about Sheriff Gary Painter. The Midland County website has a thousand word biography of him along with a picture of the lawman with his arm around former President George W. Bush. According to the site, Painter is 'a born leader of men', 'a Master Mason', 'a staunch Republican' and 'a devout Baptist'.

According to the *Conservative Tribune*, Sheriff Painter has an 'awesome message for terrorists trying to cross the border'. According to the publication, if the Sheriff finds anybody from the Islamic State of Iraq and Syria (ISIS) loitering around Midland County, he has some advice for them: 'Well, if they rear their ugly heads, we'll send 'em to hell.'

Well, in September of 2014, the terrorism threat rose considerably in Texas. According to *Think Progress*, the Sheriff told Fox News that, 'I'm saying the border is wide open. We have found copies, or people along the border, have found Muslim clothing; they have found Quran books that are laying on the side of the trail. So we know that there are Muslims that have come across, have been smuggled in the United States.'

Think Progress further reported that, 'Painter made similar comments in other media outlets where he said that ISIS has operations in Ciudad Juarez, Mexico, which borders El Paso, Texas. That claim was first published on the conservative *Judicial Watch*, but federal law enforcement told an *ABC* affiliate that it is unverified and unlikely that ISIS is in Juarez.'

The *American Patriot, Three Percent* recently published a photograph of what they said was a 'Muslim prayer rug' that was found near the Texas-Mexico border, but on closer inspection it turned out to be an Adidas shirt.

STEVEN PALAZZO

US HOUSE OF REPRESENTATIVES

GOD'S CHOSEN MAN

On July 29th 2014, a Republican Representative from Mississippi, Steven Palazzo, sent a Bible to every member of the United States Congress along with a letter telling each and every one to consult the Good Book when pondering any sort of critical decision in their life.

'On a daily basis, we contemplate policy decisions that impact America's future,' said Palazzo. 'Our staffs provide us with policy memos, statistics, and recommendations that help us make informed decisions. However, I find that the best advice comes through meditating on God's Word.'

According to the *Clarion-Ledger* newspaper, just the day before Palazzo generously passed out the Bibles, he had some interesting comments about immigrant children who have crossed the border into the United States. Palazzo said he would support changing federal law that currently allows children born to illegal immigrants in America to remain as citizens. These so-called 'anchor babies' should be deported with their parents. The Congressman obviously believes deporting children is the 'Christian thing to do'.

Another thing Jesus and Palazzo would clearly agree about is that everyone should have a gun. 'It's not God-fearing Christians going out there and committing mass murder,' Palazzo said when asked about gun control legislation. 'We're not going to sacrifice the 2nd Amendment to the Constitution just to appease special interest.'

Psalm 147:3: 'He heals the broken hearted and binds up their wounds' may comfort those of Palazzo's Mississippi constituents who are still without health insurance. He has voted over forty times to repeal the Affordable Care Act and has vowed to continue to do his best to make sure that healthcare only goes to those who can afford it.

POLISH SEJM

A GUN, A DILDO AND A CRUCIFIX

He wants the crucifix taken out of the Polish Parliament and he means it. The leader of the *Twój Ruch*
(Your Movement) party has been fighting to get it
removed since 2011. 'We're going to take the cross
case to Strasbourg (home of the European Court of
Human Rights),' said Palikot after losing his latest
legal battle in an appeals court.

The anti-clerical, left of centre, party get about
10% of the vote in elections and is the third
largest political party in Poland. Other members of
Palikot's party include Anna Grodzka, the first transsexual MP ever to be elected in Europe.
One of its platforms is to legalise soft drugs. In 2012 Palikot planned to bring a joint into
the Sejm to prove a point. He had second thoughts when threatened with arrest, but he
did burn some marijuana-flavoured incense on the parliament floor.

He supports gay rights and wants gay marriage legalised, which is not a popular
position in the staunchly Catholic country. He once appeared at a press conference
holding a handgun and a plastic dildo in order to make a point about sexual harassment
by the police. He himself was arrested and fined in 2010 for boozing it up in a public place.
Palikot also thinks the organisation that controls soccer in Poland is corrupt and brought a
severed pig's head to a press conference to make his point.

His undoing may be his ex-wife's cooperation with police investigating his complex
empire of offshore wealth amid charges of possible tax evasion.

SARAH PALIN

**FORMER GOVERNOR
OF ALASKA**

NAILIN' PALIN

Somehow in Sarah Palin's mind the celebrated Midnight Ride of Paul Revere in 1775 was all about resisting gun control. And so, some 250 years later, half of America has a gun rack loaded with multiple assault weapons and enough ammunition to take over a small country.

She put it rather elegantly when she said, 'he who warned, uh, the British that they weren't gonna be takin' away our arms, uh, by ringing those bells, and um, makin' sure as he's riding his horse through town to send those warning shots and bells that we were going to be sure and we were going to be free, and we were going to be armed.'

Despite losing her Vice Presidential bid and resigning after serving only a half-term as Governor of Alaska, she still remains popular among a certain set up slack-jawed imbeciles who still think Obama is a Nazi-Communist, Muslim foreign dictator who's out to destroy America through his weakness.

But even Fox News ended her contract, and when you're deemed too dim to sit in a Fox News studio the only alternative would be to start your own television station, which is just what she did in 2014. It promises not only to broadcast her astute political opinions but will also offer lifestyle advice from one whose family history doesn't seem to have quite reflected her conservative ideals. 'I want to help clean up the state that is so sorry today of journalism,' she told Fox News somewhat oddly, 'and I have a communications degree.'

Sarah Palin became such a national institution that there was even a porn movie about her: *Who's Nailin Paylin?* It was produced by *Hustler* magazine and directed by Jerome Tanner; you can see clips of the movie on the internet – not that it's advised. When complimented by a caller on a radio show about the quality of the 'documentary' Palin responded: 'oh, good, thank you, yes.'

PHILIPPINES ACTIVIST

THE 51ST STATE

Filipino lawyer, Elly Velez Pamatong, once filed criminal charges against Pope Benedict XVI, accusing him of human rights violations for spreading the myth of Christianity in order to trick its followers into donating money to the church.

He wrote a book in 1992 titled, *American birthright on trial: Why Filipinos are still citizens or nationals of the United States of America*. In 2004 he was arrested south of Manila for scattering metal spikes on the road in protest for not being allowed to run for president. Also found in his car at the time was a cache of military and surveillance equipment, including an M203 grenade launcher, an M-16 rifle, an Intratech machine pistol, two 45 calibre automatics, assorted ammunition, two binoculars, a sniper's telescope and a bogus American passport.

Pamatong had previously gone on television to announce he was organising the International Militia of the People against Corruption and Terrorism (IMPACT), with the intent of burning down the country's schools because they taught a web of lies to the students. He actually has some followers but not enough to qualify to run for president. His twin platform in the 2003 presidential race was to declare war against China over the disputed Spratley Islands and granting every Filipino applicant a visa to the US.

He is gearing up for the 2016 presidential elections in typical fashion. He was arrested in September, 2014, for his role in a suspected anti-Chinese bombing plot. The cops had found a van with a number of improvised explosives in it and had uncovered a plan to bomb the Chinese embassy and a number of businesses owned by ethnic Chinese. Pamatong was arrested at Manila Airport when he got off a plane coming from the southern part of the country.

KEVIN PARKER

NEW YORK STATE SENATE

ANGER MANAGEMENT ISSUES

The Democratic State Senator from New York City's Flatbush neighbourhood 'is committed to restoring the overall quality of life for the constituents of the 21st Senatorial District in Brooklyn,' or at least it says so on his website.

To his credit is helping pass the Bias Crime Bill, advocacy for the LGBT Community and work on legislation to help new mothers. That said, he's got something of a temper.

As the *New York Times* reported in January 2005, Parker, 'punched a traffic agent in the face yesterday as the agent was writing a summons for the senator's double-parked car' and was 'charged with third-degree assault, a misdemeanour, after the fight, the police said.' It further reported that, 'the police said witnesses told them that the senator flew into a rage, pushing the agent as the agent walked past him to his own vehicle to write the summons. The senator crumpled the summons and threw it in the agent's face, the police said, and then punched the agent.'

In 2010 the *New York Daily News* reported how, during a legislative committee meeting, Parker 'took several steps toward Senator Diane Savino as the two engaged in a profanity-laced argument during the contentious Democratic conference, the sources said. Parker dropped several f-bombs and called Savino a bitch.' Later that year the *Daily News* reported that 'hothead state Senator Kevin Parker erupted again Tuesday, this time with a race-based rant that rattled even his supporters.' In 2011 the *New York Post* reported that, 'Parker was sentenced today to three years' probation and ordered to pay a $1,000 fine after a Brooklyn jury found him guilty last year of damaging a *Post* photographer's camera after the lensman snapped pictures of him outside the politician's Flatbush home. Parker was also ordered to attend anger management classes and pay *The Post* back $672 to cover the cost of broken equipment.' The *Daily News*, reports that his political ally, Senator Ruben Diaz, has stated that, 'he needs help'.

FIONA PATTEN

AUSTRALIAN PARTY LEADER

LIP SERVICE

She is a former sex worker and now the leader of the Australian Sex Party (ASP), which really isn't all about sex although she does say, 'we're positive about sex'. Who wouldn't be? The ASP wants drugs legalised and to stop the Americanisation of Australian politics. By that, it means it wants the religious wing of politics done away with.

They got 250,000 first preferences in the last Australian senate election, netting about 3 per-cent of the vote – less than the 14% required to gain a seat.

Patten is also for educating Australian's youth about sex, which she says the other parties 'pay lip service to' but really don't confront the problem. The star of such cinema hits as *Turn Me On: The History of the Vibrator* (2001), *Sex Around the World* (2012) and *Satisfaction* (2007) became the ASP leader in 2009. She's also CEO of the Eros Association, which represents the sex industry in Australia.

After graduating with a degree in fashion she started her own label, Body Politic, and noticed that the most prosperous of her customers were sex workers so she thought she would try it out herself. She says she was only in the trade for a 'few months' and then went to work lobbying politicians on the behalf of her former industry colleagues.

The political issues that drive her are legalising voluntary euthanasia, doing away with the tax-exempt status of religious organisations and legalising all drugs as a means to avoid disease and overdoses. ASP is also against any form of censorship and opposes government monitoring of mobile phones and other electronic devices. In the most recent Melbourne by-election the *ASP* managed 8.7% of the vote. Many think that once the novelty of the party's brand wears off, more and more voters will take the ASP seriously.

RAND PAUL

US SENATE

PAUL V PAUL

The senator from Kentucky may end up as the Republican nominee for president in 2016. His libertarian beliefs appeal to a young, male electorate, which is a demographic his party has been unable to capture in the past three elections. But Paul knows that the key to the White House will not be his unless he starts modifying his agenda. That's why he started his flip-flop tour in 2014.

First there's Israel. Republicans attract very few Jewish voters and don't have a single Jewish member of congress, but they have an evangelical base that believes in 'the rapture' and for 'the rapture' to happen America has to be closely aligned with Israel, because that is where it all supposedly begins. The old Paul wanted to cut aid to Israel but the new Paul now supports it and wants to introduce legislation that would end Palestinian aid unless *Hamas* recognises Israel's right to exist.

He wanted to build a 2,000-mile electric fence to keep immigrants out and now he wants to find a solution that makes them legal residents. He was against taking campaign donations from lobbyists but now he's cool with it. He once said it was OK for private business to refuse to serve minorities but now thinks it isn't. He was firmly opposed to intervention against ISIS but now wants to bomb them into eternity. He was for the government staying out of the bedroom or interfering with women's issues but now wants to ban certain types of birth control and make abortion illegal.

He wanted the US not to interfere with Russian moves in the Ukraine and even criticised members of his own party for being too bellicose in their stance towards Russia, but later called the annexation of Crimea a 'gross violation of that nation's sovereignty' and added, 'if I were president I wouldn't let Putin get away with it'.

Before the 2016 primaries it's likely that most electors will get whiplash watching Rand Paul reverse every libertarian belief he once had as he seeks to woo conservative Republicans. In the process, that young demographic the party is after will likely drift away.

MAJA PAVLOVIC

CACAK CITY COUNCIL

THE IRON-PUMPING LADY

If it's class you're looking for, then Maja Pavlovic might not be right up your street. But, if you are looking for your political leader to look like she's come up on some sort of Moscow pole dancing club then you'll love Maja Pavlovic.

She won the European leg of the Women's Bikini Fitness Contest in Spain and has entered and won numerous other beauty contests. The body-building, perma-tanned blonde who was voted Serbia's sexiest politician is also a councillor in her home city of Cacak in southern Serbia and has greater political ambitions. She's also a doctor, working as a trainee cardiologist.

As a left-inclined socialist, she wouldn't have quite fitted into Margaret Thatcher's cabinet. She told the *Daily Mail* that she knew it 'may seem strange that someone from the other side of the political spectrum can be so impressed but Margaret Thatcher was a force of nature' adding that, 'Anybody that knows anything about her life cannot fail to be impressed by a remarkable woman she was, as an example to everyone.'

She told the Serbian newspaper, *Telegraf*, 'I also love politics. I want to stay involved in that and of course through my beauty contest involvement, I hope that I will get to travel and see interesting places.'

Speaking further to the *Daily Mail* about Margaret Thatcher, Pavlovic said, 'I hope like her to get to the top as well. Whether that's as a politician, a doctor or a model. Second place is not interesting.' The *Telegraf* claims that, 'people want to get sick on purpose just to get healed by her, even though she is only a junior doctor'.

DELYAN PEEVSKI

BULGARIAN NATIONAL ASSEMBLY

STOLEN LOVE

He's the husband of the blonde bombshell, Tsvetelina Yaneva, whose hit single *Stolen Love* rocked the Bulgarian music scene. He's extremely rich and a parliamentarian representing the Movement for Rights and Freedoms Party. He's also embroiled in a controversy about money, secrecy and bank runs.

In 2014 CorpBank was taken into receivership by the Bulgarian Central Bank after rumours spread on social media led to a run on the bank. It was reopened but only for those who had borrowed from the bank to repay loans. Depositors were left with losses in the millions. The central bank also refused to honour CorpBank's debt obligations.

First Investment Bank also was the victim of rumours and depositors began lining up to withdraw funds. But, as *Forbes* magazine pointed out, the government took an entirely different approach with this bank: 'First Investment Bank was provided with emergency liquidity by both the BNB and eventually the EU: the President issued reassuring messages about the safety of deposits, and the BNB called for prosecution of people guilty of spreading rumours about bank instability.' *Forbes* goes on to add, 'CorpBank was to be brought down in order to remove the current majority owner, Tsvetan Vassilev. But FI bank – the bank to which Delyan Peevski moved his money, sparking the CorpBank run – was to be protected'.

As can be imagined, this has hardly endeared Peevski to the Bulgarian people, particularly those depositors whose savings were wiped out. Then the government tried to make Peevski head of Bulgaria's security services. Reuters news agency reported that at Peevski's appointment the country 'erupted in widespread protests, which eventually brought the government down'.

WILLIE PENROSE

IRISH DÁIL

THE MAN WHO DOESN'T LIKE KYLIE

The Irish like to pretend there is such a thing as a living Irish language, which is why they call their representative to parliament a *Teachta Dála*, or TD for short. The parliament itself is called the *Dáil Éireann*, which is another example of how the Micks like to prove they are not just the western suburb of Manchester.

TDs are a fairly useless bunch but Willie Penrose has differentiated himself. First of all, he quit his position as Minister of State because the government closed an Irish army base in his home district of Mullingar. That was his 15 seconds of fame – up until 2014 when he launched into a tirade about the lack of Irish music on Irish radio stations. He'd like to see a mandatory 40% content of Irish-made toons on the airwaves, which would be popular with Irish musicians but would be exceedingly boring for the listening public.

'If they are not hearing it at all, how can we foster a love for Irish music, in whatever genre – rock, pop, country, traditional, folk, and so forth', Penrose asked an empty chamber of the Dáil Éireann in October 2014. He cited a recording made by Australian artist Kylie Minogue that he thought was unfairly classified as being Irish because it was recorded in a studio outside Dublin. While noting that the European Union doesn't allow countries to set a quota on local content of music, Penrose said angrily that broadcasters were too compliant: 'anything to portray ourselves as supplicants or poodles who must always be seen as good Europeans and always obedient.' Needless to say, if the European Union hadn't forked out the cash to get Ireland out of its banking crisis the country would be subsisting on potatoes and remittances, but that doesn't bother Penrose. He concluded his speech by saying, 'Irish country music is filling hotel ballrooms and even cruise ships, yet I do not hear much of it on RTE radio. It is about time we recognised that this is an important area.'

RICK PERRY

GOVERNOR OF TEXAS

DUMB AND DUMBER

He's a tall and good-looking guy and seemed to be ideal presidential material. That lasted about five minutes – until he opened his mouth and the true depth of his knowledge was illuminated.

Alarm bells should have gone off when it was revealed that his family hunting camp still carried the old name of *Niggerhead* well after the start of his political career.

In his bid to win the Republican nomination for president in 2012, Perry got the ball rolling by showing his understanding of Middle East politics by confusing Asia Minor with the Levant. President Erdoğan of Turkey may not be a darling of the western media but Perry thinks 'the country is ruled by what many would perceive to be Islamic terrorists' and they should be booted out of NATO.

Erdoğan astutely called Perry an 'idiot'. Perry doubled down and later said the country's leadership supported 'honour killings', adding, 'I think, you know, Turkey's got to decide whether they want to be a country that projects those Western values that America is all about.' He caused further fury in Ankara when he added, 'we need to send a powerful message to countries like Iran and Syria and Turkey that the United States is serious and that we're going to have to be dealt with.'

Perry seemed ignorant of the fact that Incirlik Air Base and Izmir Air Station were not headquarters for the Turkish Taliban Air Force but US Air Force bases that have been essential in America's operations throughout the region. The Turkish government's official response to Perry's remark said: 'figures who are candidates for positions ... such as the US presidency, should be more knowledgeable about the world and exert more care with their statements.'

Perry is a creationist, who espouses the faux scientific theory of 'intelligent design' that he believes should be taught alongside evolution in Texan schoolrooms.

He's also big on capital punishment. Since succeeding George W. Bush as Governor of Texas in December 2000, he has overseen twice as many executions than in any other US state.

KAMALA PERSAD-BISSESSAR

PRIME MINISTER OF
TRINIDAD AND TOBAGO

THE POLITICS OF LOVE

Before she became the Prime Minister of the
Republic of Trinidad and Tobago, she had to win the
race for leadership of her party, the United National
Congress, and defeat its then leader, Basdeo Panday. It was
a nasty campaign, but Kamla Persad-Bissessar waged a campaign of love not war, and handily
won the contest and the subsequent race to be Prime Minister in 2010.

In a country with a big ethnic divide between Indians and Afro-Caribbeans, she sidesteps
the religious issue, saying she is a baptised Baptist and a Hindu, a strange combination if
there ever was one. After her election she returned to her ancestral village in India in 2012.
According to the *Times of India*, she commented on her ancestors' trek, saying, 'when they
went, they had no gold, no diamond, no traveller cheque and they had no facility of cell
phone, Internet, Blackberry and Facebook. What they took with them was Ramayan, Gita
and Koran and the lifestyle, tradition, values from this land.'

Things have gone pretty well for Persad-Bissessar except for one minor problem: she
appears to get publicly shit-faced every once and a while. According to the *Trinidadian
Guardian*, 'Persad-Bissessar's real drinking problem is not whether she is a heavy drinker
who cannot hold her liquor, but that everyone, supporters and detractors alike, thinks she
has a problem and that the problem affects her ability to function.' When asked by the
Trinidad Express if she was an alcoholic, she strenuously denied it, saying, 'it is not true. It is
definitely not true. I could not work the hours and days and nights that I do should I have
had such a problem.' She told *Newsday* that the rumours about her drinking were created
by the opposition, referring to 'the propaganda, the lies, the half-truths and innuendos . . . I
deny the allegations that have been made.' That being said, sometimes YouTube videos can
speak louder than words and some of these seem to show the Prime Minister to be a little
under the weather.

EMÍLIA PIRES

EAST TIMOR FINANCE MINISTER

MISTAKEN MINISTER

There's probably a reason the government of East Timor is trying to bring in a new restrictive media law in 2014. Writing in *Crikey Media*, Jose Belo, an East Timorese journalist and director of *Tempo Semanal*, explains that the law would, 'impose large fines on media outlets or individuals that are uncertified or distribute information that is considered *undesirable* as defined by the media council.'

Perhaps the intent of that law would be to cover up scandals like the risible relationship between the East Timor's Minister of Finance, Emília Pires, and the Nigerian con man, Bobby W. Boye esq. – or whatever alias he's going under now. From 2010 until 2014 Boye worked with the Minister to help assess the tax liabilities of the big oil companies that drill off the country's coast. According to the *Sydney Morning Herald*, 'Boye's job was to issue the formal tax assessments to claw back unpaid revenue. He succeeded brilliantly, forcing the oil companies to cough up more than $350 million.' The newspaper went on further to report that, 'But as he was raking in the revenue, Boye was robbing East Timor. The shocking truth was he was a convicted felon, a charlatan and embezzler who has allegedly scammed $3.51 million from East Timor's threadbare treasury.'

Unbeknownst to Pires, 'Boye had served three years in prison in California for embezzlement in 2007 and had been banned for life by the New York Stock Exchange after defrauding clients of their stocks in 2004.' It wasn't the East Timorese government that discovered Boye's con, it was the FBI. They had uncovered the fact that he had used the proceeds to buy fancy watches, five properties in New Jersey and a Rolls Royce. They nabbed him when he landed in the US at Newark Airport in June, 2014. In 2013 *Tempo Semanal*, noted that Pires 'is under investigation for guiding Ministry of Health supply contracts to her husband.'

VLADIMIR PLAHOTNIUC

MOLDOVAN PARLIAMENT

WHO IS HE?

First of all, some background: Moldova is often considered the most depressing place in Europe. It has the highest rate of alcoholism in the world, the lowest standard of living in Europe, the most orphans and nobody smiles. It's grim and a hotbed of criminal activity, so you can imagine what the politics are like.

And then there's Vladimir Plahotniuc, who does smile a lot, because he cares about his country. He's also got another name: Vlad Ulinici, and another passport – Romanian – and lots of people asking lots of questions about him.

As reported in *Business News Europe*, he could face prosecution in the UK 'if a London court finds he is behind the transfer of shares frozen under court order' according to Patrick Boylan of Simmons & Simmons. *Euroreporter* states that Plahotniuc/Ulinici is wanted by Interpol who are 'conducting a criminal investigation into fraud related to his multiple identities'.

Whatever his name is, he is also the richest guy in the country and, outwardly, is an all round good egg and a philanthropist to boot, but *Euroreporter* asserts that the 'different names and passports were needed to conceal much more serious crimes: accusations of embezzlement, fraud and murder – stories of alleged assassinations organised by Plahotniuc have been splashed over the Moldovan press'.

In 2013 the Prime Minister of Moldova, Vlad Filat, accused Plahotniuc of involvement in massive corruption and called for him to resign. He refused. Although he's supposed to be the deputy head of the Democratic Party, it's generally acknowledged that he is the one who calls the shots because he's the guy with the money, but it wasn't enough to stop parliament from ousting him as Speaker.

Italy is also interested in Plahotniuc: the *Guardian* reports that: 'According to leaked Interpol documents he has been investigated in Italy in connection with money-laundering.'

NATALIA POKLONSKAYA

PROSECUTOR GENERAL FOR CRIMEA

PROSECUTER

She's a huge hit in Japan where a number of artists have turned her image into an anime art sensation. According to *Russia Today* Putin's propaganda outfit, she 'annexes your heart'.

At her first press call, the new Attorney-General for the 'liberated' Soviet State of Crimea wowed the audience but, as the *Mirror* reported, after the discovery of her personal pictures on social media, 'Sexy Natalia Poklonskaya's red shoes and nylon-clad legs are driving admirers wild across the world.' The newspaper further reported that, 'the pictures are now spreading across the globe but there is no doubting the luscious lovely is pouting for Putin because her politics are as red as her shoes. In an interview she gave to the Voice of Russia, she branded the Ukraine authorities in Kiev as "devils from the ashes" and made it clear she supported Crimea's new-found independence.' It's actually a vassal state of Russia.

Russia Today quoted Poklonskaya upon taking up her new gig: 'in the 12 years I've spent working in the Prosecutor General's office, I've been dealing with organised crime and put many criminals in prison.' The propaganda outfit also mentioned that, 'during her first press conference on the new position, the 34-year-old blonde didn't hesitate to denounce the coup-imposed government in Kiev.' When told that she is on a wanted list for criminal treason by the real Ukrainian government in Kiev, Poklonskaya told *RT*, 'I'm not afraid to tell the truth. I'm not a criminal. I'm not promoting Nazism, like some among the new authorities in Kiev. If they want to launch a criminal case against me, I'm not afraid of that.'

Poklonskaya left what is now the unoccupied part of the Ukraine in February, 2014, saying she was 'ashamed to live in the country where neo-fascists freely walk about the streets.' She ended up in the Crimea and in March 2014 Vladimir Putin appointed her Prosecutor-General of the 'Autonomous Republic'.

PRAYUTH CHAN-OCHA

PRIME MINISTER OF THAILAND

DICK-TATOR

You can go to jail if you say anything bad about him, which says a lot about how democratic Thailand's new dictator is. The general who overthrew Yingluck Shinawatra, Thailand's first female Prime Minister, in a military coup d'état in May 2014, is now 'Prime Minister' of Thailand but he's really nothing more than a strongman who is trying to negate the influence of Yingluck's brother, Thaksin Shinawatra, whose political parties have won every election in the country since 2001. In order to do that, Prayuth is stifling the opposition and muzzling the press.

According to the *Global Post*: 'Starting in late 2013, right-wing protest mobs were storming Bangkok's government offices, sabotaging elections and seizing major thoroughfares. Those hyper-conservative protesters were, in fact, agitating for an overthrow. They created the chaos needed to justify the takeover, the twelfth successful coup since Thailand ended direct rule by kings in the 1930s. The protesters' stated goal is the same as Prayuth's: creating *true democracy* through authoritarian rule, a confounding notion that is popular among the Thai urban elite.'

Prayuth has the newspaper editors on his side; one newspaper claimed he was the 'best looking boy' at his school. He even wrote a song, *Return Happiness to Thailand* and every radio and television station is forced to play it pretty much incessantly. King Bhumibol Adulyadej approved the takeover by Prayuth in August of 2014 but that was hardly a surprise with the general being so big on royalty.

In a sign of things to come from the paranoid Prime Minister, the *Bangkok Post* reported in September of 2014 that: 'Prime Minister Prayuth Chan-ocha hit out at anti-coup groups Thursday, saying they have resorted to using black magic against him.' The paper reported that Prayuth told a group of government officials: 'today, I have a sore throat, a pain in the neck. Someone said there are some people putting curses on me. I had so much lustral water poured over my head I shivered all over. I'm going to catch a cold.' For those not educated in the black arts, lustral water supposedly wards off curses – but it won't turn a dictator into a democrat.

JOHN PRESCOTT

UK HOUSE OF LORDS

TWO JAGS

The nickname came from the fact that when Deputy Prime Minister he personally owned one Jaguar and his official chauffeured car was also a Jaguar. He and his wife once travelled 240 metres in one once, from their hotel to the Labour conference, where he gave a speech encouraging the use of public transport.

The former cruise liner steward who talks long and loud about the 'working class' has always managed to live large on their taxes. Not that this has anything to do with Prescott's bulging waistline, which he attributes to an eating disorder brought on by stress and long hours.

Prescott was the 'Quango King' in the decade leading up to the recession and public deficit crisis. As well as being Tony Blair's deputy, he headed up a huge department, 'Environment, Transport and the Regions', that spent massively without creating a single teaching post or hospital bed. This was taken from him in 2006 when an affair with his secretary, Tracey Temple, was revealed to the press. He stayed on as Deputy PM but with a much smaller staff of 18. It later emerged in parliament that this smaller department had run up hotels and meals bills of over £52,000 ($83,000) in just nine months.

He's been in the House of Lords since 2010 and he can't keep his mouth shut. Despite standing shoulder to shoulder with Blair when he stood shoulder to shoulder with George W. Bush in the disastrous invasion of Iraq, he was shouting his opposition to any action against ISIS in 2014. In 2010 he appeared before the Chilcot Inquiry that investigated the run up to the Iraq invasion and said he had doubted the evidence of WMD all along. Although he didn't speak up against the Iraq invasion when he had a chance to, he now describes the ISIS problem as 'a regional religious dispute that we should leave to the Arab nations.' And now, without a trace of irony, Prescott is quoting his old boss as a fount of wisdom when he says, 'Tony Blair said air strikes alone won't destroy ISIS and he's right.'

RICHARD PROSSER

NEW ZEALAND HOUSE OF
REPRESENTATIVES

THE SCOURGE OF WOGISTAN

A member of the New Zealand First Party, Richard Prosser holds a seat in the House of Representatives. He also writes the *Eyes Right* column in *Investigate* magazine. As you can imagine, Prosser is hardly a fan of multiculturalism.

In one such column he wrote, 'if you are a young male, aged between say about 19 and about 35, and you're a Muslim, or you look like a Muslim, or you come from a Muslim country, then you are not welcome to travel on any of the West's airlines.' Instead of flying, he suggested that Muslims could 'go ride a camel'. He further stated that his fellow countrymen were being 'denigrated by a sorry pack of misogynist troglodytes from Wogistan, threatening our way of life and security of travel in the name of their stone age religion, its barbaric attitudes towards women, democracy, and individual choice.'

Considering that Muslims make up less than 1% of New Zealand's population, most level headed people aren't that concerned about the level of threat they pose to the country. But Prosser is anything but level headed. 'Well, I say enough is enough, I say enough pandering to an upstart minority,' he writes. 'I say enough of this cowardly, ineffectual reluctance to address the issue where it really lies. I say we stop hiding behind a facade of misplaced tolerance born of mindless fear.' There was a reason behind Prosser's rant: his pocket knife was once confiscated by airport security. Naturally, there was a bit of criticism for the self-styled 'Kiwi Nationalist' when the article came out. At first he refused to apologise, saying his writing style bore similarities to a radio 'shock jock' but he later said that it may have lacked 'balance'.

Prosser has a host of other right-wing beliefs including universal conscription and banning burqas.

VLADIMIR PUTIN

PRESIDENT OF RUSSIA

LATENTLY GAY?

George W. Bush used to call him 'ostrich legs' behind his back and sometimes 'Pootie-Poot'. According to the *Daily Mail*, 'A new biography of Vladimir Putin paints a picture of the Russian president as a traumatised man and speculates that he might be homosexual.

Moscow political scientist Stanislav Belkovsky's book *Putin* claims the rumoured affair between the president and an Olympic gymnast was an invention by his PR team and that he might be 'latently gay'. One can almost guarantee that Belkovsky's book isn't favourite bedtime reading for Russia's strongman, but perhaps he ordered the invasion of the Ukraine in 2014 because of repressed homosexual desire. But, perverse at it may seem he's certainly the heartthrob of many far-right politicians in mainland Europe and even some in America).

Here's a case in point: the ultra-conservative American politician (and spectacularly unsuccessful presidential candidate), Newt Gingrich, thinks Putin 'is arguably the most effective leader in the world today' and thinks 'Obama's foreign policy is dangerous, delusional and utterly incapable of understanding or coping with a serious leader like Putin.'

Ben Judah, writing for the *Sunday Times* has a much more nuanced take on Russia's leader, saying: 'he is driven by fear. Behind the bravado at home, the animal stunts and the Russian tricolour fluttering over warships in Crimea, lies a vulnerable, isolated and haunted man. Too many trillions have been stolen, too many oligarchs have been crushed, too many politicians humiliated, for Putin to resign without facing trial'. Putin has been getting a popularity boost at home due to his successful annexation of Crimea and comments about how he could take Kiev in two weeks. But the winter hasn't set in yet and, now with European food no longer available in the shops and prices rising for basic products, it might be time for Putin to go for broke.

NAIM QASSEM

DEPUTY SECRETARY-
GENERAL OF HEZBOLLAH

UNLIKELY ALLY

He's not the only one to be a little wary about hooking up with the 'Great Satan' to defeat the Islamic State of Iraq and Syria (ISIS). Now that the United States and its allies are fighting the same battle as *Hezbollah*, with the countenance of Israel and to the joy of Iran, there is an eerie feeling spreading over southern Beirut.

The Deputy Secretary General of the Party of God (who can argue with that) spent a good deal of 2014 buzzing between Tehran and Beirut and speaking of a supposedly secret agenda America has in Syria, as if his own paramilitary forces don't have their own plan. According to *Al-bawaba News*, he said, 'those who delve deeper into the American stance will notice that Americans accept ISIS in our region while trying to prevent it from spreading to their country. Terminating ISIS is not being considered at all.' Qassem seems to believe a combined Lebanese Army-*Hezbollah* attack on the extremists would 'wipe them out', although he should take a long look at the 1960s tanks and weapons the small Lebanese Army has at its disposal before teaming up with them. The fact is, if America and its European and regional allies could defeat ISIS, then *Hezbollah* would lose face, which would be as unthinkable as falling in love with Israel.

Bizarrely, Qassem told the Iranian Fars News Agency that, 'since the beginning, the US supported the ISIS and thought that it could use the group for confronting the Islamic Republic of Iran and the regional nations to rearrange the regional structure. They attempted to overthrow the Syrian government and annihilate it by the help of this group.'

Now, if that is not convoluted enough, Qassem has personally identified the real culprit behind the rise of ISIS: Israel. If that makes sense to you, don your keffiyeh, and march down to southern Beirut and sign up.

RUTFUR RAHMAN

MAYOR OF TOWER HAMLETS

LOVE HIM OR LOATHE HIM

It may be beyond a lot of people why the Borough of Tower Hamlets needed a directly elected mayor in the first place. It lies in Greater London, which already has a mayor in the person of Boris Johnson.

It may have just been an exercise in egotism, but the Tower Hamlets First candidate, Lutfur Rahman, seems to have taken the crown by 3,000 votes in elections that were held in 2014.

He ran against the Labour candidate, John Biggs, who cried foul after the vote was counted. A group of petitioners presented a dossier of what they called 'vote rigging' claims against Rahman in court in August of 2014. According to the *Evening Standard* newspaper, the council staff were faced with a sacking unless 'they did not obtain 100 votes each for him' through postal votes. Rahman faced a high court challenge in 2014 over the charges.

The *Guardian* sees things differently, saying, 'there had been a concerted effort by the media and political establishment to smear Rahman', adding that, 'there is a deep substrate of racism informing this.' Further to the right, the *Daily Mail* reported that, in July of 2014 while Israel was bombing the Gaza Strip, 'Tower Hamlet's Muslim mayor, Lutfur Rahman, sparked a storm of protest tonight after raising the Palestinian flag over the town hall in solidarity with Gaza.' (As if that would help.) The *Independent* calls Rahman, 'an already controversial figure accused of links to Islamic extremism.'

Perhaps the varied opinions about Rahman stem from the strange mix of people who live or work in Tower Hamlets. It's the home to some of the largest financial institutions in the world and had the biggest concentration of people of Bangladeshi descent in London. There are more than a few bankers pulling in more that £1 million ($1.6 million) per year working in the borough while four out of ten of the children living there are being raised in poverty.

MARIANO RAJOY

PRIME MINISTER OF SPAIN

ANGIE'S BOY

He has survived a serious car smash and he walked away with a broken finger when the helicopter he was riding in crashed and was completely destroyed. He's also survived in politics and now is the Prime Minister of Spain representing the Popular Party (PP), taking the job in 2011.

If Fidel Castro despises you then you must be doing something right. The former Cuban leader describes Rajoy as a 'facist' and 'an admirer of Franco'. On the other hand, Angela Merkel actually endorsed him, which would be the kiss of death for leaders in most southern European countries.

He's toned down his party's rhetoric over ETA , the Basque separatist movement, but is firmly opposed to any referendum in Catalonia where there is much support for independence. He's also done something of a good job revitalising the country's moribund economy and has led an export drive. Everything was going along just fine for Rajoy until Luis Bárcenas came along.

Bárcenas is the former PP treasurer of Rajoy's party and he had millions stashed away in secret Swiss bank accounts, which the opposition claimed was a slush fund to reward PP politicians for business friendly decisions. Rajoy addressed the accusations by claiming that any political scandal that would affect the stability of the government would drive up interest rates and destroy the economic recovery. He accused anyone that believed Bárcenas's confessions of being unpatriotic, effectively denouncing anyone who believed that corruption was rampant.

Fortuitously, Princess Cristina and her husband, Iñaki Urdangarin, the Duke of Palma, just happened to be accused of tax evasion and money laundering in 2013. The case has gripped the nation and made many forget about the allegations made against the PP. For the record, though, Rajoy is one of the few who refuse to believe the princess is guilty of any of the charges and he has publicly declared her innocent, even before the trial started.

S A RAMADASS

FORMER GOVERNMENT MINISTER

RAMADASS GOT SOME ASS

Typically, in the West, if someone is a 'confirmed bachelor' it typically means one thing. Not so with Ramadass, who is a confirmed bachelor. Ramadass represented the *Bharatiya Janata* Party in the Indian Legislative Assembly and was formerly a government minister in charge of medical education and also the minister for the Mysore district. Although he lost his assembly seat last year he hoped to pursue a parliamentary seat in Mysore district in the next election. At least he did until Premakumari put her face in the picture.

According to the *New Indian Express* newspaper, reported on the 12th of February, 2012, 'Former Karnataka minister S A Ramadass was recovering at a private hospital here (Mysore) Wednesday after a suicide bid over an affair with a woman that turned sour. The 54-year-old former *Bharatiya Janata Party* lawmaker suffered cuts in two nerves in the neck region when he tried to hang himself with a bed sheet tied to a ceiling fan in a guesthouse room. He was rushed to a hospital in an unconscious state.' (He recovered.) The newspaper further added, 'Ramadass a bachelor, took that extreme step as he was upset on learning that a woman, who claimed he married her recently, threatened to expose their relationship to the media with audio and video evidence. The incident happened within hours after the woman, Premakumari, alleged that Ramadass cheated on her after having an affair over the past five years with Premakumari assurance of marriage.'

Premakumari also claimed that Ramadass 'married' her in a private ceremony (nobody else was there) in front of a family 'deity'. The west Indian news service, *Daigiworld*, reported that as Premakumari was about to hold her press conference she got a call on her mobile and put on speakerphone for all to hear, and a man she claimed to be Ramadass told her, 'don't do anything, or else I will consume poison and commit suicide.' The news service quoted her as saying, 'Ramadass married me unofficially at his home. Now he should marry me openly and accept me as his wife'. After the dust settled and the politician got back on his feet, he told the media that Premakumari was 'mentally unstable.'

KOSOVO PARTY LEADER

#BURNISISFLAGCHALLENGE

In an upbeat article in the *Telegraph* newspaper, travel writer Tom Rowley wrote: 'Kosovo as a country once famous for war begins to embrace tourism', which brings up the question of whether the author ever actually travelled to the country he is writing about. If you are thinking about going to Kosovo: stop. It's a shithole.

This is a country where a urologist, Lutfi Dervishi, and four others were found guilty of trafficking in human organs, which they procured from duped patients and basically left to die afterwards. There are claims that senior politicians in the government trafficked in human organs during the war of liberation. Add Fuad Ramiqi to the mix and it's a sure recipe to stir up a dish of misery.

Ramiqi is leader of the hard-line Islamic Movement Unite (LISBA), which doesn't quite embrace an open attitude towards other beliefs. He was nabbed by the cops in October 2014 for being 'suspected of committing criminal offences against the constitutional order and security of the Republic of Kosovo.' What they mean by that can be summed up in one word: *terrorism*. Also picked up in the police swoop was the imam of the Grand Mosque in Priština. What LISBA wants to do is have Islam taught in schools and for women to be 'allowed' to wear the hijab in public places but Kosovo police already picked up 40 suspected Islamist militants in August 2014 who had fought for the ISIS.

80% of Kosovo is Muslim and there is a strong element of moderate spiritual Sufism in the country, but Ramiqi and his followers are exponents of Saudi-financed Wahhabism. He started leading public prayer services in the street of Priština and has called for the construction of a mega-mosque in the capital. What Ramiqi has accomplished is far from what he wanted. Instead of radicalising the youth of Kosovo, he inadvertently started the 'burn the ISIS flag movement' that swept through the region after news of his arrest became public. Instead of America's 'ice bucket challenge' the Balkans now have #BurnISISFlagChallenge.

ROBERT RANSDELL

CANDIDATE FOR
US SENATE

POETIC BIGOTRY

Who doesn't love a rhyming campaign slogan? The candidate for the US Senate from Kentucky is standing up for the repressed white majority in America: the 'sheeple' who are under the thumb of the Jews, the African-Americans, Native Americans and illegal immigrants who are really calling the shots in the Land of the Free.

It's against the law in Kentucky to take down a campaign poster so the white signs with the slogan 'With Jews We Lose' are becoming ubiquitous in the Bluegrass State.

Ransdell is a white supremacist, former organiser for the National Alliance and is waging a battle against 'anti-White lemmings'. Speaking at the University of Kentucky's 'Constitution Day' in September, 2014, Ransdell spoke of the 'need for this nation's white majority to recognize that they have ethnic interests' and complained that his message was not getting through to the public because of the 'Jewish-owned and controlled media'.

He's on the ballot as a write-in candidate facing the Republican incumbent, Senate Minority Leader Mitch McConnell, the Democratic candidate, Kentucky Secretary of State Alison Lundergan Grimes and the Libertarian David Patterson. His campaign platform calls for the dismantling of 'Jewish control' of the media, ending US support for Israel, stopping intervention in Muslim countries, deporting all Muslims living in America and instituting 'White Guard' patrols in high-crime areas. The 'White Guard' patrols would, Ransdell states, be solely defensive and intervene only when white people are being attacked.

Jews make up 0.3% of the population in Kentucky and, in real numbers, there are fewer Jews in the state today than there were in 1899.

FORMER STATE TREASURER OF SOUTH CAROLINA

THE MAN WITH THE GOLDEN NOSE

They grow 'em crazy in South Carolina, where Thomas Ravenel was once State Treasurer. He was fired by Governor Mark Sanford (of whom more presently).

In 2007 Ravenel was indicted by the federal government for purchasing less than 500 grams of cocaine with the intent to distribute the drug. He pleaded guilty and did ten months inside.

Somehow he's now starring in a reality TV series called *Southern Charm* that chronicles the lives of six friends. He's in his fifties and he's got a thing going with a 22-year-old heiress, which apparently makes good viewing. He's now thrown his hat back in the political ring and is now running for the US Senate, challenging Republican Senator Lindsay (he's straight) Graham. According to the *Daily Mail*, 'His felony conviction bars him from holding state office, but in South Carolina a felon can be elected to Congress. Ravenel presented about 16,500 signatures from registered voters on Monday. If election officials verify the signatures, he will be an independent on the November ballot.'

The paper further stated that, 'the first to cheer on the 51-year-old's run for office is Kathryn Dennis, his 22-year-old girlfriend, *Southern Charm* co-star and the mother of his child. Ravenel, a millionaire real estate developer, hasn't announced plans to marry Dennis, but the two appear to be together. Dennis has posted dozens of pictures on her social media accounts of Ravenel with his adorable daughter.'

According to the *Charleston Post & Courier*, 'Ravenel said he plans to accept the $5,000 per episode he's being paid to appear on *Southern Charm* and that nothing in federal election law prohibits it'. Just to give you a sense of how crazy politics are in South Carolina, the sitting senator, Lindsey Graham, 'demanded an invasion of Syria in 2013, claiming that Iran would nuke the Port of Charleston if American troops didn't intervene'. So Ravenel has an incumbent, a Democrat and a Libertarian to defeat, but he might just pull it off.

MARK RECKLESS

UK HOUSE OF COMMONS

THE FLIGHT OF THE LOONS (PT 2)

In 2013 it was found that only 22% of Brits knew who their MP was, which is 1% less than those who professed satisfaction with their representation in parliament. Something like 57% don't even know that they elect representatives to the European Parliament. So, when Mark Reckless announced in late 2014 that he was leaving the Conservative Party and joining the UK Independence Party (UKIP) he probably did so in the mistaken belief that his constituents would give a shit.

The political chattering class was in uproar because he was the second Tory MP that year to jump ship and join the crazies, but the people of Rochester and Strood probably wouldn't recognise their MP if passed out on his back in the public park.

UKIP wants Britain to leave the European Union and for immigrants to go home. So far, that's just about all they stand for. They are led by an amiable idiot, Nigel Farage, whose only commendable trait is an ability to laugh at himself, whereas the Conservative party is led by a privileged, private school crowd who are about as 'in touch' with their constituents as Kim Jong-un is with the people of North Korea. The Labour party are equally ineffective and the Liberal Democrats are sounding out a death rattle.

Besides missing a vote on the budget in 2010 because he was shit faced, Reckless has done little of note in his political career. In his resignation speech he could only muster up a banal 'Britain could be better' comment before he walked out of parliament only to stand again for the seat on a different party ticket. On his website, Reckless mentions that he is devoted to 'particularly trying to stop a large inflow of migrants from Romania and Bulgaria.' If he wins his seat back under the UKIP ticket he just might be able to do that because in the unlikely event that they can persuade the country to pull out of the EU, it can basically close its doors for business. Then the Romanians and Bulgarians will be the ones grumbling about British immigrants.

UK HOUSE OF COMMONS

NANNY'S BEST BOY

No British Labour Party lampoon of their Conservative opponents could ever live up to the reality that is Jacob Rees-Mogg, an Eton-educated merchant banker; long, thin and gangly with the sort of accent usually reserved for a PG Wodehouse farce.

Responding to critics, Rees-Mogg once stated that the accent of Labour's then Deputy Prime Minister, John Prescott, 'certainly stereotypes him as an oaf'. No doubt this impressed thousands of Yorkshire voters who also thought Prescott an oaf, but not for an accent similar to their own. He later admitted: 'I gradually realised that whatever I happened to be speaking about, the number of voters in my favour dropped as soon as I opened my mouth.'

In 1997, with the tactical genius that has enabled the UK's Conservatives to maintain a steady retreat from northern Britain over five decades, they decided to deploy our archetypal Southern English toff in the largely urban Scottish constituency of Central Fife just south of Dundee. Across Scotland, already joyous Labour and Scottish National Party supporters almost wet themselves with glee when it was reported that Rees-Mogg was out campaigning with his nanny and in his Bentley. 'Of course I took Nanny!' he said. 'But I didn't drive the Bentley – I couldn't afford the petrol – so it was the Merc.'

Though the locals treated him well, the Conservative vote in Fife was halved. His reward was a shot at the winnable English Midlands seat of The Wrekin, which he blew with a 1% swing against him despite his party securing a positive 3.5% nationally. But British Conservatives aren't like US Republicans: they aren't unkind to losers, especially if they went to the right school. So Rees-Mogg now has a safe parliamentary seat in his native Somerset and a bigger stage from which to open his mouth and lose his party even more voters across the nation. In the recent referendum on the future of the United Kingdom the voters of Dundee turned out to be the staunchest supporters of Scottish Independence.

CARLIE RITCH

**CANDIDATE FOR MAYOR
OF TORONTO**

MIZZ BARBIE BITCH

Who isn't up for a little hardcore discipline every once and a while? There's nothing that gets the blood flowing better than to be tied, spread-eagled to a St Andrew's cross and have a leather-clad dominatrix whip you until your whole backside is redder than a boiled lobster.

According to Toronto's mayoral candidate, Carlie Ritch, a lot of people in city hall feel the same way. She should know, because the professional dominatrix claims she has a little black book with plenty of prominent people's names in it. She's not about betraying her loyal customers, though; she wants to bring discipline to city hall.

Replacing the crack-smoking, binge drinking Rob Ford is a tall order, but Ritch thinks she's cut out for the job. She doesn't want to raise taxes, she wants to use tolls on roads to finance infrastructure repairs and she wants to convert the Canada Malting building into a concert venue. She told the *National Post* in 2014 that, 'it's about discipline, it's having control in all the right ways.'

She campaigns with a leather riding crop and teaches other women the fine arts of BDSM. Her professional website has an interesting video of her doing creative things with clothes pegs and boasts that her equipment includes paddles, straps, canes and speculums and she is 'looking for submissives to play with, egos to annihilate, wills to crush.'

She told the *Star* newspaper that the reason she was running for mayor was, 'we stand up and say that, you know what, we may be a dominatrix, but at the same time we have morals and principles and we have boundaries.' The mother, grandmother and dominatrix might just be the person to make Toronto even more interesting now that Rob Ford has hung up his hat.

VORELBURG STATE ASSEMBLY

THE CASE OF THE MISSING GNOMES

Gnomes are a big thing in Austria. When a couple marries and buys a house the first thing they do is buy a gnome for the garden. Michael Ritsch thought he could use gnomes to turn around the electoral fortunes of his political party. The SVP (Social Democratic Party) chief in the Austrian province of Vorarlberg isn't going to step down even though he seems to be losing a fighting battle against the OeVP (Austrian People's Party). The left-wing SVP only got 10.9% of the vote in the 2009 election whereas the anti-immigrant Freedom Party garnered 25% of the ballots and the OeVP got 50.8%.

In 2014 Ritsch thought some new thinking might be in order and came up with the idea of 'coolmen' instead of the traditional campaign poster. The coolmen were quirky gnomes, adorned with sunglasses and hats and hung from lamp posts around the streets of the province. Ritsch had 20,000 of them made, and they were popular up until the day 400 of them disappeared on August 24, 2014.

Ritsch wasn't amused by that in the slightest. 'I suspect our rival party OeVP to have removed the gnomes', he said in a statement to the media. He immediately went to the police and reported the theft. A spokesperson for the OeVP issued a statement strenuously denying that the party had anything to do with the theft and cleverly suggested that the gnomes may have just got fed up with the left-wing politics of the SVP and walked off the job. But Ritsch wasn't having that and came out and said, 'All of our gnomes are 40 centimetres tall. The thieves must have needed more than just one truck to steal them'. He also pointed out that the missing gnomes were replaced by OeVP campaign posters. The SVP wisely spent $660,000 on the gnomes and the money actually came from the Austrian government, which subsidises campaign expenses for the parties.

JOSÉ RIVERA

NEW YORK STATE ASSEMBLY

DA BRONX

He represents the Borough of the Bronx, a rough and tumble place that has a large Hispanic population. He considers himself a progressive, a stand up guy for the working man and someone who helped organise the thousands of drivers of 'gypsy cabs' that roam the streets of the city that never sleeps. He's also known for a few other things.

According to the *Village Voice*, 'The newly elected leader of the Bronx Democratic party, state assemblyman, José Rivera, was once such a rolling stone that city investigators found he never lived at three different Bronx addresses he claimed as legal residences over a five-year period. Although no action was ever taken against Rivera, the city's Department of Investigation reported in 1987 that he not only lied about where he lived but also failed to disclose an old gun conviction that sent him to jail for a seven-month stretch back in the late 1950s.'

That was a while ago, but Rivera got in the news in 2014 for an entirely different matter. According to the *New York Daily News*, 'A video emerged Tuesday of 77-year-old José Rivera (D-Bronx) lewdly chatting up young women during a visit to the Dominican Republic.' The newspaper reported that he asked one younger woman, 'what are your body measurements?' and then asking another woman, 'Do you happen to have a little sister?' The video also shows Rivera joking with a street vendor about drinking a mamajuana, a concoction of rum, wine and tree bark that is supposed to be an aphrodisiac. The *Daily Mail* reports that 'after swigging the concoction he says in Spanish he feels strong enough to get laid with all those young ones.'

He's not worried that his antics will affect his election chances, though. According to the *Norwood News*, 'Rivera, known for his hats and propensity to film gatherings, represents a district that has the second lowest voter turnout record in the Bronx within the last decade'.

PAM ROACH

WASHINGTON STATE SENATE

'ROACHED'

Even her fellow Republicans think she has a problem. In 2010 she was banned from the Republican Caucus because of 'anger management issues.' She's not only a nut, but an angry one at that. According to the *Seattle Times*, Roach was sent a letter from the Republican leadership that said, 'it would be best to physically separate you from the caucus staff and from other Republican Senators while we are working on the floor.' The newspaper further quoted unnamed sources as saying she could go 'from zero to ten on the angry scale' in an instant and victims of her vitriol describe it as being 'Roached.'

Roach is fighting back, claiming it is all a vast conspiracy against her. She told North West Public Radio that, 'this is the largest, most concentrated effort to ruin somebody's name in the legislature that has ever happened in state history.' Like any good Republican with an anger management issue, Roach proudly packs an AR-15 assault rifle, which is the 'civilian equivalent' to the M16 that the US military uses. According to KOMO News, Roach, who organises a legislative shoot out every year at a firing range near the capital, is against Initiative 594 that would require some background checks on the nutcases who feel they need to purchase numerous assault weapons. '594 has been devised to make it much more difficult for people, for individuals, to exercise their 2nd amendment rights,' she said.

The *Associated Press* reported that Roach's behaviour hasn't improved after counselling and, during a recent argument with another senator, she was 'exceptionally loud and angry, and using highly inflammatory, accusatory, hostile, personal attack language' for up to ten minutes. Maybe her anger management issues are partly the motivation for opposing Initiative 594: Roach's background check just might result in her precious AR-15 being taken from her hands.

ART ROBINSON

CHAIRMAN OF OREGON
REPUBLICAN PARTY

PSEUDOSCIENTIST

In an article published in *Access to Energy* Robinson recommended a unique solution for the disposal of nuclear waste: 'wastes dumped into the deep ocean will soon reach the bottom, where they are less hazardous than nearly any other place on Earth'.

Art Robinson is crazy in ways too crazy to measure. He's running again in the 2014 elections for the US House of Representatives and will probably lose by a landslide again, just like he did the previous two times. He wants to abolish the public (state) school system and remove all taxes on energy. He wants to abolish the Federal Reserve banking system and is a signatory to *A Scientific Dissent from Darwinism*.

Robinson is also an AIDS denier and published yet another article where he wrote: 'AIDS may be little more than a general classification of deaths resulting from exposure to homosexual behavior.'

Rachel Maddow interviewed Robinson on MSNBC and used some of his own quotes to question his beliefs and the Republican candidate imploded in a rather spectacular fashion, claiming later that he was 'stitched up'. Among his stranger scientific positions is his advocacy for 'hormesis', which is a belief that low-level radiation doses are good for health and Robinson believes it should be used to 'enhance' Oregon's drinking water.

In his past he co-wrote *Fighting Chance: Ten Feet to Survival* with Gary North, a far right Christian economist who believes that economic study 'must begin with the biblical story of creation'. The book was about surviving a nuclear war.

Considering he spent over $1 million running against his Democratic opponent, Peter DeFazio, and lost by over 20% of the vote, there's little chance this nutcase from Oregon will show up in the US Congress in 2015.

DEBBIE ROBINSON

AUSTRALIAN PARTY LEADER

Q-TIP

Politics *as a business* used to be strictly an American thing.

The way it works is you gin up the public about shit that's not going to happen and get them on the bandwagon and their wallets opened up and get them to buy books about imaginary threats to society. Regnery Publishing in America virtually cornered the market on right-wing books until the other publishers woke up and started their own imprints for books that addressed imaginary problems. *Take no Prisoners* by David Horowitz is a new release by Regnery and, according to the publisher, 'Horowitz says it's time for conservatives to take the gloves off—and take our country back.' There are dozens of books like Horowitz's published every month in America; they all tell the same story, and they sell like hotcakes.

Debbie Robinson is head of the mysterious anti-Islamic 'Q-Group' and is now running for office in Australia for the Australian Liberty Alliance party, which has just been registered in Western Australia. Its avowed goal is to stop the Islamisation of Australia, as if that's going to really happen. It's got the backing of the Dutch nutcase, Geert Wilders, so you know it's all bollocks. 'Many of you are disappointed with current political parties and have had enough of politicians who sell out western civilisation,' said Wilders when speaking about the founding of the party.

Speaking of any links between the 'Q-Group' and the new political party, Robinson said there were no direct links but, 'individuals connected with the society are in the process of forming a political movement.' Wait till next year when Robinson comes out with her own book about 'taking the country back' from extreme Islam. The fact that she has no political experience won't matter and it's better for sales if she loses. If she won, the ominous threat of Islam taking over Western Australia would be revealed for what it is.

DIMITRY ROGOZIN

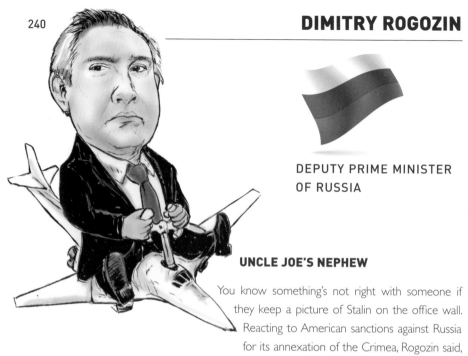

DEPUTY PRIME MINISTER OF RUSSIA

UNCLE JOE'S NEPHEW

You know something's not right with someone if they keep a picture of Stalin on the office wall. Reacting to American sanctions against Russia for its annexation of the Crimea, Rogozin said, 'after analyzing the sanctions against our space industry, I suggest that the USA bring their astronauts to the International Space Station using a trampoline.'

It wouldn't be so bad if he was just a random Russian who has a distate for the west, but Dmitry Rogozin isn't a nobody: he's the Deputy Prime Minister of Russia. When told his plane couldn't fly over Romania, Rogozin said this: 'upon the US request, Romania has closed its airspace for my plane. If they don't allow me to pass through again, next time I'll fly on board a Tu-160 (the world's fastest nuclear bomber).' The US government has banned him from travelling to the United States and frozen all his financial assets there.

He's big on Twitter and posted a message recently showing Vladimir Putin holding a small leopard and Barack Obama holding a small white dog. This demonstrated, according to Rogozin, a 'difference in values' and also clearly indicated that the Russian president was 'manlier' than his American counterpart. Rogozin also holds a post as Head of the Military-Industrial Commission (the defence industry) and is frequently pictured examining assault weapons. One of his pet projects is to change back the name of Volgograd to Stalingrad – although even his boss seems too rational to support the move.

In his former job as Russia's ambassador to NATO, Rogozin spent much of his time photographing himself shooting things while his wife, Tatiana Rogozina, recorded and released a pop album (it was awful). She still likes to sing at diplomatic receptions although not many diplomats want to be seen with Rogozin.

MINISTER OF ECOLOGY AND ENERGY

DELIGHTFUL BUT DIM

America may have Bachman and Palin but France has Ségolène Royal. Although they may hold different political views, there's no denying that they're all pretty hot looking. Royal may win hands down in terms of class and sophistication but in terms of mental acuity she's in the same ballpark.

Ségolène lost her 2007 bid for the French presidency to Nicolas Sarkozy who is famously married to the hot ex-model and singer, Carla Bruni, who's also on the dim side.

Ségolène's ex-partner and father of her four children (they never married, regarding the institution as too bourgeois for their socialist credentials) is the unpopular and charisma-free French President, François Hollande. He left Ségolène for Valerie Trierweiler, who wasn't nearly as hot, then dumped her for actress, Julie Gayet, who is both hot and vacuous. It makes for interesting reading but France's situation might be improved if its politicians paid a more attention to running the country than scratching their libidos.

In 2013, Ségolène thought the country needed a moral boost, so she posed as the legendary French revolutionary figure, Marianne, in Le Parisien Magazine, trying to recreate Eugene Delacroix's famous painting, Liberty Leading the People. This generally prompted howls of laughter and derision from the public but Hollande was so impressed he appointed her Minister of Ecology and Energy, a post for which she is thoroughly unqualified.

She recently published a book, Cette belle idee du courage (A Grand Vision of Courage), in which she attributed a quote to Franklin Roosevelt, that was actually uttered by Theodore Roosevelt. During her presidential campaign she travelled to Lebanon and met a member of Hezbollah who criticised both the 'Nazi-like' attitude of Israel and the US administration that he said suffered from a case of 'unlimited dementia'. She astutely replied that she agreed with a lot of what he said, 'notably your analysis of the United States'. She followed this up by appearing to endorse the independence of Quebec on a visit to Canada.

In 2014 the Telegraph reported that despite her egalitarian affiliations she'd upset civil servants in her ministry with an edict that staff should stand up when she passes; an usher would precede her to announce her presence.

The list goes on… but she does know how to dress and loves the camera.

MOHD ALI RUSTAM

MALAYSIAN SENATE

CHINESE BASHER

Malaysia is a multi-ethnic country, with Malays making up about 60% of the population, ethnic Chinese composing about 23% and ethnic Indians making up about 7%. It's not a perfect society in that the Chinese and the Indians often don't share the same faith as the Malay population, who are almost overwhelmingly Muslim. But the minorities do vote and it doesn't help a politician to insult them.

Mohd Ali heads the *Perbadanan Usahawan Nasional Berhad* (PUNB) party and is the former chief minister of the Malaysian state of Melaka (Malacca) and now a Federal Senator – though he lost his run for the Vice Presidency in 2013, probably because of some of the things he said.

According to the *Malaysian Insider*, 'Mohd Ali allegedly said that the Chinese were behind all illegal businesses in the country', saying, 'we (Muslim Malays) can't have casinos, 4D, Toto, gambling, lottery, massage parlours, ah long. These are all illegal. And the Chinese are the ones dabbling with all the illegal businesses.' He defended his remarks to the *Insider*, saying, 'I am just saying that the Chinese can run certain businesses that are haram (forbidden) for Muslims – casinos, lotteries, gambling and ah long. It is haram for Muslims to run these businesses although they have the permits to do so.'

In 2012 Mohd Ali also threw something of a fit at Malaysia's first gay marriage. According to *Gay Star News*, 'the chief minister said that Reverend O Young Wen Feng (also known as Ngeo Boon Lin) and his husband Phineas Newborn III are clearly challenging the laws and the values of our country, especially in the month of Ramadan'. The news site went on to add that, 'Newborn, an American musical producer, commented about being part of the first publicised gay marriage celebration in Malaysia, saying: "We're thankful to be able to make Malaysian history"'.

FORMER PRESIDENT
OF GEORGIA

NOT HIM AGAIN

He was the darling of the neoconservatives and, when he poked the bear a bit too hard and started to suffer the consequences, it was the US Senator, John McCain, who uttered one of the most stupid statements of his life: 'we are all Georgians now'.

The founder of the United National Movement served as President of Georgia for two terms, from 2004 to 2013. He was voted in on a platform of reform and economic liberalism but he had two thorns in his side throughout his tenure in office: Abkhazia and South Ossetia. These regions broke off from the rest of Georgia and aligned themselves with Russia whilst Saakashvili sought better ties with the West and NATO. Georgia was one of the biggest contributors to the 'coalition of the willing' in the Second Iraq War.

On the 7th of August, 2008, in response to harassing artillery fire from South Ossetia, Georgia invaded the breakaway region and sparked the Russo-Georgian War. Many in the West thought the Georgian Army, with its NATO quality weaponry and some training could stand up to a Russian advance. They were really wrong. It lasted all of five days. The Russian 58th Army routed the Georgian forces and occupied a good part of the country until they withdrew in October.

When Saakashvili was booted out of office in 2013, he took a teaching job with Tufts University in America. Now he's plotting a triumphal return to Georgian politics and he's found the perfect place to do it from: his uncle's apartment in Brooklyn. Back home he has a couple of prosecutors waiting for him to show his face so they can slap some embezzlement charges on him, but the now rotund ex-president says they are politically motivated. Saakashvili thinks the Russian invasion of the Ukraine in 2014 will galvanise opinion in Georgia around him.

TAKUMA SAKURAGI

INAZAWA MUNICIPAL
ASSEMBLY

CRYSTAL PALACE

They're known as the Senkaku Islands in Japan and the Diaoyu in the People's Republic of China. The uninhabited islands are claimed by both countries, particularly now that there's evidence that there may be significant oil reserves in the waters surrounding them.

Takuma Sakuragi, a member of the Inazawa Municipal Assembly in Aichi prefecture, has been vocal in his belief that the Senkaku Islands belong to Japan and that may be reason he went on trial in August of 2014 for drug smuggling, or it may not.

It seems unlikely that someone over 70 would attempt to smuggle 3,289 grams of crystal meth into Japan, but the cops nabbed him at Guangzhou's Baiyuan International Airport on October 31st, 2013 with luggage given to him by a Nigerian, Gemadi Hassan, containing women's platform shoes stuffed with 28 bags of the drugs. He's being tried with Aly Yattabare, from Mali, and Mohamed Soumah, from Guinea. Sakuragi claims it's a politically motivated frame-up.

The accused has been re-elected five times to his local assembly and has served since 1995. Anyone found guilty of possessing over 50 grams of meth is subject to the death penalty in China. The People's Republic has no problem with executing foreigners for drugs. It executed four Japanese drug runners in 2010, as well as one Briton and put another Japanese to death in 2014 for drug related charges. One of the Japanese it pulled the plug on was over 65 and had 1.5 kilograms of meth on him.

Working in Sakuragi's favour is evidence he was duped by the Nigerian, Hassan, and lost over $700,000. His Finnish wife took the stand in his trial and testified that he is a 'good Christian, a decent politician and a lousy businessman'. The prosecution is calling for the death penalty in Sakuragi's case and the defence is hoping for an acquittal.

SCOTTISH PARLIAMENT

THE LAST KING OF SCOTLAND

The man who almost brought an end to one of the world's oldest and most stable democracies does have a degree of charisma or he wouldn't have become Scotland's First Minister. But, all in all, he really is a brusque, pompous ass who actually thought he could hoodwink the Scots into taking a walk on the wild side.

He's the son of civil servants, he married a civil servant (17 years his senior) and he's been getting paid by the British government for years, so it's pretty obvious he's not a risk taker by nature. Furthermore, he actually likes country and western music and, more astonishingly, believes that renewable energy actually works. He also counts Rupert Murdoch as one of his BFFs. So what's not to like about Salmond?

He likes to live large off the British government, for one thing. He blew a few grand of its money to go to a golf tournament in Chicago. He used to claim up to £400 on expenses from Westminster each month, although he seldom bothered to go there. He opposed NATO intervention into Serbia saying it was, 'an act of dubious legality, but above all one of unpardonable folly,' even though the world was bearing witness to daily scenes of ethnic cleansing.

He sold the voters on the idea that an independent Scotland would be readily welcomed into the European Union knowing full well that other countries with separatist movements, like Spain and Belgium, would have thought long and hard about Scotland's admittance. He argued that Scotland could keep the pound knowing full well that the decision would not have been up to the Scots to make. He argued that independence was the best way of safeguarding the National Health Service – a British institution brought about by a Welshman – even though the funding and management of the NHS in Scotland was already in his own remit under existing devolved powers. In the end he blew £13.3 million to find out what everyone knew all along: that the Scots are too smart to break up what they themselves had such a major role in creating.

MARK SANFORD

US HOUSE OF REPRESENTATIVES

THE LOVE MACHINE

South Carolina is one of the reddest states in the US and it's the home of Parris Island, which is where anyone east of the Mississippi receives their basic training in the United States Marine Corps. The state bristles with military installations: it's where men are men, the women stand by their man and Democrats are sissies. It's also a state that continuously re-elects Lindsey (he's straight) Graham to the US Senate and recently elected the former governor, Mark Sanford to the US House of Representatives.

The latter individual should have been run out of the state on rails solely on a question of good taste. First of all, he once had a sizzlingly attractive wife in the person of Jenny Sanford. Granted, she's a bit zealously religious which might have precluded some interesting marital activities, but those are issues that could be worked on.

But that's not what Sanford's about. When he was governor he did a disappearing act in June of 2009 for six days. His staff, who were left in the dark, told reporters that the governor was 'hiking the Appalachian Trail', which has since become an all purpose euphemism for cheating. He didn't tell anyone where he was going but he returned with a sheepish grin and an Argentinean señorita, Maria Belén Chapur, and promptly dumped his wife. In turn, Jenny Sanford did a photo spread in *Vogue* just to show Sanford what an idiot he was and likened his cheating heart to a 'pornography addiction'.

Sanford's term as governor expired in 2011 and in 2013 he ran for the US House of Representatives and won. In September of 2014, in an act of exceedingly bad taste, Sanford announced on his Facebook page that he was dumping his Argentinian babe because of ongoing child custody disputes with his ex-wife. He wrote a 2,346 word explanation to his constituents about the matter, explaining that, 'in as much as you sign my paycheck and you have elected me to represent you in Washington, I think I owe you my thinking on this personal, but now public matter.' That could be true but it also may be a way for the 'love machine' to lay the groundwork for a new, hotter and younger babe in his life.

PEDRO NUNO SANTOS

PORTUGUESE ASSEMBLY OF THE REPUBLIC

DEBT BOMB

'We have an atomic bomb that we can use in the face of the Germans and the French: this atomic bomb is simply that we won't pay,' said Nuno Santos on the floor of the Portuguese Assembly in 2011. The vice-president of Portugal's parliamentary Socialist Party said this as his country's economy shrank by 3% after accepting a €78 billion bailout under severe austerity conditions.

According to the *Telegraph*, 'Nuno Santos said Europe's southern states should join forces to resist the austerity dictats and contractionary policies being imposed by the core powers.' Described as part of a new generation of socialists, Nuno Santos, wants his to be much more strident in their opposition to the ruling party. 'It was discontent against inequalities that brought me into politics,' he told the Portuguese publication *iJournal*, adding that, 'what I have to say is true: most of the problems the Portuguese have are not solved in our country.' (He believes they reside with Brussels.) 'The country must flatly reject the austerity, which is killing our economy: we have to say enough . . . there is no going back and it has unnecessarily destroyed much of our economy,' says Nuno Santos. 'Debt is our only weapon and we must use it to impose better conditions, because recession itself is what is stopping us complying with the (EU-IMF Troika) accord. We should make the legs of the German bankers tremble.'

Nuno Santos also advocates legalising prostitution – which is a big deal in a Catholic country like Portugal – and he's for gay marriage and adoption by same-sex couples saying, 'already there are many same-sex couples who raise children and studies indicate that it does not interfere with the child's growth.'

NICOLAS SARKOZY

FORMER PRESIDENT OF FRANCE

LITTLE BIG MAN

A short man with a short temper. He once said of his rivals 'I'm going to fuck them all in the ass' – and in his meteoric rise to power, culminating in his election as head of state in 2007, he did.

His outbursts – rare in French politics, where politicians have traditionally been known for being obtuse and intellectual – inevitably make the headlines. Perhaps his most famous was during riots on Arab-dominated council estates: he said he would clean the neighbourhoods with a Kärcher pressure cleaner and called the inner-city youths 'scum'. He is also remembered for reacting to a heckler in 2008 with the retort, 'Piss off, you poor twat!'

A recent scandal has been labelled 'Air Cocaine'. According to Le Point, the scheme involved ferrying 'nose candy' from the Dominican Republic in private jets operated by a close friend of Sarkozy. Add to that accusations from Mediapart that his 2007 campaign was financed by Muammar Gadhafi, serious assertions that he wire-tapped judges' phones, and his involvement in an illegal campaign kickback scheme via a PR firm run by two associates of his, and it's clear that 'Sarko' (as he is universally known in France) has been a busy boy. Allegedly.

He's known as the 'king of bling' for his love of Rolex watches, his celebrity wife Carla Bruni, and his friendships with celebrities and billionaires. According to Marianne, Sarkozy's costly 2008 divorce proceedings was funded by the generous Emir of Qatar, who went on to buy up half of Paris – and, funnily enough, got France's vote to host the 2022 World Cup in the Gulf Emirate. Coincidentally.

Sarkozy was portrayed in Jacques Chirac's memoirs as 'irritable, rash, overconfident and allowing for no doubt, least of all regarding himself'. Like Bonaparte before him, though, the short man with a short temper may soon be returning from exile – polls say he has the best chance of anyone on the right of beating far-right Marine Le Pen in 2017.

DANA ROSEMARY SCALLON

FORMER IRISH
PRESIDENTIAL CANDIDATE

THE QUIET AMERICAN

It pays €250,000 a year and it comes with its own house, a palatial mansion surrounded by 1,752 acres of Phoenix Park, near central Dublin. Oh, let's not forget about the staff. Just ring a bell and every whim will be catered to. You may ask what the catch is. Well, there really isn't one. The job is meaningless, you don't really have to do anything and you get to travel for free.

The office of the President of Ireland is mainly ceremonial. It sounds ideal for any American woman, like Dana Rosemary Scallon, except she forgot to tell the Irish people of her secret nationality when she decided to run for president. She has both an Irish and an American passport.

The former MEP and winner of the 1970 Eurovision Song Contest for her rendition of All Kinds of Everything was something of a darling to a certain generation of Mick.

She told the Irish Independent that her secret nationality would be an advantage to the country, saying, 'If I'm elected President I will be in a unique position to strengthen our bonds with the US while making sure our relationship with Europe is based on friendship rather than colonisation.' According to the Irish broadcaster, RTE, 'Scallon's sister, Susan Stein, told a court in Iowa in 2008 that a decision was taken in 1997 not to make the fact public because she said it wouldn't look very good if the people of Ireland knew she was an American citizen.'

Despite the fact that the singer thought the citizenship issue shouldn't be an issue, the voters disagreed. She lost large. Then came a sex scandal involving her brother. According to the Belfast Telegraph, 'John Brown, a brother of the singer-turned-politician (Dana Scallon), faced five counts of indecent assault in the 1970s against two girls under the age of 16, who cannot be identified for legal reasons.' Brown was cleared of the charges and later told the Express newspaper that, 'when this came out in 2011, it was to derail her presidential campaign, that was the purpose.'

GUDRUN SCHYMAN

PARTY LEADER

FUNNY FEMINISM

The *Guardian* says she 'comes across like a fusion of Germaine Greer and Ken Livingstone.' In a country that holds egalitarianism as its ideal, Sweden has been slipping backwards in the last decade with a real wealth disparity forming, although nothing to match the US or the UK.

Schyman's new party, the Feminist Initiative (FI) is shaking the foundations of the centre-right alliance that has governed the country for a considerable time. The former leader of the Left Party was one of the biggest stars on Sweden's version of *Strictly Come Dancing* and counts among her supporters Benny Andersson from *Abba*, the *Cardigans* and Nina Persson. She had to resign her leadership of the Left Party when it emerged that there were expense irregularities in her tax returns. She has fought a long battle with the bottle and famously was caught on camera hopelessly pissed at a film premiere in 1996 but she wants to ban booze at the *Riksdag*, Sweden's Parliament.

In the 2006 elections the FI won only 0.68% of the vote, and this dropped to only 0.4% in 2010. The 2014 Swedish elections could be the party's high point and might put Schyman back in parliament but they need to capture at least 4% of the vote for that to happen and that looks unlikely.

While in parliament previously for the Left Party she tried to institute a special 'man tax' that would cover the cost of shelters and treatment for abused wives. In the run up to the 2010 elections, another of her stunts to promote equality of pay for the sexes was to burn 100,000 kronor ($14,000) in the streets. She is most remembered for her 2002 'Taliban' speech in which she said of discrimination towards women: 'the same standard, the same structure, the same pattern, is repeated as well in Afghanistan under the Taliban... as in Sweden.'

AYELET SHAKED

ISRAELI KNESSET

GREEN EYED GIRL

With her sultry looks and mesmerising green eyes, the youngish member of the Knesset for the Jewish Home Party is hardly what you would expect in a politician but the packaging is doubly misleading. The *Independent* reported how Shaked posted some rather shocking statements on her Facebook page in July, 2014.

According to the newspaper, she wrote: 'behind every terrorist stand dozens of men and women, without whom he could not engage in terrorism. They are all enemy combatants, and their blood shall be on all their heads. Now this also includes the mothers of the martyrs, who send them to hell with flowers and kisses. They should follow their sons, nothing would be more just. They should go, as should the physical homes in which they raised the snakes. Otherwise, more little snakes will be raised there.'

A week earlier she had written, 'this is not a war against terror, and not a war against extremists, and not even a war against the Palestinian Authority. The reality is that this is a war between two people. Who is the enemy? The Palestinian people. Why? Ask them, they started it.'

The *Jewish Home Party* doesn't believe in a two state solution to the Middle Eastern problem, they believe the Jews are 'divinely commanded' to rule the Land of Israel, and that land contains both the 1967 borders of the country and the West Bank. According to the *Charleston Gazette*, Shaked may be the Palestinians' best friend: the newspaper reported how Antony Lerman, former head of the Institute for Jewish Policy Research, said that Jewish American support for Israel is weakening greatly because the government is increasingly dominated by 'extreme religious Zionists and the strictly Orthodox, aided and abetted by Jewish racists in the Knesset like Ayelet Shaked, a Jewish Home Party member who recently called for the mothers of Palestinian 'snakes' to be killed.'

CHANDRA NARINE SHARMA

GUYANA PARTY LEADER

MONSTER OR HERO?

The leader of the Justice For All party in Guyana is all about empowering the poor and disenfranchised. According to the *Guyana Times*, his political platform calls for addressing the, 'allegedly high Value Added Tax, the high cost of living, poor wages and working conditions, and the need for a more robust approach to address the problems facing the sugar and bauxite industries.'

Sharma's not only a politician; he owns a television station in the small South American country. He seems a nice enough bloke but he's got some serious legal problems. According to the *Kaieteur News*, he was nicked in the 'wake of revelations that a 13-year-old girl in a sworn affidavit signed by Justice of the Peace and Commissioner of Oaths to Affidavits Lachman Narine, dated April 12, 2010, recounted a most harrowing tale of repeated rape and sexual molestation of four sisters over several years.'

That was some years ago, but the wheels of justice seem to turn slowly in the former British colony, either that or charges of rape can sometimes be trumped up by a government out to get someone. A year later, Sharma was still free and threatening to close his television station down because the government thought it was too controversial. *Kaieteur News* reported in 2011 that, 'the station closed for a month a few years ago, after a woman during a call-in programme had made what authorities viewed as shooting threats against President Bharrat Jagdeo. It was then closed for four months after Sharma aired footage showing government officials partying during the 2005 floods.' In 2012 the rape allegations seem to have been forgotten but Sharma lost another appeal by the courts to have his television station suspended. In 2013 Sharma was committed to stand trial for the 2010 rape charge but he remained free on $2 million bail.

In 2014, the *Guyana Chronicle* reported that, 'after suffering multiple strokes, the veteran broadcaster (Sharma) returned to the airways to host his popular call-in program, *Voice of the People*. Sharma's health deteriorated following allegations of sexual impropriety by under-aged girls. The matter is still before the High Court.'

SHWE MANN

SPEAKER OF THE
MYANMAR PARLIAMENT

WARLORD

In US diplomatic cables from 2007, published by WikiLeaks 'Shwe Mann appears to also have crony business connections and complicity in human right violations', adding that, 'while he may not be as notoriously corrupt as some of his colleagues, Shwe Mann has solid connections to regime business cronies'.

A lot changed seven years later when, in 2014, he was Speaker of the *Pyithu Hluttaw*, the lower house of the Myanmar parliament, and he announced he was running for president in the 2015 elections.

Of course, that is an honour that the Nobel Laureate Aung San Suu Kyi would like to have, but the country's clique of ruling generals have fixed that. Under Clause 59(f) of the newly written constitution anyone with a relative who has a foreign nationality is not allowed to run for president. That rules her out of the equation because Suu Kyi's recently deceased husband was British and her two children, that he brought up because she was under house arrest for decades, are British nationals. Shwe Mann, who will run for the Union Solidarity and Development Party, is therefore a shoe-in for the job.

Calls have been made to make an exception in the case of Suu Kyi and the USDP seemed at first to oblige by setting up a committee to determine if the public wanted change. Shwe Mann set up a Constitutional Amendment Implementation Committee after Suu Kyi's party, the National League for Democracy, gathered five million signatures on a petition urging repeal of Clause 59(f). Not surprisingly, they concluded that the 'people' wanted to keep Clause 59(f) by an overwhelming percentage notwithstanding the fact that Suu Kyi had been elected to parliament by an even more overwhelming percentage.

The former army divisional commander (more like warlord) had a business whereby he tightly controlled the chemical fertiliser business in the Irrawaddy Delta region of Myanmar and gave allotments of it to rice farmers in return for an unspecified portion of their crop. He also had a construction business and is rumoured to be worth billions of dollars.

VOLEN SIDEROV

BULGARIAN
PARTY LEADER

ATTACK!

He's against just about everything and so is the party he leads, Атака (Attack). The Bulgarian politician, author and newspaper editor has been accused of being anti-Muslim, ultranationalist, anti-Turkey, anti-Semitic, racist, anti-Roma, anti-globalisation and anti-NATO. The *New York Times* once described his persona as 'a studied imitation of Hitler.'

According to the *Sofia Globe*, he and his party are 'apparently headed for political oblivion'. It's not because right-wing politics have gone out of style in Bulgaria, it's because there's a new kid on the block: the *Natzionalen Front za Spasenie na Bulgaria* (National Front for the Salvation of Bulgaria) and its leader, Valeri Simeonov, says anyone from Attack is welcome to join their party provided they're not 'people with mental health problems'. Both parties believe in enshrining the Orthodox Church into the Bulgarian constitution and believe foreign banks and foreign companies should be kept out of the country.

Before reinventing himself as a politician he was a photographer, posed nude for a magazine and studied theology. He wrote two books: *Bumerangut na Zloto* (Evil's Boomerang) and *Vlastta na Mamona* (Mammon's Power), both of which are about supposed Zionist and American conspiracies for world domination and how the Freemasons secretly run the world.

That's when he got his TV gig and started a short show that had the same name as the political party he leads. Атака was a 15 minute ultranationalist rant on Roma crime, the ineptness of the government and the supposed 'Turkification' of the country. It was hugely popular, allowing Siderov's party to gain 21 seats in parliament in 2005. He ran for president in 2006 but failed to capture more than 26% of the vote. Since then things have gone downhill for Siderov. Speaking to the BBC before the elections he said the decline in his share of the vote was 'because of the media blackout placed on the Attack party' and because he 'was misrepresented as an extremist and as a dangerous man.'

GABOR SIMON

HUNGARIAN NATIONAL ASSEMBLY

MILLIONS OF MYSTERIOUS FORINTS

First of all, there are *two* Gabor Simons in Hungary's National Assembly – or there were two a while ago. The first Gabor Simon seems to be a fairly innocuous character. He was born in 1972 and is a jurist and a politician. The *other* Gabor Simon is the interesting one and a source of some mystery.

The former Vice President of the Hungarian Socialist Party was nailed by the *Magyar Nemzet* newspaper in March of 2014 for having about a million dollars hidden in an Austrian bank account. He almost immediately resigned from his post and was lifted by the police for suspicion of forgery and tax evasion. The *Budapest Times* reported that 'later it turned out that he also had an account containing HUF 75 million ($350,000) at Magnet Bank in Budapest. This account was opened with a fake Bissau-Guinean passport in the name Gabriel Derdak.'

Magyar Nemzet newspaper found out that the fake passport was procured from Tamás Welsz, a Hungarian businessman who arranged fake ID for over 500 other prominent Hungarians. According to the *Budapest Times*, 'it was revealed that Simon had a personal safe at Welsz's apartment in Érd (a suburb of Budapest), containing several millions in cash, fake passports … and numerous documents used to cover up the Austrian bank account.' Interpol had a warrant out for Welsz relating to a forgery charge in Panama despite the fact that he had very publicly bought Sólyom Airways. He was arrested but released due to the lack of an extradition agreement between Panama and Hungary and he died in police custody (apparently from natural causes) but not before handing over all his confidential files.

Meanwhile, Simon is under house arrest but, according to the *Budapest Beacon*, has 'accused the government of conducting a show trial and vowed to defend himself and others against the charges.'

ABDEL FATTAH AL-SISI

PRESIDENT OF EGYPT

THE NEW PHARAOH

That democracy thing didn't work out so well for Egypt in the end. If Mohammed Morsi's Muslim Brotherhood hadn't been so spectacularly incompetent, arrogant, dictatorial and dangerous, al-Sisi would still be sitting in a military barracks wondering about his eventual retirement. Now he's a globetrotting president calling on America to take the fight to the Islamic extremists all over the Middle East and brokering deals between *Hamas* and Israel.

He should be concerned. There's still a lot of residual violence in Egypt as supporters of the Muslim Brotherhood are being brutally suppressed and the ISIS have called on their followers to destroy the, 'guards of the Jews, the soldiers of Sisi, the new Pharaoh of Egypt'.

Al-Sisi was sworn into office as President of Egypt in June, 2014, but he had actually been running things for more than a year before since the military took over the country. In a decision he would later regret, Morsi actually appointed al-Sisi as head of the Egyptian military high command.

After al-Sisi took power he became instantly popular and was basically drafted into running for president. He captured 22 of the 23 million votes cast in the election. Since he took office he cut fuel subsidies, slapped taxes on foreign cigarettes and booze and began a colossal job to widen the Suez Canal. He's got a thing going on with Vladimir Putin and has strengthened relations between Egypt and Russia. He's also got a little secret going on in Libya, along with the United Arab Emirates, where he supported the moderates against the extremists with targeted air strikes.

At home, his government has sentenced thousands en masse to prison, made it a crime not to stand for the national anthem, jailed three *Al Jazeera* journalists for reporting the truth, banned unauthorised demonstrations and has 'disappeared' a number of opposition members.

DENNIS SKINNER

UK HOUSE OF COMMONS

THE BEAST OF BOLSOVER

He's a conviction politician, he's an unrepentant, old school socialist, he represents the place where he grew up in Derbyshire and he once did a real job for a living (he was a coalminer) – any one of those qualifications makes Dennis Skinner a rare specimen in British politics these days.

He once said that he would retire at the age of 65, that to do otherwise would be to 'take another man's job', So far, he's gone 18 years beyond that, but nobody could ever accuse him of riding the gravy train: Skinner has arguably had the best attendance record in the House and yet frequently listed as claiming the least in expenses. He's always spurned paid trips abroad, anything smacking of patronage and even the House of Commons bars – he prefers to meet visitors in the canteen.

He's also democracy's most prolific and vituperative heckler and his sneering harangues have become legendary. Sometimes they're funny; often they're just bile and battery acid. He called one former cabinet minister 'slimy' and 'a wart' and another a 'pompous sod'. He accused Prime Minister Margaret Thatcher of being the sort who would bribe judges 'to save her own neck'.

Skinner's staunchly against the monarchy, and the annual opening of Parliament has always triggered a response – usually directed at 'Black Rod' the liveried official sent to summon MPs to the House of Lords for the Queen's speech. When a new Black Rod, the diminutive retired general, Michael Willcocks, made his first appearance, Skinner cried: 'They've short-changed us! He's nowt but a midget!'

For decades he was something of a hate figure for everyone who didn't share his politics. Now that's changed as the Brits are increasingly disposed to see their legislature as a bland, self-serving tribe, and after his 44 years in the House, even his annual anti-monarchy quips have become as much a part of the cherished parliamentary ritual as the braying of the royal fanfare. 'I shall miss you Dennis,' said Willcocks on his last day in office as Black Rod, seven years after the 'midget' jibe. And the truth is: so will they all.

MIKE SONKO

KENYAN SENATE

MR GENEROSITY

He is Kenya's hip-hop senator and he's in the press virtually every day. Known for his generosity and dubious past, his list of past girlfriends is as long as his arm and his style of dress could only be called unique.

In late 2014 he was sporting a hairstyle that read, 'Respect our Prezzo', in reference to the news that President Uhuru Kenyatta would attend hearings at the International Criminal Court in October to answer charges that he committed crimes against humanity. Sonko offered to fly 20 young people to The Hague to support Kenyatta.

Sonko made his money in transportation by buying fleets of *matatus* (mini-vans) to ferry people around Nairobi. How he made the money to buy the vans is open to question. It is rumoured that he was previously big in the drug trade and did a stint in the notorious Shima La Tewa prison before he went 'legit', but he strenuously denies he is involved in narcotics in any way.

He's got three children by three different women and is rumoured to have more on the way by more women. He was recently ordered by a Nairobi court to take a DNA test to determine if even more children were his. Sonko's sartorial style is eclectic, ranging from business suits to hip-hop gear and lots of bling dangling from his neck. He was once kicked out of parliament for wearing sunglasses and earrings.

His most embarrassing moment was when he photo-shopped an image of Nelson Mandela hugging Mohammad Ali. Sonko put his face in the picture over Ali's and posted it to his Facebook page. It was such an amateurish job that it made him a laughing stock of in Kenya. To win back the public's approval he bought 1,500 tickets for a crucial football match and gave them away.

Besides being loose with cash and having a dodgy reputation, he is enormously popular in his district for delivering jobs and opportunities, although nobody is quite sure what his political beliefs are, if any.

IIONA STALLER

PARTY LEADER AND FORMER MEMBER OF THE ITALIAN CHAMBER OF DEPUTIES

LA CICCIOLINA

She says modestly of herself, 'I'm an historical figure; I moved the boundaries of common decency.'

That's an understatement for a woman who got her tits out to make a point in the Italian Parliament. She's combined porn and politics in Italy for decades, and she isn't even Italian by birth.

She was a Hungarian chambermaid when she met her Italian husband, Salvatore Martini, and married him when she was 25.

The actress in over a dozen hardcore films was elected to the Italian Parliament in 1987 with the *Partito Radicale*, a libertarian group. In the run up to the First Gulf War, she offered to have sex with the Iraqi leader, Saddam Hussein, in return for his withdrawal from occupied Kuwait. She made the same offer in 2002 before the American invasion of Iraq and again to Osama bin Laden in 2006.

After she lost her bid for re-election in 1991, she ditched her husband and took up with the American artist, Jeff Koons, who painted a series of extremely explicit photorealistic images of her for an exhibition in San Francisco in 1992. Staller ran for mayor of the Italian town of Monza in 2002 and Milan and 2004, but lost by wide margins. She also explored a political career in Hungary but couldn't generate any electoral enthusiasm.

In 2012 she formed the Democracy, Nature and Love Party (DNA), which stood in the 2013 elections. The party's platform supported gay marriage, a minimum wage, pledged to reopen closed brothels and 'eroticise liberal and secular culture.'

FRANK-WALTER STEINMEIER

GERMAN BUNDESTAG

SPINELESS

It takes a uniquely gutless asshole to say, 'it takes a lot of courage not to meet with the Dalai Lama these days'. Steinmeier is the same guy now that he was in 2007 when he opposed the additional sanctions against Iran that actually brought them to the negotiating table over their nuclear program.

The smug Social Democrat is the Minister of Foreign Affairs for Germany under Chancellor Angela Merkel. He's never met a Russian he didn't like, including the lovable Vladimir Putin. When the United States, France, Britain and a lot of the rest of the world grew alarmed by Putin's land grab in the Crimea in 2014 and his involvement in the eastern part of Ukraine, Steinmeier was unfazed, saying: 'I found that some things that came out of Brussels, from NATO headquarters, in these last few weeks weren't always helpful.'

As far as sanctions being imposed on Russia, Steinmeier wouldn't want to see the lucrative luxury car market dry up in Moscow just because some human rights were violated or that a wall of armour had been driven right up to the border of the Ukraine. In May 2014, the minister said he welcomed 'Putin's constructive tone to negotiations'. Maybe his opinion of the Russian autocrat is shaped by Steinmeier's old boss, Gerhard Schröder, who once referred to Putin as a 'flawless democrat'. With the largest population in Europe and a GDP almost twice the size of Great Britain, Germany responded to the ISIS attacks by sending a planeload of military equipment while the United States, Britain and France conducted hundreds of air strikes. The Luftwaffe has 428 aircraft but, when it comes to using any of them in concert with the country's allies, Steinmeier dismisses the notion saying, 'for us there is no question of it'.

AUSTRIAN PARTY LEADER

MEGA RICH

He's the 19th richest man in Canada, so what's he doing trying to build a political future in Austria? The answer, in short, is that it's just another hobby of his, like his interest in thoroughbred racing. The *Times Union* newspaper of Albany, New York, reported in August of 2014 that Stronach 'would welcome the chance to acquire the New York Racing Association's franchise and run Saratoga, Belmont and Aqueduct race courses' and 'he has invested $1.5 billion in racing and now owns Santa Anita Park, Gulf Stream Racing and Casino, Pimlico, Golden Gate Fields and Portland Meadows tracks.'

Stronach is not untypical of a lot of plutocrats around the world: he likes to dabble in politics. The founder of Magna International, an automotive parts manufacturer in Ontario, also puts some money into founding the Stronach Institute in Vienna and has started his own political party, Team Stronach. The institute and the party are against the euro, anti-EU and for classical *laissez-faire* liberalism. The really wealthy typically gravitate towards that vision because it goes hand-in-hand with lower taxes. He was born in Austria but moved to Canada in 1954 to make his fortune. Both Bill Clinton and the former CNN celebrity interviewer, Larry King, have endorsed Team Stronach, although how much difference this makes to the typical Austrian voter is anybody's guess.

Besides wanting to do away with the euro and bring back the Austrian schilling, the party also endorsed a 'flat tax' of 25%, regardless of income. That means Stronach can keep more of his money to buy racehorses. The party is not exactly a stunning success, polling about 10% of the vote in elections and most Austrians think the billionaire will give up on the effort once he gets bored.

JOHN SULLIVAN

CANDIDATE FOR GLOUCESTERSHIRE COUNTY COUNCIL

WELL DONE THE RUSSIANS!

The UK Independence Party (UKIP) does attract a different breed of politician – the type that is not afraid to be stupid and demonstrate it in public.

John Sullivan, who has probably never been to a gym in San Francisco – or even Brighton, seems to think that regular, physical exercise is the key to preventing rampant homosexuality.

According to the *Telegraph* in April of 2013, 'the candidate for the Newent Division of Gloucestershire County Council is alleged to have referred to the Victorian belief that physical exercise released tension and thus avoided homosexuality.'

The *Daily Mail*, described how Sullivan claimed 'in a Facebook post that regular physical exercise "prevents" children from becoming gay' and he 'applauded Russia for banning gay pride marches in Moscow', posting 'well done the Russians' on his Facebook page.

According to the *Gloucester Citizen*, 'During an increasingly tense twenty-minute live showdown (in May of 2014), Mr Farage (the leader of UKIP) was put on the spot by LBC host James O'Brien after former county council candidate for Newent, John Lyndon Sullivan suggested shooting gay men.'

The newspaper went on to report that Sullivan, wrote online that: 'I rather wonder if we shot one poofter, whether the next 99 would decide on balance, that they weren't after-all? We might then conclude that it's not a matter of genetics, but rather more a matter of education.'

Sadly, Sullivan was not elected to the Gloucester County Council but he came in a respectable second.

TAN JEE SAY

SINGAPORE PRESIDENTIAL CANDIDATE

MARTYR COMPLEX

There are over 5 million people packed into the island state
of Singapore and they're a blend of people from all over the
world: ethnic Chinese, Malay, Indian, Australian, European and
whoever. It's also a country that sprang from nowhere. It was
nothing up until 1819 when Sir Stamford Raffles founded an outpost for the East India
Company, so there's no such thing as a 'native' but Tan Jee Say has founded a new political
party, the Singaporeans First Party (SFP).

Considering that the country is a *de facto* one party state with the People's Action
Party (PAP) dominating the political scene since 1959, it takes either courage or a great
deal of naivety to found a new opposition party. Tan ran for president in 2011 on the
Singapore Democratic Party (SDP) ticket on a platform that promised more service sector
job growth, lower taxes, a minimum wage and the creation of a national wealth fund to tide
the country over during economic downturns. (Singapore is one of the wealthiest nations
in the world.)

The PAP isn't that crazy about real democracy so they set requirements to run for
office that are often unattainable, but they allowed Tan to run and he came in third place
with a respectable 25% of the vote. He has just published a book, *A Nation Awakes: frontline
reflections*. His manifesto states that, 'Singaporeans First will remake society with policies that
turn us into masters, not slaves, of economic growth' and remove the 'high dependence on
multinational corporations and foreign labour'. These are lofty goals but Tan must know that
he will never become president of Singapore because the PAP would, frankly, never allow
it. He surely knows the history of Chee Soon Juan, the leader of the head of the Singapore
Democratic Party (SDP). Chee was arrested dozens of times, fired from his job and sued
by two prime ministers. Tan may have a martyr complex that is sure to be satisfied in full
before the next presidential elections in 2016.

MARCO TAPIA

GOVERNOR OF GUALACEO

HARDBALL POLITICS

It doesn't pay to cross any of President Rafael Correa's friends and allies, as Marco Tapia has learned. Tapia was once a rising star in the Ecuadorian canton of Gualaceo for President Correa's *Alianza PAIS* party where he gathered 2,500 signatures on a petition for Correa to campaign in the region in 2006 and wholeheartedly supported the relative unknown, who was eventually elected in 2007.

Tapia was awarded with the job of chief of staff for Cuenca's governor, which was an important post because it's the country's third largest city and the capital of the Azuay province. But Tapia wanted more, so he ran in the primary for the job of Governor (mayor) of Gualaceo. He first had to beat Paúl Manuel Íñiguez Ríos, a very close friend of the increasingly authoritarian president Tapia had helped to office. Tapia nailed the nomination by an eight to one margin and got Íñiguez seriously pissed off. To mollify his friend, the president appointed Íñiguez to the equivalent position of chief justice of the Supreme Court.

Íñiguez is obviously a guy who thinks revenge is a dish best served cold, so he waited a couple of years and then, in 2014, he initiated legal action for 'libel' against Tapia, alleging that the politician had set out to destroy his reputation in a campaign speech that the then would-be mayor made in which he didn't mention Íñiguez by name.

Tapia was convicted of the bizarre crime of 'aggravated insult', fined $250,000 and sentenced to three months in prison. To add insult to injury, Íñiguez, filed a separate suit asking for $5 million in damages. Tapia filed an appeal against the criminal case that was 'abandoned' in a decision made by three judges in his absence. The mayor held a press conference, saying, 'I think there is no justice in this country,' and promised to take the case to the International Court of Human Rights.

SHASHI THAROOR

INDIAN PARLIAMENT

MR TWATTER

He's an accomplished author as well as a politician. Known as Mr Twitter in India, he has 2 million who follow his regular tweets and his life got even more interesting in 2014.

Here's a tale of suspected spies, love affairs, jealousy and an untimely death – or maybe none of the above. In 2010, Tharoor 'tied the thali' to Sunanda Pushkar, a Dubai-based entrepreneur. By 2014, Mr Twitter was a government minister and also seemed to have become close to Pakistani journalist, Mehr Tarar, who some think has another job as a spy.

On January 15, 2014, a series of romantic messages supposedly sent by the journalist to Tharoor were posted on his Twitter account. Both politician and journalist stated publicly that the messages were bogus and meant to damage their respective reputations, but Sunanda Tharoor then declared that she had broken into her husband's account and made the messages public because – she claimed – Mehr Tarar was stalking Tharoor and was a member of Pakistan's intelligence agency, ISI.

Then came a 'joint statement by Sunanda and Shashi Tharoor' on the Minister's Facebook page claiming they were very much in love and that Sunanda had been ill of late. Next day, January 17, Sunanda was found dead in a hotel room in New Delhi. Initial reports indicated suicide but they were later revised to death by unnatural causes. The autopsy revealed not only high levels of drugs and alcohol in her body, but also indicated some physical injury. A media fire storm followed.

According to *India Today*, Sunanda's caretaker told the magistrate looking into the mysterious death, 'I had gone along with the couple to Thiruvananthapuram where they got into a heated argument over Tarar. We later returned on 15 January afternoon but on the way back they again started fighting'. According to the *Times of India*, 'Journalist Nalini Singh, who claimed to have spoken to Sunanda hours before her death, has said in her statement to the magistrate that Sunanda had told her that her husband, Shashi Tharoor, was going to marry Pakistani journalist Mehr Tarar'.

SUTHEP THAUGSUBAN

PARTY LEADER

YELLOW SHIRT

Thailand's politics are deeply dysfunctional and part of the reason for that is people like Suthep Thaugsuban. Although it may seem confusing at first, it's actually quite simple to understand Thai politics: it's a struggle between the 'haves' (yellow shirts) and the 'have-nots' (red shirts). The yellow shirts support Thaksin Shinawatra and his younger sister, Yingluck, both of whom held the post of Prime Minister (Yingluck was the first female in Thailand to hold the office). They are both leaders of the *Pheu Thai Party*, which represents the poor and rural population. Thaksin was overthrown by a military coup in 2011 and Yingluck faced the same fate in 2014. They were naturally charged with abuse of power, but in reality they just got in the way of the country's elite and the military.

The most fervent of the Shinawatra haters is Suthep Thaugsuban and he is the leader of the yellow shirt movement. He also faced charges of murder, including that of an Italian journalist, that were conveniently dropped in 2014. Former Deputy Prime Minister Suthep, leads the *People's Democratic Reform Committee* and has blabbed about his collusion with the military in the effort to rid Thailand of the Shinawatras.

US diplomatic cables released by WikiLeaks mention Suthep being held in suspicion of corruption by members of his own party. In 2013 he quit the *Democrat Party* and resigned from parliament to focus entirely on unseating Yingluck Shinawatra. He and his followers took possession of government buildings and were subject to an arrest order. The anti-government protests in 2013 that Suthep helped organise were incredibly expensive to maintain. (Estimates vary, but the best guess is $1.7 million per day.) The goal of his '*Reform Committee*' has never been to hold new elections that he knows could never be won. The 'reform' he wants is to end democracy in Thailand so the elite can rule the country permanently.

ELENI THEOCHAROUS

EUROPEAN PARLIAMENT

NOT HAREM MATERIAL

2014 was not her best year. The Greek Cypriot MEP, Eleni Theocharous, has been accused of being too thin-skinned by a judge who recently threw out her defamation case against *Politis*, the daily morning newspaper read by anybody who is somebody in Cyprus.

The article in question was an opinion piece about her objections and her *no* vote on the 'Annan Plan' referendum (after Kofi Annan), a UN-backed resolution that would have created a federal state compromising both the Greek and the Turkish side of Cyprus (the Turks approved it by 65% but only 24% of Greek Cypriots voted for it).

According to the *Cyprus Mail*, the article was inspired by the contents of an interview in which she said: 'if implementation of the Annan plan depended exclusively on my personal "yes", I would rather commit suicide.'

The offending article in *Politis* said, 'the super-patriotic MEP also tried to project her bravery in the interview, declaring that she would rather do the dance of Zalongo (commit suicide) than join the harem of Ali Pasha. I would like to assure her that there was no way she would end up in a harem.' That wasn't what bothered the elderly MEP. The joke went a bit further when the rather ungallant author wrote: 'in October, I visited the harem at Dolmabahce Palace in Constantinople. I was impressed with its size and luxury as well as with the very strict selection criteria for the harem's 120 women. The prettiest women of the Ottoman Empire were chosen. I think it is obvious that Dr Theocharous would never have set foot in the harem. At best, she could have got a job as domestic helper in the eunuchs' quarters next door.'

The judge basically said that if she couldn't stand the heat she shouldn't be in the kitchen and ordered her to pay all costs for the legal action.

THOM TILLIS

NORTH CAROLINA HOUSE OF REPRESENTATIVES

MAN-SPLAINER

The Republican nominee for the 2014 race for the US Senate in the state of North Carolina thinks there's a demographic problem in America: as opposed to the black and Hispanic population, Tillis thinks the 'traditional' Americans just aren't reproducing fast enough.

Tillis, in a debate with his opponent in 2014, said he wanted to 'make America great again' but, in his role as Speaker of North Carolina's assembly, he has managed to lower the public approval rating of the House to just 18%.

Even though Carolinians are paying for the Affordable Care Act through their federal taxes, Tillis has stopped the expansion of Medicare for 500,000 of the state's residents, he has cut off unemployment insurance for 170,000 people and forced those that still qualify for assistance to take drug tests in order to pick up their weekly cheque.

He earned the nickname 'man-splainer' for his condescending attitude towards his female opponent, Senator Kay Hagan. To counter his weak image among female voters, Tillis came out with a proposal to sell birth control over the counter but not allow it to be covered by insurance, as it is mandated under federal law.

He's also steered the state into signing a deal with the Spanish development company, Cintra Infraestructuras, to expand the highways in return for charging tolls that could cost commuters $20 every weekday, which is deeply unpopular with Carolinians. Tillis oversaw the lowering of taxes for the wealthy but opposes raising the minimum wage. In terms of those voters who are on social benefits, Tillis has stated that 'we need to divide and conquer people on public assistance'. He's also big on restricting voters' rights by pushing a bill through the legislature that requires photo proof of citizenship in order to access the polls.

QUINCY TIMBERLAKE

KENYAN PARTY FOUNDER

VOODOO

The founder of the Platinum Centraliser and Unionist (PlaCenta) Party lives in exile now in Brisbane, Australia but says he is going to run in Kenya's 2017 presidential elections.

That might now prove to be something of a challenge: on Tuesday, September 2nd 2014, Timberlake was arrested by the Brisbane police and charged with the murder of his son.

Timberlake denied the charge and applied to the Supreme Court for bail. According to the *Brisbane Times*, Timberlake was, 'accused of murdering his three-year-old son trying to rid him of aliens and demons.' His wife, the former television presenter, Esther Adongo Timberlake, was charged as an accessory to the crime.

In July of 2014 Timberlake was treated at Brisbane's Prince Charles Mental Health Hospital and his wife subsequently told the police that he had mental health problems. According to the *Times*, 'Mrs Timberlake told officers her husband was pushing on the boy's stomach repeatedly because he believed he had been possessed by aliens and demons' and she told the court that Timberlake was speaking as if he was attempting to save him 'from alien embryos implanted in his stomach'.

Timberlake claims to have fled Kenya to avoid political prosecution but the reality is much different: he fled the media storm surrounding the Finger of God Church. Far from being a *bona fide* politician, Timberlake is a failed rap star and convicted conman. He took money from various artists to arrange special deals with major international brands and television networks. The deals didn't exist. The Finger of God Church, to which Timberlake and his wife belonged, was deemed to be an 'illegal society' by the government and was shut down. Timberlake was put under arrest on a number of charges before he fled the country.

DAVE TOLLNER

NORTHERN TERRITORY ASSEMBLY

WHOLE LOTTA GAYNESS GOIN' ON

In the old days, Australian politicians were much more hilarious; that was before *moderation* caught on. The Northern Territory Deputy Chief Minister, Dave Tollner, seems to be something of a refreshing throwback to the good old days when alcohol fuelled the political debates down under.

His nickname in the legislative assembly is 'Dopey Dave'. Although both members of the Liberal party, Tollner and his colleague, Gary Higgins, aren't talking to each other after Tollner called Higgins's son a 'shirt lifter' and a 'pillow biter', both dated references to homosexuality. Higgins son, Joshua, works as an aide for an Aboriginal member of the Northern Territory legislative assembly, the Community Services Minister, Bess Price.

Three days after making the comment, in August, 2014, Tollner said it was 'friggin' nonsense' to think he would resign over the incident. He resigned the next day.

Shortly after that, Tollner gave a press conference and told reporters that his mother had left his father for another woman when he was younger and that he has a nephew who is gay – so, it was plainly clear he couldn't be homophobic and he had 'no issue with gay people at all'.

A week after resigning Tollner asked for his job back. He then threatened to resign from the Liberal party if they didn't reinstate him, saying, 'I've got a bunch of colleagues sitting behind me throwing knives in my back. Well I can't operate in that environment.' The Labour opposition has called Tollner a 'one-man wrecking ball' but his Liberal boss says he is simply 'tired… and needs a rest'. Tollner is still waiting to get his job back, but has backed down on his threat to leave the party.

CARLOS TREVIÑO

MINISTER IN THE STATE OF QUERÉTARO

PLANET OF THE APES

The Head of the Ministry of Social Development for the Mexican state of Querétaro from 2006 to 2009 and a member of the *Partido Acción Nacional*, party since 2000, isn't a big fan of the beautiful game. Treviño is not the first PAN official to mix football and trouble: two party officers were arrested and jailed in Brazil during the 2014 World Cup for inappropriately touching a woman on the street and beating up her husband. Also in 2014, some PAN members of parliament were suspended for partying with prostitutes.

But, in terms of racism, Carlos Treviño could easily win the party's crown. According to the *Guardian*, 'The tone of the commotion over Ronaldinho's surprise signing for the Mexican club Querétaro has moved from general enthusiasm to outrage in response to a Facebook post by a local politician calling the Brazilian legend an ape.'

Treviño wrote on his Facebook page in September, 2014, 'I try to be tolerant but I DETEST FOOTBALL and the dumbing down phenomenon it produces, I detest it all the more because people obstruct and flood the main avenues, causing me to spend two hours getting home ... and all to see AN APE ... A Brazilian, but an ape nonetheless. This has become a ridiculous circus.' The *Guardian* further reported that, 'Treviño's post also promoted his own right-wing National Action Party to announce it would launch an inquiry. The party's regional chief, José Baez, said he would be seeking the politician's expulsion from the party.'

In an interview with TVC Deportes, Treviño, who is also a professor in American history at the University of Querétaro, explained that the comment was brought about when 'a taxi driver complained to me he had gone for two hours without collecting a fare because all the fans had come to see this ape.'

DONALD TRUMP

CONTENDER?

JACKASS: THE REALITY SHOW

He's not quite a politician yet but he fancies himself as one, which can only be good news for Democrats.

The orange-haired clown considers himself something of a political pundit and has spent the last few years focusing his remaining brain cells on such issues as Barack Obama's real place of birth. The problem with 'the Donald' is not with 'the Donald' but with a media so polarised and so mentally challenged that they turn to a phoney who will spout any sort of utter nonsense to gin up their audience.

In a real country with a real media that wouldn't happen. That being said, Richard Branson has been telling people he's going to send them into space any day now since about 2004 and the rich and famous are still, supposedly, buying tickets for their chance to be an astronaut and the media in Britain still cover every announcement he makes about impending flights.

A common rule of thumb in life is that when people tell you they're smart, they aren't. Smart people don't have to say this: 'Let me tell you, I'm a really smart guy.' Astute business people don't have to say this: 'I didn't go bankrupt.' People who aren't assholes don't have to say this: 'I'm not a schmuck.' And attractive and charismatic men certainly don't have to say this: 'You know, it really doesn't matter what (the media) write as long as you've got a young and beautiful piece of ass.'

Trump still teases the Republican Party, hinting that he might make a run for the presidential nomination, but he has consistently pulled out just before the deadline arrives and the bad press really picks up. The scary thing is that some people might be dumb enough to actually vote for him.

OLEH TYAGNIBOK

**UKRAINIAN
SUPREME COUNCIL**

TOP 10

He made the Simon Wiesenthal Centre's top ten hit-list as early as 2012. Based in Los Angeles, the organisation monitors anti-Semitism and hate speech globally, and picked out the leader of the Ukrainian *Svoboda* (Freedom) party along with such other notables as former Iranian President Mahmoud Ahmadinejad.

According to the centre, 'Oleh Tyagnibok has called for purges of the approximately 400,000 Jews and other minorities living in Ukraine and has demanded that Ukraine be liberated from what he calls, the Muscovite Jewish Mafia.' There's something particularly adrift with that statement: according to the *World Jewish Congress*, there are only about 250,000 Jews remaining in the Ukraine. Nevertheless, Tyagnibok has a problem with them.

According to the BBC, in 2005 he sent a letter to the president of the country asking for an investigation into 'criminal activities of organised Jewry in Ukraine'. Yup, you can always spot a genuine anti-Semite: they're always convinced of an international Jewish conspiracy of some sort or other.

Nutcases like Tyagnibok capture an undue amount of media attention and they are the types that *Russia Today* points to when they claim the Ukrainian government has been taken over by neo-Nazis. The popular vote doesn't lie, though: Tyagnibok's party got just 1.3% of the vote in the last elections. According to the *International Business Times*, the Russian government has opened a criminal investigation into Tyagnibok, which is probably a propaganda effort to keep the fringe of Ukrainian politics in the news. According to the newspaper, Russia believes 'Tyagnibok supported Chechen separatists in the 1990s and is now being prosecuted for organising an armed gang', which is somewhat unlikely when you consider that Tyagnibok is as fervently anti-Muslim as he is anti-Semetic.

YULIA TYMOSHENKO

**FORMER PRIME MINISTER
OF UKRAINE**

THE GAS PRINCESS

How is Yulia Tymoshenko connected to the Hollywood actor, George Clooney? It just so happens that George's new sweetheart, Amal Alamuddin, represented the former Ukrainian Prime Minister, after she was convicted of embezzlement in what many think was a politically motivated trial for violations during the negotiation of a gas supply agreement with Russia.

Despite Alamuddin's undeniable charm, Tymoshenko remained incarcerated until the events of 2014 and the Euromaidan Revolution allowed the laws used to convict her to be retroactively repealed.

Tymoshenko was a heroine of the Orange Revolution (that's the one that didn't work out so well in the end) and was responsible for the ousting of the then president, Viktor Yanukovych. He came back to haunt her and defeated her handily in the 2010 election. (It was probably rigged.) She was put in prison a year later. According to the BBC, 'in April 2013 the European Court of Human Rights ruled that her pre-trial detention had been arbitrary and unlawful, though the judges did not rule on the legality of her conviction'. She was a spectacularly beautiful woman before she was imprisoned and she played that to her full advantage but she suffered severe back pain in prison and was released in a wheelchair.

Her popularity has diminished greatly as a lot of the mud that was thrown against her by her political opponents seems to have stuck, particularly accusations of tax evasion in the 1990s. She now leads the *Batkivshchyna* (All-Ukrainian Union or Fatherland) party and has been calling for the imposition of martial law in the eastern part of the country of which parts are in revolt against the Kiev government. According to a recent poll, Tymoshenko's party will likely get around 8% of the vote in the 2014 election. Two prominent members of *Batkivshchyna*, the Prime Minister and the Speaker of the Ukrainian Parliament, have announced that they are quitting the party.

NILS UŠAKOVS

MAYOR OF RIGA

MINI-PUTIN

The Mayor of Riga is not who you would expect him to be. He's a Russian speaker in a country where the majority speak Latvian. According to *Delfi: The Lithuanian Tribune*, the 'Mayor of Riga, Nils Ušakovs has been put forward as a Prime Ministerial candidate for Latvia's 12th election this year. The leader of the left-wing Concord (Harmony) Centre Party and former journalist, Ušakovs presides over the party that is better known for its support of ethnic Russians in Latvia.'

Just like the James Bond super villain, Ernst Stavro Blofeld, the mayor often is photographed stroking his favourite cats, Kuzia and Muris (they both have Twitter accounts that chronicle their day-to-day life for the losers that get into that stuff).

As *VoxEurope* reports, 'It is no secret to anyone that Nils Ušakovs travels regularly to Moscow and meets with Russia's economic and political elites. A few years back his correspondence with Alexandre Hapilov, an employee of the Embassy of Russia who was suspected of espionage, was revealed. The Concord Centre does not deny its close links with United Russia, the party in power in Russia.'

According to *LSM: Public Broadcasting for Latvia*, Ušakovs sparked a bit of controversy when he was interviewed in Moscow and said, 'for us at the moment, President Vladimir Putin is the best one we could have because, if he wasn't there, then power would not go to Navalny (opposition leader Aleksej Navalny).' He went on further to add, 'The presidents that could be in his (Putin's) place would not bring stability to the neighbourhood.'

Although most Latvians would doubt that Putin has brought much stability to the neighbourhood, Ušakovs enjoys a 73% approval rate for his job as mayor. To put the fear most Latvians have of Russia into perspective, in April of 2014, the Latvian government blocked access to the popular Russian TV channel. According to the *Wall Street Journal*, Ušakovs' party, 'Concord Center, whose political platform is to create a bridge between the Latvians and Russian speakers in Latvia, has recently lost support' making it unlikely that Ušakovs will be the next Latvian Prime Minister.

KEES VAN DER STAAIJ

NETHERLANDS HOUSE OF REPRESENTATIVES

TODD AKIN IN DUTCH

It's a common myth that, since the Dutch allow the sale of pot and there are legal zones for prostitution, they are a liberal people. They're not. Many look down their noses at anyone who frequents a 'coffee shop' or furtively sneaks out of a hooker's hole in the wall. They may seem more tolerant publicly, but at home they can be more conservative than most Europeans.

That's why a nutcase like Kees van der Staaij can hold public office in the Netherlands. First of all, he represents the *Staatkundig Gereformeerde Partij* (Reformed Political Party), a Calvinist Protestant party that, up until a few years ago, didn't allow women to join and only changed course because the government ruled it unconstitutional. It's the oldest political party in the country and has never held any real power because it refuses to cooperate with the other parties.

As you can imagine, they are very pro-life and anti-abortion. That's why van der Staaij makes statements that make the former American Congressman, Todd Akin, look smart. During an interview with the Dutch broadcaster RTL, van der Staaij said it was a 'fact' that women rarely get pregnant when they are raped. Although he said he felt sympathy for rape victims, he didn't get the impression that many abortions were the result of rape and he said his party remains opposed to legal abortions.

Like a lot of Christian fundies around the world, van der Staaij buys the 'rapture' bullshit hook, line and sinker, and thus he has to be a supporter of Israel because that's where the 'rapture' will begin. He recently visited the country to denounce any effort to disinvest in Israel because of its actions in Gaza and the West Bank. This was because a Dutch company, Vitens, recently cancelled a joint venture with an Israeli company because it believes Israel has violated international law, a move that drew the condemnation of the Dutch Foreign Office. 'The purpose of this whole visit was to undermine this type of action,' said van der Staaij.

ARNOUD VAN DOORN

FORMER PARTY VICE-CHAIRMAN

WILDERS RIGHT, AFTER ALL

Geert Wilders has been warning Europe for years that the Muslims will eventually take over and everybody just thought he was another racist nutcase. Then his Number 2 Man, Arnoud van Doorn, proved him absolutely right.

Van Doorn is the former vice-chairman of the Freedom Party (PVV) and, up until May, 2014, a member of The Hague City Council. But he wasn't in the post representing the PVV, he was serving as an independent.

Van Doorn had helped Wilders produce and distribute the short film, *Fitna*, which was basically a hate-filled rant against Islam. *Fitna* was what made Wilders the darling of the extreme right in Europe. It's now just an embarrassment to van Doorn, because in 2013 the Dutchman did the unthinkable: he converted to Islam.

Being a modern kind of bloke, van Doorn outed himself on Twitter, writing, 'there is no god but Allah and Mohammed is his prophet.' That caused quite a stir and much press interest. He then told Al Jazeera that, 'According to some people I am a traitor, but according to most others I have actually made a very good decision.' The journey from Islamaphobe to a believer takes some explaining, particularly if you've once been one of the ones stirring up the pot.

Van Doorn knew if he was going to talk the talk he better walk the walk, so he went off to Mecca to do the Hajj. On his way he told the *Saudi Gazette*, 'I thought of the grave mistake which I had made by producing that sacrilegious film. I hope that Allah will forgive me and accept my repentance.' As if to further confirm Wilders's belief that the Muslims are hell bent on taking over Europe, van Doorn's son, Iskander, announced in 2014 that, 'I bear witness that there is no God to be worshipped but Allah and I bear witness that Muhammad (peace be upon him) is His servant and last messenger.' To add insult to injury, van Doorn said he is now going to launch a pro-Islamic party to counter the anti-Islamic PVV.

HARSH VARDHAN

LOK SABHA (INDIAN PARLIAMENT)

KEEP IT IN YOUR PANTS

Dr Mahinder Watsa is India's leading sex expert. The ninety-year-old, who writes for the *Mumbai Mirror*, was profiled by the *New York Times* in October of 2014 and cited examples of letters he received questioning whether or not a woman could get pregnant if she and her man masturbated together or if a man who had a penis the size of a cashew could do anything to make it larger.

That's why it's refreshing to have someone like Dr Harsh Vardhan, the modern-thinking Indian Minister of Health and Family Welfare, who thinks sex education in the country's schools should be banned entirely and that teachers should concentrate on teaching about India's unique culture or, better yet, yoga.

He already came out with a statement saying that condoms should be replaced by marital fidelity (because that works out so well), but his comments in 2014 about banning sex education and making yoga compulsory, caught many in the country by surprise.

Obviously Vardhan hasn't taken a stroll in Kamathipura neighbourhood lately or read the Kama Sutra (someone should tell him that *Cosmo* recently updated the content and added even more positions).

His opposition to condoms is almost inadvertently hilarious. He issued a statement in 2014 saying, 'condoms promise safe sex, but the safest sex is through faithfulness to one's partner' and 'government campaigns in India should focus on safe sex as a holistic concept which includes highlighting the role of fidelity to single partners.'

After being almost universally condemned for his comments about banning sex education, he clarified the remarks to say he is against 'vulgar sex education' but maybe he would just like to ban sex altogether.

OLEG VARGON

DONETSK INSURGENT

UNCOMMONLY CRAZY

The Prussian general, Carl von Clausewitz, once said that war was merely the continuation of politics by other means. If that's the case, then Oleg Vargon is not only the commander of the 700 men who make up the pro-Russian Svarog Battalion that fought in the Donbas region of the Ukraine throughout 2014, he's also one of the most bizarre and scary political figures in the world.

Vargon and his band are fighting to establish the so-called Donetsk People's Republic in the east of the country and his fighters think they are helping to establish what will become a Russian empire stretching from the Pacific to the Atlantic oceans. It gets crazier from there. They believe Jesus Christ was a Slav and things like AIDS, Ebola and the Third Reich are 'Jewish creations'.

They're pagan too. Vargon told the *Times* newspaper that his troop of men 'have the cosmic right to take up weapons' and that 'Russians are victorious liberators from rotten parasites and fascists and other scum'. Regarding the Slavic forces he is battling, Vargon told the newspaper that, 'they are un-people. By the level of their evolutionary development they haven't reached the level of people.' He and his followers worship the wooden idols of pre-Christian gods at the military base they train at and study Cyrillic symbols to decipher their hidden meanings.

Vargon told the *Times* that before the Russian Empire can be restored to former grandeur, 'it's important to go through this killing off process first because the cancerous cells have to die. This is the evolutionary road.' Meanwhile the 'country' Vargon is fighting for, the Donetsk People's Republic, is shaping up just like the Russian president, Vladimir Putin, wanted and announced in 2014 that it had no intention of holding elections.

SAMPATH VIDANAPATHIRANA

FORMER CHAIRMAN OF PRADESHIYA DISTRICT COUNCIL

VISIT SRI LANKA, THE WONDER OF ASIA

He was a council chief in Pradeshiya district of Tangalle, which is a tourist city in the south of the island of Sri Lanka for the ruling Freedom Alliance Party. Up until July of 2014, he was a free man – even though he had murdered a Briton and participated in the brutal gang rape of his Russian girlfriend.

That wasn't his first murder either. This victim, Kuram Shaikah Zaman, was a Jewish doctor who fitted prosthetic devices in the Gaza strip for the International Red Cross and he was on a holiday in 2012 with his girlfriend, Victoria Alexandrovna, when he made a well-intentioned mistake.

Vidanapathirana arrived at a resort hotel where Zaman was staying and got into an argument with the manager, which soon turned into a brawl. Zaman tried to break it up but Vidanapathirana and four others turned on him with broken bottles and assaulted him. When he tried to get away Vidanapathirana pulled out a gun and shot Zaman dead. Then they went to work on his Russian girlfriend, repeatedly raping her. When they were done and had left, an ambulance took her to intensive care where she recovered from blunt force trauma to the head.

One would assume that Vidanapathirana would have been instantly locked up but that's not how the police in Sri Lanka treat a politician. Vidanapathirana spent the following two years after the murder enjoying immunity because of his connections to the family of President Mahinda Rajapaksa. Vidanapathirana had previously killed an elderly woman in the run up to the 2010 elections but was let off because the police decided he was 'mentally unstable'. In fact, he was a well-known psychopath that was a suspect in numerous murders.

He was eventually found guilty for the Zaman crime and sentenced to 20 years hard labour in 2014 but there is now a movement to free him. There's a Facebook item that calls Vidanapathirana a hero who fought British imperialism and urges politicals to unite and force his release.

EUROPEAN PARLIAMENT

PUTIN'S POODLE

It's a name that just rolls off the tongue, once you remember it in its entirety: Viscompte Philippe Le Jolis de Villiers de Saintignon or, as he is known in the French satirical press, Le Fou du Puy (referring to a fantastically popular and utterly tasteless Christian theme park he created).

Much to de Villiers disappointment, being a Viscount or having an aristocratic background means little in today's France. He'd like it to return to the good old days and his definition of that means kicking out everybody who isn't white, Christian or native French. Multiculturalism isn't something that de Villiers does, except when he takes a trip abroad.

He is fantastically popular in the Department of the Vendee where he regularly won elections to the National Assembly by wide margins. He leads the *Mouvement pour la France*, which is somewhat like the anti-immigrant party, *Front National* but with a bit more class. He calls himself a 'rooted conservative' and *The Economist* calls him an 'ephemeral Catholic monarchist.'

The worrying thing is that he's been sucking up to Russian President Vladimir Putin lately like a lot of right-wing European politicians who all seem to have a man-crush on him. 'People in Europe do not think the same as their leaders and do not share the opinion of those who issue commands from Brussels,' de Villiers said to the Russian 'news' agency, ITAR-TASS after he met with Putin. He further said that, 'Europe is linked not to the United States but to Europe, including Russia.' According to ITAR-TASS: 'Philippe de Villiers said that in the hearts of many Europeans a politician like Vladimir Putin was a much more respected figure than most European leaders.'

His latest deal with Putin will not endear de Villiers to many Ukrainians. According to the *Moscow Times* newspaper, 'Putin has signed off on plans for French businessman and politician Philippe de Villiers to build historically themed amusement parks in Moscow and on the Crimean peninsula.'

NATALIYA VITRENKO

UKRAINIAN PARTY LEADER

MADAME LAROUCHE

She may not actually be married to him, but the perennial Ukrainian presidential candidate is a big fan of Lyndon LaRouche, an equally strange American conspiracy theorist and perennial presidential candidate. In fact, on LaRouche's own publication, the *Economic Intelligence Review*, Vitrenko wrote an article in which she said, 'LaRouche met with Speaker of the Ukrainian Parliament Oleksandr Moroz; he met with members of the Parliament from the Socialist Party . . . And he told them what should be done and what should be avoided', says Vitrenko. 'LaRouche exudes love for humanity, but the IMF came in with dollars and bought off politicians, officials, and members of Parliament. Then came privatization, in which essentially, the whole economy was put on the auction block for peanuts.'

Instead of closer cooperation with the EU, Vitrenko thinks the Eurasian Union is a splendid idea. This would put the country in the company of such forward thinking democracies and vibrant economies as Russia, Belarus, and Kazakhstan, instead of the totalitarian states in the European Union, like Great Britain, Germany and France. Speaking of what has been happening in the Ukraine to PressTV, the Iranian media outfit, Vitrenko said, 'Washington and Brussels . . . used a Nazi coup, carried out by insurgents, terrorists and politicians of Euromaidan to serve the geopolitical interests of the West.'

Representing the Progressive Socialist Party of Ukraine she once garnered 11% of the vote in the presidential elections but now she's down to less than three. She nearly got killed in 1999 when two grenades were thrown at her during a political rally.

During a tour of Europe to raise the spectre of a 'Nazi takeover' in Ukraine she said, 'the will of the majority of the population in Ukraine is being grossly flouted, because the majority favours Ukraine's increased integration with Russia, and does not want Nazism in Ukraine.' It's to be wondered how popular that view is now.

UDO VOIGT

MEMBER OF THE
EUROPEAN PARLIAMENT

UH, OH . . .

There are neo-Nazis all over the world, but since they are
such a fringe minority, not many people worry about them
too much. But Udo Voigt is different: he's German and he's been
elected as an MEP to represent his country in Brussels.

He's got a strange view of history, perhaps shaped by his father who
served as an officer in the Wehrmacht. Voigt also did his time in the German military, albeit
during more peaceful times. He represents the *Nationaldemokratische Partei Deutschlands*,
who think that Germany should take back the land it lost in the Second World War and
doesn't recognise the border with Austria, believing it to be part of 'a greater Germany'. It
naturally opposes the European Union. Despite this, the EU pays a salary of €8,000 a month
to Germany's only neo-Nazi holding public office.

In an interview for *Junge Freiheit*, Voigt described Hitler as a 'great statesman' but
conceded he was 'ultimately responsible for the defeat of Germany'. He's also said that
the Federal Republic of Germany 'was founded on the bayonets of the allies and Germany
today is ruled by collaborators'. *The Times of Israel* describes Voigt as 'the new face of
German fascism' and *Reuters* news agency quotes a party pamphlet as saying, 'an African or
Asian can never become a German because giving them a piece of paper will not change
their biological genetic makeup.' The government has tried to ban the party repeatedly
but that is a difficult task given Germany's liberal constitution.

Voigt himself has been arrested for distributing racially charged material but was given
only a suspended sentence. The *Guardian* newspaper reports that, in an interview he
gave to Iranian journalist, he claimed that 'no more than 340,000' Jews were killed by the
Nazis in the Holocaust. He's also suggested that Rudolf Hess, Hitler's former deputy, be
posthumously awarded the Nobel Peace Prize.

GABOR VONA

LEADER OF THE
JOBBIK PARTY

HUNGARIAN FOOLASH

What is it with neo-Nazis and uniforms? Is it the lure of dressing up in some bizarre outfit that draws young men into the Nazi mentality or does the brain rot begin before the uniform is donned? *Magyar Gárda Mozgalom* (Hungarian Guard Association for Protection of Traditions and Culture) was the neo-Nazi group that Gabor Vona founded in 2007. It had a nice Germanic *Volk* ring to it, reminiscent of the cultural aspirations of the Nazi Party in Germany. *Magyar Gárda* was a paramilitary group that many compared to Hitler's Brown Shirts. It was banned by the Hungarian courts in 2009 because it violated the rights of minorities. It largely faded but Gabor Vona didn't disappear at all.

Although the Roma people probably only make up 5-10% of the population of Hungary and many have integrated fully into society, Vona wants to get rid of them all – and a few other people too. He's now the leader of *Jobbik Magyarországért Mozgalom* (Jobbik, the Movement for a Better Hungary), which has been described as a neo-Nazi, anti-immigration, anti-gay, anti-Roma and anti-Semitic. They have 23 seats in the National Assembly and 3 seats in the European Parliament.

According to the *Guardian*, Vona endorses 'capital punishment and chemical castration for some criminals'. The paper also states that 'Vona has advocated segregation for Hungary's 800,000 Roma', although he denies that and said before the recent elections: 'even the honest Gypsy will do better if Jobbik gets to govern.' Of course he worships Vladimir Putin and spoke at Moscow University in 2013, later stating that it was 'clear that Russian leaders consider Jobbik as a partner'. According to *Foreign Affairs*, Jobbik thought the referendum to annex Crimea 'exemplary' and also states that 'there have been persistent rumours that Jobbik's enthusiasm is paid for with Russian roubles.'

BNP LEADER

ER . . . WALKER

Maybe racism has passed its sell-by date in Britain. The British National Party (BNP) is the UK's answer to France's *Front National,* Germany's National Democratic Party and Greece's Golden Dawn, with two exceptions: they're far worse than any of them; they're on their way out rather than up.

What mass protest vote the BNP ever had has now been soaked up by UKIP, which has an elected MEP, Amjad Bashir, who can actually say: 'here I am, of Asian birth, of Asian parentage, Muslim, and I have been selected by this so-called racist party'. UKIP has 24 MEPs and came in first in the European elections of 2014 and so far two Conservative MPs defected to the party in the same year. It looks set to contest almost all seats in the next British elections.

The BNP, in comparison, holds two local council seats and lost its one European Parliament seat in 2014. Furthermore, its previous party chairman, Nick Griffin, not only went bankrupt to the tune of £120,000 ($194,500), but in May of 2014 declared that the party could only be described as 'racist'. (This from Nick Griffin!)

Then along came Adam Walker who accepted the job of BNP chairman in July 2014. As can be imagined, Walker brings a history to the job. He's been banned from teaching for life by the then Minister for Education, Michael Gove, for an incident that happened in 2011. At the time Walker was a teacher at Kepier Sports College, in Houghton-le-Spring, a town in County Durham, England. After school he was provoked by three children between the ages of 10 and 12. He chased them in his car, verbally abused them and slashed the tires of their bikes. He was suspended from teaching for two years by the National College for Teaching and Leadership and given a 6-month suspended sentence by Durham Crown Court and a 12-month driving ban. Gove upped the punishment to a lifetime ban, which Walker appealed but lost. In a sign that it's same-old-same-old for the BNP under Walker's leadership, in a 2013 speech to the party, he described Britain as a 'multicultural shithole'.

MARK WALKER

CANDIDATE FOR THE US HOUSE OF REPRESENTATIVES

ELECT AN IDIOT

The sad news for the 6th Congressional District of North Carolina is that Mark Walker will likely be their new Congressman in 2015.

The Republican candidate is a Pastor of Arts and Worship at Lawndale Baptist Church in Greensboro, North Carolina and doesn't have a clue about the world around him. He occupies a zone of intelligence that falls somewhere between vacuous and imbecilic.

At a Tea Party event in the summer of 2014 he pondered the response he would give to the problem of illegal immigration, specifically the immigrants that cross the border between Mexico and the US. After thinking long and hard about the subject, Walker suggested, 'if you have foreigners who were sneaking in with drug cartels to me that is a national threat and if we've got to go laser or blitz somebody with a couple of fighter jets for a little while to make our point . . .' When asked if that meant he would declare war on Mexico, he said, 'we did it before, if we need to do it again, I don't have a qualm about it.'

The problem with the voters in his district is they consume Fox News like crack cocaine and have convinced themselves that somehow Mexican drug cartels are just on the verge of teaming up with dangerous Jihadists and launching a serious attack on the United States. Whereas in more sane parts of the country Walker's comments would have disqualified him in the eyes of the voters, the right-wing blogosphere lit up when Walker talked of bringing the full might of the US Air Force down on the heads of the Mexicans. 'At least he has a plan,' wrote on Greensboro blogger.

They also like his education. Walker has a bachelor's degree in Biblical Studies. That goes down well in the Bible Belt.

PRESIDENT OF NAURU

BROKE AS A JOKE

Speaking before the United Nations about global warming in February 2014, Waqa summed it up nicely when he said, 'we celebrate this special year with the sombre knowledge that unless action is taken soon some islands won't make it to the end of the century. The President of Nauru since 2013 wasn't joking. In money terms, Nauru didn't make it until the end of 2014.

The tiniest nation in the world sports a population of only 10,000 people but was somehow able to raise over 29 million dollars in the international debt market. A New York hedge fund, Firebird Management, holds that debt and wants to be paid back. They won a court case in 2012 and in late 2014 they froze the assets held in Nauru's Australian bank, Westpac.

According to Finance Minister, David Adeang, after the final payment to the island's 1,200 government employees is paid, Nauru will have to shut down its airlines, close its hospital and schools, shut down its courts and cut off all electrical power. About the only income the Nauru generates is as a dumping ground for 1,200, mainly Afghan, asylum seekers who have tried to immigrate to Australia in a deal brokered between Waqa and the Australian Prime Minister, Tony Abbott.

Waqa already survived a vote of no confidence in early 2014 for sacking and deporting a number of Australian judges, which would have normally earned the rebuke of Australia's government but, as the Australians aren't keen on absorbing the immigrants, Abbott turned a blind eye to the problem. Australia already cuts a $29 million cheque to the country every year as a thank you for holding the hapless refugees in an 'offshore processing centre' (holding pen).

In 2013, Waqa began cozying up to Vladimir Putin, trying to end travel restrictions between the two countries so that Nauru's offshore banks could profit from the money Russians used to stick into Cypriot banks and also to get more foreign aid.

LENAR WHITNEY

US CONGRESSIONAL CANDIDATE

THE RUNNER

Whitney is the sort of Republican candidate that even makes other Republicans hide their heads. The Louisiana State Representative now has her sights set on Washington and is running in the 6th District for a seat in the US House of Representatives.

The Cook Political Report is a widely respected non-partisan analysis of American politics and also somewhat of a predictive tool. It's also a means for candidates to raise their profile as Cook meets and interviews thousands of politicians each year on both sides of the aisle. Whitney jumped at the chance to be interviewed by the organisation and met with David Wasserman who has since written about the interview for the *Washington Post*, describing the Louisianan as 'the most frightening candidate I've met in seven years'.

Wasserman questioned Whitney about her assertion that the earth was cooling instead of warming and asked her to cite just one scientific expert that agreed with her. In response 'she froze and was unable to cite a single scientist, journal or news source to back up her beliefs.' When he asked Whitney if she believed Obama was really born in America, she claimed it was a matter of 'controversy' before her two aides rushed her out of the room before she really stuck her foot in it. According to Wasserman, 'it was the first time in hundreds of Cook Political Report meetings that a candidate has fled the room.'

She later said that Wasserman was out to get her in the interview and 'liberal shills like [him] want to destroy us' and claimed his attitude was 'belittling'. Whitney does have a ten minute YouTube video out in circulation titled *Global Warming is a Hoax* where she says, 'any 10-year-old can invalidate (the warnings of climate scientists) with one of the simplest scientific devices known to man: a thermometer.' She's also a 'light-bulber', and thinks the law that President George W. Bush signed into law that mandates the use of low-energy light bulbs is some grand liberal conspiracy.

VINCENT WIJEYSINGHA

**FORMER MEMBER OF THE
SINGAPORE PARLIAMENT**

COULD THERE BE A CONNECTION?

There is such a thing as 'coming out' and there is also
something called being 'kicked out'. Sometimes the
two things go together.

Representing the Singapore Democratic Party
(SDP), Wijeysingha ran for election to the parliament in 2011, garnering almost 40% of the
vote. In June of 2013 he announced, via a Facebook posting: 'Just in case Fabrications about
the PAP (Singapore's ruling People's Action Party) was wondering, yes, I am going to Pink
Dot (gay pride event) tomorrow. And yes, I am gay.'

Like prostitution, homosexual sex acts are illegal in the island state. (Don't worry, there
are plenty of hookers in the dark corners of Orchard Road at night and *Travel Gay Asia*
says the Tantric Bar on Neil Road is 'probably the most popular gay bar in Singapore'.)
Nevertheless, two months after he announced he was gay, the SDP sadly announced he
was leaving the party to pursue LGBT interests.

In 2014 Wijeysingha announced that he had been abused by Roman Catholic clergy
in his youth. According to *SG News*, he said he 'came into unfortunate contact with a priest
who would engage in play wrestling and attempt to touch [his] crotch in the process'
and 'he once brought me to his bedroom and took a stack of pornographic magazines
from his wardrobe to show me'. He went on to say that he didn't want to make a 'specific
allegation of abuse against a priest' and 'it was an attempt without any conclusion and
therefore I consider myself neither to have been abused nor damaged subsequently.'
Wijeysingha, who says he is Catholic, 'the church cannot hold a position on both sides of
the argument that homosexuality is evil but homosexual people are not. This is essentially
nonsense.'

GEERT WILDERS

DUTCH HOUSE OF REPRESENTATIVES

THE PRINCE OF BLONDNESS

It seems every far right politician across Europe has some sort of crush on the Dutch politician, Geert Wilders. Perhaps it's because he can spout bigoted rubbish with a bit more élan than most, who just sound like shrill haters. Or maybe they just dig his long, dyed-blond hair.

According to the *Guardian* newspaper Wilders described Islam as a 'force of darkness' that has helped make Rotterdam and Paris look like 'suburbs of Cairo.'

He is the leader of the *Partij voor de Vrijheid* (Party for Freedom) and a member of the Dutch Second Chamber. He made a film about Islam, *Fitna*, in 2008. It was only 17 minutes long and it was a diatribe linking Islam with terrorism, but it got him a lot of international attention.

Due to frequent death threats, he has a personal security detail and lives something of a reclusive life although, like Julian Assange, he doesn't like to be out of the public spotlight for long. That's possibly the reason why he recently called on 'everyone' to join him in an 'anti-Islamic' march in the Schilderswijk neighbourhood of The Hague, shortly after his party struck out in the European elections of 2014.

The PVV were widely expected to achieve great things in these elections but they made no further gains, coming fourth with only three of the Netherlands' twenty-six seats. In fact, the PVV's support has fallen by a third since its electoral zenith in 2010. Some have attributed this to high profile defectors who blamed Wilders's ego and autocratic leadership. Others think his decision to team up with Marine Le Pen's *Front National* Party in France was a step too far.

Wilders told the *Telegraaf* newspaper that if permission was not given for the anti-Islamic march in The Hague he would march alone carrying the Dutch flag, 'even though my personal protection force will not think that is a good idea.'

JULIE WILLIAMS

JEFFERSON COUNTY BOARD OF EDUCATION, COLORADO

1984

She was elected in 2013 and now she wants to change things for the better by making the teaching of American history more patriotic. The mother of two did not run on a party ticket but defeated her opponent by a two to one majority.

Jefferson County comprises the western suburbs of Denver. It is a prosperous, 99% white area of the country and the parents, for the most part, want their children to be taught to respect law and order and to love their country.

Of course, that means leaving a lot of the bad stuff out of the history books, including the civil rights struggles, the displacement and slaughter of Native Americans, slavery and most of the dozens of wars the country has fought around the world. According to *Chalkbeat Colorado*, Williams says, 'there are things we may not be proud of as Americans but we shouldn't be encouraging our kids to think that America is a bad place.'

A lot of the students that the new plan would affect aren't that crazy about Williams's ideas and they took to the streets in September 2014. Students from six large high schools protested at what they saw as an attempt to censor their education. If Williams is successful the school board will set up a committee to review the coursework and assure that it 'promotes citizenship, patriotism, [the] essentials and benefits of the free-market system, respect for authority and respect for individual rights [and doesn't] encourage or condone civil disorder, social strife or disregard of the law'. Williams was one of three conservative school board members elected in 2013. As there are only two others opposed to the measure it seems likely that the proposal will pass.

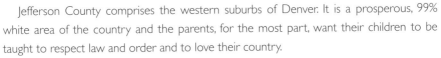

LALU PRASAD YADAV

FORMER MINISTER

GUNDA RAJ

Prasad is an old-fashioned kind of Indian politician. Whenever there's a cookie jar open, chances are you'll find his hand stuck in it. Prasad used to be Chief Minister of the Indian state of Bihar from 1990 to 1997 and Minister of Railways from 2004 to 2009.

He's a charming, charismatic crowd puller that some accuse of fostering criminality in his home state. His most famous brush with the law was his alleged involvement in the 'fodder scam' – a scheme whereby animal medicines and farming equipment was 'supplied' to non-existent cattle herds. It was an ongoing wheeze that lasted for years and netted its masterminds something over $210 million.

The allegations against Prasad forced him to resign as Chief Minister but he cleverly arranged for his wife to take over the job, which led to accusations that she was acting as his surrogate for her term in office.

He has been bunged up in jail and under arrest in guesthouses for the past ten years but the wheels of justice ground on and he was eventually convicted in 2013 by the Central Bureau of Investigation court and sentenced to five years in the clink. This being India, though, he's still a free man and out on bail pending appeal. Due to the conviction he's not allowed to be an MP any longer and he is barred from running for office for six years. In 2014 he had a cardiac operation but quickly recovered.

While he was still active in politics he used a clever political trick in the 2005 elections to woo Muslim voters. He was accompanied by an Osama bin Laden lookalike that stood by him onstage while he made speeches attacking the United States. During the 15 years Lalu Prasad and his wife governed Bihar, the economy of the state plunged to the bottom of all the states in India. Crime and the use of private armies also increased as did the private fortune of Lalu Prasad Yadav.

**FORMER PRESIDENT
OF UKRAINE**

MISSING PRESIDENT

One of the many things you could say about Viktor Yanukovych is that nobody could ever claim that he has good taste.

He fled the Ukraine in February, 2014, now lives somewhere in southern Russia and still considers himself president of a country that has issued an arrest warrant for him on a charge of mass murder. He and his cronies plundered the treasury before they left, so he's not short of a few bob, although his cringe-worthy mansion is a site of fascination for his countrymen who must hide their heads in shame when they see the awful collection of kitsch he left behind.

Of course, when Yanukovych first disappeared, the propaganda outfit, *Russia Today* were in no doubt what had happened: the Americans were behind the president's disappearance: 'Has he not been hidden by people who are very adept at covering tracks? That is to say, by the Americans.' Even they couldn't keep up the facade when Yanukovych popped up in Russia a week later calling for Crimea to be returned to the Ukraine.

Yanukovych's troubles began in November 2013 after he scrapped a cooperation agreement with the EU seeking closer ties – and money – from Russia. The Euromaidan demonstrations began and, after he ordered the shooting of dozens of protestors, he hopped on a plane and made off to Putin's homeland (not exactly to open arms).

Where he is is a matter of mystery, but in August, 2014, a Macedonian newspaper, *Nova Makedonija*, reported that 'Oleg Mitvol, leader of the Russian party with no parliamentary representation, *Alliance of Greens-People's Party*, said Yanukovych and his associates were in Bulgaria. Mitvol said he had met the associates of Yanukovych in a Bulgarian resort. According to the Russian politician, they asked for a place to reside in a Slavic country and not a long time ago asked to become Bulgarian citizens.'

AHMED RUFAI SANI YARIMAN

NIGERIAN SENATE

WHAT A GUY

He would be locked up in most countries, but not in Nigeria. The Senator representing the Zamfara State in northwest Nigeria was elected on the All Nigeria People's Party ticket. The region Yariman represents falls under Sharia Law, in an accommodation with the mainly Christian southern part of Nigeria, which operates under Common Law.

According to *Your Daily Muslim*, a Nigerian news site focusing on Islamic issues, 'Nigerian Muslim senator Ahmed Rufai Sani Yariman is a pervert of the highest order. Not only did he marry an underage girl (allegedly thirteen), he used his political background to get himself excused of any wrongdoing, and has also fought against marriage reform laws that would end child marriage. Why did Yariman do it, aside from being a creepy paedophile?'

According to the BBC, 'the senator is reported to have paid a dowry of $100,000 to the child's parents – and to have brought the girl into Nigeria from Egypt' and 'newspaper reports have also accused the senator of having previously married a 15-year-old girl in 2006'. Yariman denied that the girl was thirteen but would not reveal her age. He told the BBC in April of 2010, 'I don't care about the issue of age since I have not violated any rule as far as Islam is concerned. History tells us that Prophet Muhammad did marry a young girl as well. Therefore I have not contravened any law. Even if she is thirteen, as it is being falsely peddled around. If I state the age, they will still use it to smear Islam.'

Although never properly investigated for the alleged underage marriage, Sani has faced problems since. In 2013, according to the *Daily Post* newspaper, 'the former Zamfara State Governor, and a serving Senator of the Federal Republic, Yariman, was arrested in Kaduna State over alleged inciting comments on a live radio programme run by the Federal Radio Corporation of Nigeria, Kaduna.'

DMYTRO YAROSH

UKRAINIAN PARTY LEADER

PRAVYY SEKTOR

He's been put on the 'wanted list' by Interpol, although that was at the request of Russia, so you might take that with a pinch of salt. Yarosh is the leader of *Pravyy Sektor* (Right Sector) who are either a gang of neo-Nazi thugs or national heroes, depending on which side of the border you live on.

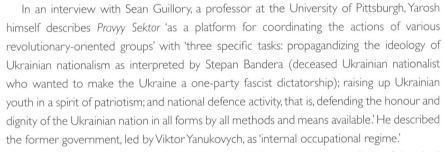

In an interview with Sean Guillory, a professor at the University of Pittsburgh, Yarosh himself describes *Pravyy Sektor* 'as a platform for coordinating the actions of various revolutionary-oriented groups' with 'three specific tasks: propagandizing the ideology of Ukrainian nationalism as interpreted by Stepan Bandera (deceased Ukrainian nationalist who wanted to make the Ukraine a one-party fascist dictatorship); raising up Ukrainian youth in a spirit of patriotism; and national defence activity, that is, defending the honour and dignity of the Ukrainian nation in all forms by all methods and means available.' He described the former government, led by Viktor Yanukovych, as 'internal occupational regime.'

During the Euromaidan Revolution, Yarosh told *Time* magazine that *Pravyy Sektor* had amassed enough weapons 'to defend all of Ukraine from the internal occupiers' – by which he means the ruling government – and to carry on the revolution if negotiations with that government break down.' According to *Time*, the *Pravyy Sektor* 'ideology borders on fascism, and it enjoys support only from Ukraine's most hard-line nationalists, a group too small to secure them a place in parliament'. Yarosh told his interviewer that his goal was to 'steer the country in a new direction, one that would make it truly strong, not dependent on either the West or the East.' He doesn't like the US, the European Union or Russia. He thinks America has an agenda for the Ukraine, that the EU would push liberal policies like gay marriage, and that Russia's appetite is too small for just taking Crimea.

LELAND YEE

CALIFORNIA STATE SENATE

UNCLE YEE

According to the *San Jose Mercury News* things aren't looking up for the Democratic Californian State Senator, Leland Yee. He was supposedly an 'award winning gun control advocate' and the first Asian American to become speaker of the California Senate. The *Mercury News* reported that a Federal Grand Jury has concluded that 'he was part of an organized crime operation in which he sold legislative votes and influence for piles of money, just as he was earlier accused of conspiring to traffic in guns.'

Yee was set up in an FBI sting operation, taking $60,000 to influence a vote on workman's compensation legislation that would affect the National Football League. He was reportedly enthusiastic about taking the money and doing the job, telling the undercover agent that 'we gotta juice this thing'.

His accomplices include Raymond 'Shrimp Boy' Chow, the Mafia Don in San Francisco's Chinatown. Yee's Mafia handle was 'Uncle Yee' and he was known for trading bags of cash for government influence. In a fit of brilliance, he tried to get an undercover FBI agent to help him pull an international arms deal.

What makes that particular potential crime worse is that he wanted to provide assault weapons to rebel groups in the Philippines, some of which make Al Qaeda look like the good guys. Yee faces a federal racketeering charge which is only reserved for the most powerful Mafia figures. He has been suspended from the California Senate but is still collecting his salary. In elections that were held after the indictment against Yee was handed out, he collected over 300,000 votes: not enough to win but he placed third in his district, which says something about how much Americans pay attention to politics.

MILOS ZEMAN

PRESIDENT OF THE
CZECH REPUBLIC

DRUNK AS A SKUNK

He likes his booze but claims he never gets drunk. 'If anyone has ever seen me drunk in my life, tell me when,' the Czech president said during his latest campaign. He's been filmed on numerous occasions when he certainly looked like he had a few too many drinks but he's always claimed that his stumbling was more to do with a 'virus' rather than alcohol, which has prompted many in Prague to post late night videos of themselves succumbing to the same illness that Zeman seems to suffer with regularity.

Refreshingly, for a Central European politician, Zeman isn't anti-Semitic. In fact, he's a big fan of Israel. 'The only holiday of independence which I can never leave out is the celebration of the independence of the Jewish State of Israel,' he said in a speech he gave in Brussels in 2014. He's also a big fan of Vladimir Putin and has stated that he thinks Russia should join the European Union, which rather sounds like something somebody would say when they've had one too many. The self-described 'tolerant atheist' isn't a big fan of Arab Muslims, though: 'The enemy is the anti-civilisation spreading from North Africa to Indonesia,' Zeman said in 2011.

He's also a climate change denier and thinks Kosovo is a terrorist state run by a narcotics peddling criminal group. Nor is he a supporter of the LGBT movement, once denying a professor a university appointment because of his involvement in gay rights. He's unabashed about cigarette smoking and beer drinking and said his campaign ran on *becherovka*, a particularly nasty Czech herbal liquor. Despite his drinking, the enormously popular Zeman seems not likely to end up like Boris Yeltsin, the last really drunk world leader.

TATYANA ZHDANOK

EUROPEAN PARLIAMENT

VLADIMIR'S VOICE

Tatyana is old school. That's in the sense that she opposed her own country's independence and longs for the days of Soviet rule.

She's not allowed to run for the Latvian parliament, but she can run for the European Parliament where she holds a seat under the European Greens – European Free Alliance party.

She's an anathema to most Latvians and, according to the Baltic News Network, Zhdanok 'spreads Russian propaganda.' Being a hard line communist in Latvia has its difficulties but, with a Russian-speaking minority that feels diminished by the Latvian speaking community, she can muster enough votes every few years to go to Brussels and live on the EU 'gravy train.'

She's barred from running for the Latvian parliament because she was a member of the Communist Party when it called for a coup against the government in 1991. The reasons for her opposition to Latvian independence may be understandable if you are aware of her Jewish background and the role Latvian Nazi collaborators played during the Second World War.

She was one of the 'observers' for the 2014 Crimean 'vote' to leave Ukraine and join Russia. She is a member of the EU-Russian Speakers Alliance and has backed the Kremlin wholeheartedly against Ukrainian nationalists. Her big issue now is to get the Ukrainian 'Right Sector' classified as a terrorist organisation under the dubious claim that they committed genocide during the 2014 riots in Odessa. She has appeared on the Kremlin's mouthpiece, *Russia Today*, a number of times calling for the group to be banned and claiming that the Ukrainian leadership is riddled with neo-Nazis. In response to EU condemnation of Russia's actions in Ukraine, Zhdanok claims the 'resolution is another proof of growing Russophobia, which, in my opinion, has already become a legal phobia in the European Union.' She further warns that 'Russians can tolerate many things, but, as with a spring, it is dangerous to push too hard.'

VLADIMIR ZHIRINOVSKY

RUSSIAN DUMA

'RAPE HER HARD!'

It's not easy to deny something when it's been caught live on camera, but the rabid Russian politician, Vladimir Zhirinovsky, is still trying to squirm out of an outrage filmed in April 2014. According to the *Mirror*, when asked a relatively softball question about the Ukraine crisis from Stella Dubovitskaya of the state owned news outlet, *Russia Today*, Zhirinovsky physically pushed two male aides towards her and told them to 'rape the woman hard'.

'Go and kiss her, grab her,' he added. When a female reporter from Interfax tried to stop Zhirinovsky he asked her, 'what are you doing intervening here, you lesbian?' Just in case everyone in the room didn't get the fact that he's crazy, he shouted 'Christ is risen, truly he is risen!' before leaving the press conference. He said he was sorry afterwards. If you like full-on crazy politicians, Russia is the place.

Zhirinovsky ran for Prime Minister in 1993 promising free vodka for men and better knickers for women. The leader of the *Liberal Democratic Party of Russia*, thinks America is full of 'cocksuckers, handjobbers, and faggots'. According to *Vice* magazine he once described the former American Secretary of State, Condoleezza Rice, as 'a black whore who needs a good cock ... one of our divisions will make her happy in the barracks one night.' The platform of the party he leads wants to re-establish Russia as a great world power. *Vice* also describes Zhirinovsky as 'belligerent, racist, sexist, homophobic, nationalist sociopath' and 'insane clown prince of Russian politics'. He often gets in pushing matches or fights during debates and has threatened to take Alaska back from the United States as a place to put the Ukrainians. He's not allowed in a lot of countries in the world but he can take comfort in the fact that Russians readily buy his branded vodka and ice cream.

JACOB ZUMA

PRESIDENT OF
SOUTH AFRICA

THE POLYGAMOUS PRESIDENT

Why can't women have four or five husbands? It would actually make much more sense, particularly from the woman's point of view. It's called polyandry, not polygamy, and it only happens in certain societies in the Himalayan Mountains and, where it does occur, it typically involves two brothers marrying the same woman.

But, that's a long way away from KwaZulu-Natal, the traditional home of the Zulu, where successful men traditionally take more than one bride. Zuma has been married six times and now has four wives (one died and one divorced him). It's a difficult choice as to who the lucky woman is when the President of South Africa goes on a state visit, although he's not much of a travelling man, particularly now that another potential trial awaits him.

His previous trial was more sensational and demonstrated his keen knowledge of medical hygiene. He got off from a rape charge when the judge ruled that the sex was consensual. Zuma did admit he had unprotected sex with the woman and knew she was HIV positive, although he took a shower afterwards to make sure he didn't contract the disease – because that works. He sang the revolutionary ditty *Awulethu Mshini Wami* (ring my machine gun) throughout the trial, as did his supporters.

The upcoming trial involves releasing something called the 'spy tapes', which are recordings that purportedly show that accusations of massive corruption against Zuma were fabricated by rivals in the *African National Congress* to cause him political harm. One would think he wouldn't be fighting to keep the tapes under wrap, but that isn't the case at all, which raises any number of questions. He has been accused of using something like $20 million to spiv up his home, but a man with four wives has to have somewhere to hang his hat.

THE MADNESS RANKINGS

NORTH AMERICA

1. ROB FORD, Former Mayor of Toronto
2. LOUIE GOHMERT, US Congressman, Texas
3. PAUL LEPAGE, Governor of Maine
4. PATRICK BRAZEAU, Canadian Senator
5. WAYNE LAPIERRE, National Rifle Association
6. SCOTT DESJARLAIS, US Congressman, Tennessee
7. SALLY KERN, Oklahoma State Representative
8. NATHAN DEAL, Governor of Georgia
9. PAUL BROUN JR, US Congressman, Georgia
10. MARION BARRY, Councilman, Washington DC

CENTRAL AND SOUTH AMERICA

1. NICOLAS MADURO, President of Venezuela
2. DESI BOUTERSE, President of Surinam
3. HORACIO CARTES, President of Paraguay
4. DANIEL ORTEGA, President of Nicaragua
5. CRISTINA FERNANDEZ DE KIRCHNER, President of Argentina
6. RAFAEL CORREA, President of Ecuador
7. ROSAURO MARTINEZ, Congressman, Chile
8. OLLANTA HUMALA, President of Peru
9. PERCY FERNANDEZ, Mayor of Santa Cruz, Bolivia
10. ENRIQUE FLORES LANZA, Minister of the Presidency, Honduras

WESTERN EUROPE

1. JEAN-MARIE LE PEN, European Parliament, France
2. BROOKS NEWMARK, Member of Parliament, UK
3. MORTEN MESSERSCHMIDT, European Parliament, Denmark

4. BRUNO GOLLNISCH, European Parliament, France
5. GIANLUCA BUONANNO, Chamber of Deputies, Italy
6. GEORGE GALLOWAY, Member of Parliament, UK
7. JANUSZ PALIKOT, Member of Parliament, Poland
8. JEAN-LUC MÉLENCHON, European Parliament, France
9. GEERT WILDERS, House of Representatives, Netherlands
10. JUSSI HALLA-AHO, European Parliament, Finland

EASTERN EUROPE

1. VLADIMIR ZHIRINOVSKY, Vice Chairman of the Duma, Russia
2. ALEXANDER DUGIN, Party Leader, Russia
3. EDUARD LIMONOV, Party Leader, Russia
4. OLEG VARGON, Party Leader, Ukraine
5. GABOR VONA, Party Leader, Hungary
6. FUAD RAMIQI, Party Leader, Kosovo
7. VLADIMIR PUTIN, President of Russia
8. ALEXANDER LUKASHENKO, President of Belarus
9. KRISZTINA MORVAI, European Parliament, Hungary
10. VIKTOR ORBAN, Prime Minister of Hungary

AFRICA

1. TEODORO OBIANG MBASOGO, President of Equatorial Guinea
2. JULIUS MALEMA, Party Leader, South Africa
3. ROBERT MUGABE, President of Zimbabwe
4. ISAIAS AFWERKI, President of Eritrea
5. JOSEPH KABILA, President of the Democratic Republic of Congo
6. AYO FAYOSE, Former Governor of Ekiti, Nigeria
7. EPAFRAS MUKWIILONGO, Party Leader, Namibia
8. YOWERI MUSEVENI, President of Uganda
9. GOODLUCK JONATHAN, President of Nigeria
10. VICTORIA HAMAH, Former Deputy Minister, Ghana

ASIA

1. KIM JONG UN, Supreme Leader of North Korea
2. ABU BAKR AL-BAGHDADI, Self-styled Caliph of the Islamic State
3. NAFTALI BENNETT, Knesset of Israel
4. BUNG MOKTAR, Parliament of Malaysia
5. AYELET SHAKED, Knesset of Israel
6. ISLAM KARIMOV, President of Uzbekistan
7. JOSEPH ESTRADA, Mayor of Manila, the Philippines
8. RYUTARO NONOMURA, Former Assemblyman, Hyogo, Japan
9. DAUREN BABAMURATOV, Party Leader, Kazakhstan
10. HUN SEN, Prime Minister of Cambodia

AUSTRALASIA AND OCEANIA

1. TROY BUSWELL, formerly Assembly of Western Australia
2. FRANK BAINIMARAMA, Prime Minister of Fiji
3. GEORGE CHRISTENSEN, MP, Queensland, Australia
4. LARISA LEE, Northern Territory Assembly, Australia
5. RICHARD PROSSER, Member of Parliament, New Zealand
6. DEBBIE ROBINSON, Party Leader, Western Australia
7. KIM DOTCOM, Hacker and activist, New Zealand
8. DAVE TOLLNER, Northern Territory Assembly, Australia
9. MARK LATHAM, Former Opposition Leader, Australia
10. FIONA PATTEN, Party Leader, Victoria, Australia

. . . AND THE WORLD

1. KIM JONG UN, The Fat Boy with the Bomb
2. VLADIMIR ZHIRINOVSKY, Vice Chairman of the Duma, Russia
3. ABU BAKR AL-BAGHDADI, Self-styled Caliph of the Islamic State
4. TEODORO OBIANG MBASOGO, President of Equatorial Guinea
5. JEAN-MARIE LE PEN, European Parliament, France

6.   JULIUS MALEMA, Party Leader, South Africa
7.   NICOLAS MADURO, President of Venezuela
8.   ROB FORD, Former Mayor of Toronto
9.   ROBERT MUGABE, President of Zimbabwe
10. LOUIE GOHMERT, US Congressman, Texas

MADNESS MEDALS TABLE

RANK	STATE	APPEARANCES
1.	USA	63
2.	United Kingdom	27
3.	France	11
3.	India	11
5.	Australia	10
5.	Russia	10
7.	Italy	8
8.	Canada	7
9.	Ukraine	6
10.	Czech Republic	5
10.	Mexico	5
12.	Hungary	4
12.	Ireland	4
12.	Israel	4
12.	Nigeria	4
12.	Philippines	4
12.	Poland	4

SPECIAL AWARDS

The *John F Kennedy Award for Sexual Prowess* has to go to **Boris Johnson**, London's mayor, who has had so much fun that he's now probably facing a permanent hosepipe ban on the home front.

The honour of winning the *King George III Trophy for Unquestionable Insanity* belongs to ... **Vladimir Zhirinovsky**, the donkey-riding Russian politician who thinks it's fine to recommend rape as a way to hush up awkward journalists.

The sought after *Dan Quayle Award for Utter Stupidity* in politics goes to none other than the British Member of Parliament, **Brooks Newmark**, for sending a snap of his willie to a man he thought was a girl he never met.

The dashing and sexy **Kim Jong Un** wins the coveted **Lord Lucan Where-the-fuck-is-he? Award** after disappearing from the public scene for months on end and then reappearing with a limp.

The highly prized **Neville Chamberlain Award for Appeasement** goes to none other than **Philippe de Villiers**, Vladimir Putin's very own French bitch.

The **Caius Caligula Megalomania Trophy** goes to **Teodoro Obiang Nguema Mbasogo**, Equatorial New Guinea's immortal god and never-ending nightmare.

As widely expected, the **Herbert Hoover Award for Economic Incompetence** goes to… Argentina's **Cristina Fernández de Kirchner**.

The prized **Tomas de Torquemada Award for Religious Fanaticism** goes to … **Abu Bakr al-Baghdadi** who's seldom seen a head he didn't want to take off.

The **Rodrigo Borgia Award for Family Values** goes to a loving father and husband… **Islam Karimov**.

Two for the Road…

BARACK OBAMA

PRESIDENT OF THE
UNITED STATES

KENYAN, SOCIALIST, NAZI DICTATOR, AND A SISSY TO BOOT

Imagine an America without death panels, a place where Christmas was still a holiday, when Americans didn't have to have a microchip implanted in them, an America before the guns were confiscated and, most poignant of all, an America with a White House, not a Black House. It wasn't that long ago.

The end of the nation as we knew it began at the same place the War on Christmas was started: a meeting room in a nameless office building in Mecca. Around the table sat an odd assortment: Jews, radical Muslim terrorists, of course the French, the Queen, the Freemasons, homosexuals, the New World Order, the UN, the Illuminati and ACORN. Horse trading began immediately. The Muslims wanted the Caliphate extended up through Mexico and into the deep American South, the Jews wanted to bring about the Protocols of the Elders of Zion, the French wanted to make America more European, the New World Order wanted to take the guns away, the UN wanted to subjugate the country, homosexuals wanted heterosexuality to be discouraged, the Queen wanted to replace the dollar with a world currency controlled by the Royal Family, the Illuminati wanted Christianity abolished and ACORN was just there for the money.

What the people sitting around the table needed was a man to secretly implement their plan. They scoured the world and finally found a candidate in a small village in Kenya. A devout Muslim and an avowed communist, he seemed ideal. He had a different name but they changed that to honour one of their heroes, Saddam Hussein. On a day in early 2007, Barack Obama was created and launched his bid for the presidency. The clever Kenyan knew he couldn't win in a fair race, but he had a secret weapon in ACORN, who were able to 'create' millions of voters. It was a long struggle but on a cold January morning in Washington DC, Barack Hussein Obama was sworn in as president and the country changed forever. The next day the painters arrived at the White House and started the job of painting it black.

HEAD OF THE
VATICAN STATE

THE MAN WITH THE POWER

Imagine being governed by a man who is incapable of getting stuff wrong; who is officially infallible?

He's the weird absolute ruler of a tiny micro-state in Europe and also 'chosen by God' to lead a crazy cult that has millions of adherents around the world. He hasn't got a surname: his handle is just Francis, although his real name is Jorge Mario Bergoglio and he hails from Argentina, but he'd rather keep that low key.

He runs a big pyramid scheme out of the Italian city of Rome where he's convinced millions to worship some guy who was born a couple of thousand years ago 'to a virgin' and 'rose from the dead' after the Romans did him in.

Sound bizarre? There's more. If you've done something wrong, even seriously bad stuff, he can absolve you – which is presumably why the President of Zimbabwe keeps popping over for a hug – and if you hallucinate and think you've seen something you haven't, he can make you a saint, but only after you're dead.

The cult has gatherings every week around the world and the leader of each cell gives a speech. Everyone shares one glass of wine and some crackers at every meeting. If you don't have 'special' water poured on your head at some point in your life you are doomed, and if one of his minions doesn't 'bless you' after you've kicked the bucket, then you're going down instead of up. The cult has a book that is required reading for every member. Every cell of the cult gathers money and sends it to Francis every week.

He has his own bank and a private army that comes from another country. He's into washing people's feet for some bizarre reason and doesn't have sex, even with himself, alone, with the lights out.

Brian O'Connell is an author, editor and journalist. He has worked throughout Europe, Africa, the Middle East, the United States and Australia and has published articles in over 30 newspapers including the *Sunday Times*, the *Evening Standard*, the *Wall Street Journal*, the *Irish Independent* and numerous other newspapers and magazines. He has worked as an editor on three magazines as well as editing numerous books and periodicals at *Le Soir, Wolters Kluwer* and *Sdu Uitgevers*. Brian has appeared on television and radio in the United States, England, Ireland and Belgium. He is also the author of six books. He is American by birth but has spent the vast majority of his adult life wandering the globe. In his personal time he is an avid sailor, an amateur historian, a fisherman, a beer connoisseur and an all around reprobate. He lives in Oxford and, to the best of his knowledge, has two children, both of whom deserved a much better father.

Norm Chung is an illustrator and former games artist who has worked for Ignition Entertainment, Rebellion and Awesome Play. He has worked on games such as *Pool Paradise, Mercury, Aliens vs. Predator Requiem* and *Speedzone*. He began freelancing in 2010 and has since produced a variety of work in both traditional and digital media. *The Fat Boy with the Bomb* will be his first published book.

Norm was raised in a Chinese Takeaway in Derbyshire and although he still enjoys being in the kitchen, he demonstrated his chosen career path at an early age, by scribbling on the walls, furniture and appliances of his parents' business. In his personal time he is a keen martial artist and, although he trains really, really hard, his 5-year-old daughter still walks all over him. He is based in Oxford and considers himself blessed for his wonderful family and his awesome friends.

I was sitting in a wine bar in Oxford on to my second bottle of plonk when I came up with the idea of *The Fat Boy and 299 Others*. When I explained the idea to a few of my friends over the course of the next few days I could tell by the blank expressions on their faces that they were singularly unimpressed. That's when I realised it needed some punch and a visual aspect to it.

I got in touch with Norm Chung and met him at the Jam Factory in Oxford. Despite his tortured expression, he finally agreed to illustrate the book so we got together and came up with ten representative pages, wrote an introduction, packaged it into a PDF and sent it off to various publishers.

Ed Handyside from Myrmidon got back to us relatively quickly and we arranged to meet in Paddington station in London. I explained to Ed that I was a bit of a leftie, in the American sense, and wanted to have a real go at the right-wing 'tea party' nuts in America. I thought he would feel the same, because, after all, how many people in publishing – especially 'Geordies' – aren't lefties? That's where I was wrong. Ed is anything but a leftie. He's a libertarian who thinks the main job of government is to just stay out of everybody's face, would like it to be easier to own a gun in Britain and would probably vote a straight Republican ticket if he was American.

I knew we would have a problem when he began to wince when I mentioned how I would take down Rand Paul and his ilk. During the long process it has taken me to finish this book he's accused me of being too cruel to the Irish, too easy on the Democrats and the Labour party, too offensive to UKIP and has lectured me for hours on the shortcomings of the British political system. For the most part he's been right, but when he threatened to not publish the profile of Barack Obama we almost came to blows. I think he has flushed many other profiles down the toilet as well. In fact, I have probably written far more than 300 in total, but I lost count long ago and for some reason there always seemed to be fifteen short of the total. I rightly began to think Ed just enjoyed tormenting me for the hell of it.

In the process, any chance of a friendship with Norm has gone out the window as our cordial working relationship gradually degenerated into pure hatred. He told me to fuck off when I suggested we work together again.

ACKNOWLEDGEMENTS

My social life has taken a turn for the worse as well. Every time I bring up the book in my local pub people seem to drift away, unless of course I buy a round of drinks; then they act intrigued until they take their first sip and then seem to immediately find someone else more interesting to talk to.

You would think that being a published author would at least get you laid, but that hasn't worked at all either. In fact, the last hot babe I tried to chat up, by telling her about the fascinating book I was writing, actually broke out into laughter and turned her back on me. I know this is where I should thank everyone who worked with me on this project but, honestly, Norm, Ed, all the guys down at the pub and particularly that woman who laughed at me can all fuck off.

Brian O'Connell,
November 2014